It's Been A Long, Long Time

Marianne Lods

May you enjoy
the journey,

Marianne Lods

It's Been A Long, Long Time

Copyright © 2010

By Marianne Lods

Registration Number TXu 1-688-833

It's Been A Long, Long Time

Is dedicated to the memory of my parents, to the members of the Belgian Resistance and to all of the Allied Armies especially the American GI's.

A special remembrance is to my sister, Michele Nadine Morgen, who went back to Belgium with me in 1999.

Acknowledgements

My thanks go to my father for saving every souvenir and document from his life during the Great Depression and his U.S. Army service. I thank my mother for telling me the tales of her life in the Belgian Resistance and for leaving behind the Gestapo papers that serve as proof of life-altering events. I thank them both for saving over 300 letters giving me a window into their love and lives which I will always treasure.

Special thanks go to my Aunt Francine Haughey who shared momentous events of their lives in WWII whenever I asked questions.

I really appreciate the time of Olivier Van der Wilt, curator of Breendonk Memorial, and to my friends in Brussels, Michel Picavet and Claire Renders, for being a part of my journey through the past.

I am grateful to retired journalist, Joyce Vanaman, who edited the original manuscript and gave me solid advice that set me on the right path in order to fulfill my desire to publish.

Thanks go to Alirio Pirela for designing the cover for this book which captures its ominous essence, bravery and above all, the love that is the fabric of the entire story.

Much gratitude goes to my husband, George, for understanding the importance of almost every Sunday for four years being spent on research and writing.

Lastly, I thank my brother, Serge Morgen, for his perspective as a child during the occupation of Belgium and for his encouragement to keep on writing.

It's Been A Long, Long Time is a true story about members of my family, their friends and enemies. Some characters are fictional and were added as needed to complete particular scenarios. Locations and dates are mostly accurate; however, I took liberties with Allied military bases located in southern England as official U.S. records of the location of the 347th Advanced Engineers could not be found.

TABLE OF CONTENTS

Part I

Part II

Prologue

Suzanne sat on a stool in the small, dark cellar with the baby lying on her lap. Serge was almost one year old but was still small and couldn't walk. He had been so ill with one ear infection after another. The recent mastoid surgery forced her to stay in her house even though the Germans were approaching from the east.

Moisture from her hair dripped onto her lap every so often. Her mother had poured cooking oil onto her beautiful long, blonde hair before they descended to the cellar. She feared that the invaders would rape a beautiful woman. There had been much rape during the First World War, and Eva feared that her eldest daughter, Suzanne, would become a victim of the Nazis.

Her younger sister was in the cellar, too. She was only 13. As a school girl, she should have been enjoying herself on this beautiful spring day in May 1940. Instead Francine was stuck in this God awful, dingy cellar waiting.

Waiting for what? The British troops had been stationed all over their little "city" in the suburbs of Brussels. They were knocking on doors early in the afternoon telling anyone that was left they had been ordered to retreat. The Brits had a machine gun installed only a few houses east on their street. It was right next to the large tree that made a natural round-about on the cobbled little Rue Virgile.

When the soldiers reached number 31, Suzanne's house, a corporal tried to explain in French, that they were ordered to leave. Their commanders knew these small squadrons could not stop the massive number of German troops that were entering the capital of Belgium. Suzanne was advised to leave.

She couldn't. Not with the baby still so weak after his operation. Serge was such a sweet little boy. Why did he have to suffer so, she wondered?

1

Eva and Francine came running into the house from the back door right after the corporal left. They lived next door to each other and Eva was terrified. She said they must go into the cellar and hide. That's when she thought about the possibility of rape and grabbed cooking oil from the pantry. She ordered Francine to bring a few blankets, to gather a couple of flashlights, and some wine. Eva already had a basket prepared with cheese and bread in case they were in the cellar for several hours. Suzanne also picked up some diapers, a sweater for Serge and two little blankets.

******

They were in the cramped cellar among the wine bottles and root vegetables for about an hour when Francine, who was sitting next to the door, thought she heard something. Over her mother's protests, she opened the door just a tiny bit.

Everything was very still. It seemed as though there was not even a bit of air outside. And then, she heard the sound again. It was light and sweet, the sound of many voices singing in another language. She didn't understand the words. The singing became louder, and she flung open the door to really hear it.

There was no sound of trucks or guns. There were the sounds of the singing voices and, then, she could hear the sound of marching feet.

Her mother tried to hold her back but Francine was determined to see, and she crept alongside of the house as far as the gate and kept herself hidden from the street by a large bush. The singing was really audible now; so was the marching.

The voices were sweet, but could not drown out the sound of boots pounding on the stone pavement. They must be at the top of the street, Francine thought. There were hundreds of soldiers marching right down Rue Virgile and making their way to the nearby Chausee Ninove leading them into heart of Brussels.

2

Francine watched the soldiers in uniforms they had become familiar with in the newspapers and in the newsreels at the cinema. There were thousands of German troops coming from the vast fields that lay to the north and east of them and they were pouring down into every neighborhood in this section of greater Brussels known as Anderlecht. There was no army to keep them out. What happened in Poland eight months earlier was happening to them now.

Even their own men were not able to stay here. Their brother, Ivan, and Suzanne's husband, Maurice, had left a few weeks before with their friend, Amand, for southern France. They hoped to join the French Free Army. The three men had taken their bicycles and headed south as so many other Belgians had. Along the way they were joined by many refugees fleeing and thinking that somehow they could escape the grasp of Hitler's armies.

There weren't enough of them. The Belgian Army was pitifully small and ill equipped. Even joining forces with France and England they could not defend the entire country of Belgium.

After the troops passed and Francine couldn't see them any longer, she ran to the cellar door. "Come out! There's no reason to hide down there. They are already gone and must be on the chausee by now," she said.

Suzanne stood up with Serge in her arms and went up the steps with her mother right behind her. They walked into her garden. The vulnerable little family still felt frightened but there was also relief. There had been neither gunfire nor artillery and nothing was destroyed.

They entered the house and went into the dining room. Francine went to the radio. Soon they would find out what would be happening next. The three women knew for certain that their lives were going to change forever.

Suzanne thought of her husband, her son, of herself and wondered what their destiny would be.

3

Part I

Occupation

After 18 days of resistance, the German occupation of Belgium began on May 28, 1940. City Hall became the headquarters of the commanding military officer of the German Army. It only took a few days of organization to set up a rationing system for the citizens of Brussels. The governing bodies of the city's sectors were removed, but the municipal employees remained at each of the administrative offices. They disseminated directives and ration cards from the Nazi regime to the public. The experience gained in Poland and other eastern countries now occupied made the establishment of the Nazi government in the West effortless.

Eva and Suzanne went to the city hall in Anderlecht to receive their ration cards. There was a long line of people mostly women and old men waiting for hours for their first ration books. Younger men didn't take a chance of being noticed fearing they would be pulled aside and given orders to go to work for the Germans. News had already spread that those young men without families would be sent to work in German factories.

Francine had stayed at home to take care of Serge. A month had passed since his ear surgery and he was getting better rapidly. The baby was finally free of pain and bubbling with laughter. Suzanne entered the house and went over to him. His smile and gibberish sounds lit up the room. He held his arms out so his mother would lift him out of the bassinette. Suzanne kissed his cheeks and laughed with him. This was the high point of the day she and her mother just spent, and it changed the mood of the women.

Francine asked about everything that had happened at city hall. Eva recounted the hours of waiting, whom they had seen from the neighborhood and the rules of the ration books. For the moment, the rations seemed adequate for the size of the two households.

Having enough nourishing food for little Serge was a priority.

"We have the garden for food, too," Francine reminded them.

"Yes, of course," Eva agreed. "We already have the spring vegetables growing and we'll have plenty of fruit from the trees in the summer. Everything will have to be canned to help us survive through the winter," Eva reflected knowing very well what it meant to live through a war as she had from 1914 to 1918.

Suzanne listened to them while she changed Serge's diaper and was glad that the conversation was positive and not at all the gloomy talk she and her mother had exchanged on their way home from city hall. Eva had been sure they couldn't possibly live on the rations allotted. Suzanne was angrier about having to deal with the *Boche* than how much food they could buy. The hair on the back of her neck bristled as she approached the desk of the Nazi clerk that questioned her.

"And where is your husband, Frau Morgen," the clerk asked after she described her household was just her child and her.

"He left me some time ago, monsieur," she lied.

"Why would he do that?" he asked while eyeing her beautiful face.

"Because he didn't want a child, I suppose. He's lazy and doesn't want to support a family," she said.

People in the line near her stared and listened intently. Many realized she was putting on a show to make certain that there was no husband to take away and send to Germany. Even though most of the men being sent away were single, no one knew how long it would be before husbands and fathers would be ordered to a train station for deportation.

Finally the clerk looked her in the eyes and said, "If your husband were with you, you would be entitled to more rations, frau. Seeing that it is just you and a baby your rations will be much smaller."

"I understand. I hope there will be a larger ration for milk and eggs so the baby will receive proper nutrition," Suzanne said coolly.

"There's enough," the clerk answered smugly. "You'll have to make do, frau." He handed her the ration book.

Suzanne took the book and turned away without another word to the clerk. Several Belgians in line smiled thinly at her as she walked past them to join her mother at the back of the hall. Her head was held high but her skin was crawling. Being called *frau* made her sick to her stomach.

When they reached the outdoors, she took several long deep breaths and told Eva what had happened.

"You did the right thing, Suzanne. Let them think Maurice is gone for good. I did not tell them about your brother, either."

"Did they ask about Ivan, *Maman*?"

"They knew I had three children. I explained that you were here for your own household and the records show you are married. When they asked about Ivan, I told them he had taken a job on a commercial fishing boat and I hadn't heard from him in months," Eva explained to her daughter. "What will happen if Maurice and Ivan come back from France, Suzanne?"

"Oh, *Maman*, I really don't know. They will have to hide," her voice trailed away.

Suzanne finished the diaper change and sat at the table. Francine made the coffee, and they had bread, butter and jam with it. They had been at the city hall since the morning and missed dinner. All of them ate hungrily now and enjoyed the coffee.

As they finished the little meal the front bell rang, and Francine got up to answer. She saw the postman when she opened the door.

"Mademoiselle," Monsieur DuBois greeted Francine. "May I speak to your sister, please?"

"Suzanne, the postman wants to talk to you," Francine said.

6

Suzanne was startled and handed Serge to her mother and went to the front door. "Yes, Monsieur DuBois, what is it?"

"I have a letter for you," he hesitated, "from France."

"Oh, wonderful," Suzanne exclaimed.

"Madam," the postman interrupted and spoke just above a whisper. "The letter has not gone through the censors."

"Oh," Suzanne paused. "That is good. I didn't even think about censors. How did it get through?" she asked.

Monsieur DuBois had known this family since they had come to rue Virgile and knew they could be trusted. "There are people working on the inside to make sure certain mail gets delivered without the *Boche* seeing it," DuBois said. "Many men have gone to France and are now trying to let their families know what is happening," he explained.

"Thank you, monsieur," Suzanne said very quietly.

"Make sure you destroy the envelope in case your house is ever searched. Postal workers could be in jeopardy if they are found out."

"Of course," she again said quietly. "I'll burn it tonight."

"*Merci, aurevoir.*" The postman turned and left for the next house.

Suzanne leaned against the door for a moment after shutting it. She looked at the postmark. It was from Toulouse. Suzanne crossed the room and picked up a knife at the table to open the letter. She began reading with Francine and Eva staring at her.

"My dearest bebe,

I am in Toulouse and have found a job in a factory. I decided to work while keeping up with the news from Brussels. It is hopeless to think that I can ever be in the French Army. They are so disorganized. None of us had any luck. Amand and Ivan are already on their way back to you.

They will be very careful upon their arrival not to bring any suspicion upon the family. I will stay here until I think it is safe to return. I hope it is not too long, my bebe. You and the child are in my thoughts and in my heart every moment. There is no way you can be in touch with me but I will try to let you know what is going on if it is possible. It is only a matter of time before France falls to the Germans. I hope you are safe and that Serge is feeling better after the surgery. Be strong, my love. You must be strong for the two of us. I will come back to you, I promise.

Your loving bebe."

Suzanne brushed away the tears that were falling upon her cheeks. Finally Eva spoke in a whisper, "Suzanne, what is it?"

"It is all right, *Maman*. Maurice is safe. And so are Ivan and Amand," she sat down and read the letter out loud.

"The news is good, Suzanne. They are safe!" Eva exclaimed.

"Where will Ivan stay, *Maman*?" Francine asked.

"I don't know. Perhaps he will stay with his friend Amand when they get back. He can't come here. The *Boche* will find out and deport him," Eva said fearfully. How could she think they were safe? Safe for the moment but for how long?

Suzanne decided not to tell them what the postman had said about the censors. She feared one of them might repeat it. It would be harmless gossip, but it could cost jobs. It could cost lives, she thought in horror!

Right at that moment Suzanne realized that not only had their circumstances changed, but they had no idea of how much danger was surrounding their day to day lives. She would have to think twice about every move she made.

The joy of learning her husband was safe and would return to Brussels faded quickly with the sobering thoughts of the Nazis governing them every moment of this ugly war.

8

It had been raining since they had sat down to supper in the dining room of Eva's house. A chill had enveloped them as the storm grew in intensity but Suzanne and Eva knew they could not waste fuel during the spring and summer months. Each week, they bought their ration of coal and stored it in their cellars. Being chilly now would allow them more warmth when the cold north winds would begin to descend upon them from the North Sea in November.

The radio was on and Beethoven's *Emperor's Concerto* was the main program for this evening. Eva was knitting while she hummed along with the radio. Suzanne had put Serge in the little crib next to the cold fireplace, and he was sleeping soundly. Francine was leafing through the latest issue of *Paris Match* while Suzanne displayed the Tarot cards the women often read throughout the week. As she reshuffled the cards, there was a loud noise in the rear of the house. It sounded like a metal trash can had been knocked over. Eva stood up and placed the knitting on the table.

The shutters on the windows were closed and so she went to the kitchen to peer out of the curtained back door. Just as she approached the door, the handle turned. Eva stood still. Although the radio emitted the notes of the concerto, the house was silent. The door was flung open.

Ivan stood on the threshold surprised that his mother was standing only a couple of feet from him. She stepped back as he moved forward and shut the door behind him.

"*Maman*," Suzanne's voice was concerned.

Finally, "Everything is fine," Eva said loudly. "It's your brother."

Ivan kissed his mother's cheeks three times and then walked into the dining room. Francine jumped up and ran around the square walnut table and threw her arms around Ivan's waist. He patted her head and gave her shoulder a squeeze. Suzanne stood and looked incredulously at her brother.

"Why are you so surprised?" he wanted to know. "Did you think I would stay in France with no army to join? They are in a mess there. Worse than here, I think."

"Ivan, is it safe for you to be here?" Suzanne queried.

"No. It's not safe anywhere. I need to get a good night's sleep and find some places to hide if it becomes necessary," Ivan said with authority.

"Where will you hide?" his little sister wanted to know. "How long will you hide?"

Eva interrupted. "You don't need to know where he will hide."

"That's right, Francine. And as far as how long; well, how long will this war last?" he answered without knowing the answer. "I'm afraid it will be for a very long time."

"Tell us, Ivan, what happened when you left here. Tell me about Maurice," Suzanne was almost in tears.

"Did you get a letter from him, Suzanne?" Ivan asked.

"Yes. A very brief letter telling me you were all safe and that you and Amand were returning and that he was working in Toulouse," responded Suzanne.

"That's right," Ivan said. "When we left Toulouse, he was working in a factory. He wants to wait and see what the *Boche* have in store for regulations regarding Jews here in Brussels before he comes back. Maurice is safer there, I think." Ivan looked at his older sister and saw the sadness in her eyes. "Maurice will come back here, Suzanne. He told me to tell you that was a promise."

Suzanne nodded and wiped away a tear. She blew her nose and when she spoke her voice was clear and strong. "I know he will. Now, please tell us everything that happened."

"I will, but first I must ask for some supper. I haven't eaten anything since early this morning," he said as he took off his jacket and got seated at the table.

"Of course, Ivan," his mother answered. "How stupid for not thinking about that right away. Francine, come and help me fix your brother a big plate."

Suzanne leaned close to Ivan and squeezed his hand. "Tell me, Ivan, is Maurice really all right?"

"Yes, he is. He's in no more danger in Toulouse than any Frenchman. He'll be coming home, Suzanne," Ivan said sincerely.

"How is the baby? I see him sleeping through all of this and he seems fine."

Suzanne smiled. "Yes, he is much better now. I think he is finally over all of the infection and will get stronger throughout the summer. He should gain weight and be healthy as winter approaches.

"Good," Ivan replied.

Eva and Francine brought two plates loaded with bread, butter, and cheese. There were also radishes from the garden. Eva took the bottle of red wine they had started early from the buffet and a glass and placed them in front of her son.

They waited patiently while he ate and drank down a glass of wine. Ivan slowed down as he buttered a second piece of bread and began to recount the journey from Brussels to Toulouse.

The three men had set out on the Chausee de Waterloo on their bicycles, crossed the Meuse River and had reached Namur by evening. They spent that night at the family's cousin, Germaine DeJardin. She was very happy to see them and willing to help in any way. There was no danger on the road or in the towns and villages because it was May 1 and the invasion by the German army was more than a week away.

From Namur they took the road to Felenne in order to spend the night with Ivan's Uncle George. Felenne's location in the Ardennes Forest along the French border made George knowledgeable about the

11

political condition of northern France. The next morning George DeJardin joined the men on his bicycle and pedaled to the border and guard station. He knew them and told them his relatives were on their way to join the French Army in the south. The guards let them pass and they waved good bye to Ivan's uncle.

The roads were well protected here in the French Ardennes and they wound their way up hills and coasted downhill giving their leg muscles much needed rest. They were entirely on their own once they had left Bolgium. There were no other relatives to give them food and shelter.

Although the daylight was already long lasting, Amand suggested they camp in a small woods about 40 kilometers north of Paris. They had bread, cheese and wine in their knapsacks and found shelter in a tight grove of young trees. Maurice wanted to build a fire, but Amand warned against it. A fire could bring unwanted attention to them. That night as they drank the wine they talked about what might lie ahead of them. They would follow the national road toward Paris and then go through the city quickly. Amand thought it was best to be on the road south as fast as possible.

When they reached the national road in the morning, they were amazed at the sight. Hundreds of people were walking, bicycling and driving towards Paris. There were families sitting on farm wagons with large work horses pulling them. Mothers and their children were walking carrying only small suitcases. Old men and women were walking trying to keep up with their children and grandchildren. But there were mostly young men like themselves heading to join the ranks of the army in desperate hope of thwarting an invasion of the Germans into their beloved France.

They pedaled in single file to get around the people walking, and after a few kilometers, they realized there were thousands of them not just hundreds. Maurice was the tallest of the three men and he got a good look at the road ahead when they reached a fairly steep decline. He saw the road snake ahead and it was filled with humanity for as far as he could see.

Maurice was shocked by the sight and hollered over his shoulder to Ivan and Amand, "Look ahead; we may not reach Paris today."

As Ivan and Amand got their turn of the long view ahead they both let out a long whistle. Amand shouted to them, "There are a lot of refugees. I think many of them are hoping for safety in Paris. We'll be able to pick up speed once we've gotten on the other side of the city."

Maurice and Ivan shouted out their agreement and the three men kept pedaling, albeit more slowly than before. Ivan was thinking about finding a decent meal at a café and spending the night in one of the large parks. They could continue south the following day.

When they finally reached the center of Paris they were absolutely exhausted. The horde of people they had been with for the entire day had scattered upon their arrival into the city. The families were all in search of relatives and started turning down the narrow streets of this great city. The men traveling together continued towards the center of Paris.

Ivan suggested stopping at a pleasant looking café and his brother-in-law and good friend agreed immediately. It was dusk and the temperature was mild. They took a table outside so they could watch their bicycles from the table. Normally, you would not need to do so at a café, but times were difficult and a bicycle could be very desirable right now. After taking turns in the wash room, they ordered steaks and frites and the house red wine. All of them were ravenous and ate quickly.

They ordered a second bottle of wine and drank more slowly. With cigarettes in one hand and wine in the other, they finally began to unwind and talked about the experience of that day. Maurice commented that they would probably never see anything quite like that exodus again, but Amand disagreed. "I think we will continue to see things that we never imagined," he said. "We have no idea of what lies ahead of us," Amand concluded.

His friends were quiet. They knew he was right. None of them knew what would happen to them on this journey or on any future journeys.

Ivan finished recounting the tale of their travels by telling his mother and sisters that the next two days were uneventful and they finally reached Toulouse. There were thousands of young men from all over France, Belgium and even northern Italy wanting to find an army that was organized and ready to embrace them into service.

What they found was chaos. They asked for directions; whom to see, where to sign up. The answers always lead to a dead end. It was as if no one was in charge. They camped out with hundreds of other men that evening in a park in the center of Toulouse thinking that the army officers would be more organized in the morning.

During the next two weeks Maurice, Ivan and Amand realized there was no army to join. Their trip had been wasted. While they were in Toulouse, Belgium had been invaded and her small army had defended her with honor, but in the end it was no match for the Nazi troops, panzers, and artillery. The men knew their city had been taken without incident.

Maurice felt confident that his family was safe, and so he decided to stay and work in Toulouse until he could determine his fate in Brussels. News had gotten out about the ghetto that had developed in Warsaw for the Jews right after the occupation of Poland began. If the same happened in Brussels, Maurice knew he would not be able to return. Reason should have told him that couldn't take place. There just weren't enough Jews living in Brussels to warrant a ghetto.

Ivan and Amand decided to head back for Belgium very soon. Their return voyage took a lot longer because they spent several days in Paris. They were looking for work so that they could stay, but with the huge influx of refugees from all over Europe, it was impossible.

The story of their trip ended and Ivan poured another glass of wine for himself. Suzanne looked at her brother for a long time and then she asked, "How will we keep Maurice safe once he comes home?"

Ivan turned to his older sister and looked at her for a few moments before answering. "What makes you think he can be safe? Do you think I will be safe? Or Amand? Any of us for that matter," he sounded irritated and angry.

"Forgive me, Ivan. I know it is dangerous for you and all of the young men, but I must think about the welfare of our little family and we need Maurice," Suzanne emphasized.

Ivan paused before he spoke to his sister again, "I understand. You have the baby to think about. Maurice will have to be careful, Suzanne."

"I also have to think about *Maman* and Francine. Maurice helps look after all of us, Ivan. Without him I really don't know how we will manage to get through this," Suzanne said.

"We're all going to get through this. Listen, all of the men will be hiding from the Nazis. We may need different identities. We'll figure it out," Ivan spoke hastily. He needed to reassure his sister. Ivan realized he had frightened her, and he was sorry about it now. He stood up and put an arm around Suzanne's shoulder. "We will find a way to outsmart them. I promise you."

Suzanne gave her brother a thin smile and squeezed his hand. Ivan would be concealing his identity and whereabouts, and she would have to be very strong.

Eva had remained remarkably quiet throughout the discussion. She knew that her family would have to be clever and quiet. No one outside of their two houses must ever know where Ivan and Maurice would be. Francine was a child, but Eva felt that she understood how serious this situation was. Tomorrow she would

15

explain the gruesome consequences if the Germans found out anything more than what they believed now.

For now she thought it best for all of them to get some sleep. "Ivan, I think it will be safer for you to sleep here at Suzanne's. If they come looking for you, you won't be in your own bed and that may give you time to leave quickly," she said with authority.

"Why, *Maman*, you are right and quite clever," her son responded. "Fine. Let's go to bed. I will get up very early and slip out before anyone is on the streets. Good night." Ivan kissed each of the women and bounded up the stairs to the back bedroom.

Surprise Visitor

Suzanne was in the kitchen washing a large bowl of strawberries. The day before she and Francine had walked to Dilbeek and went into the woods to pick the small wild berries that were so sweet they needed no sugar. She had baked a cake and had managed to buy cream on the black market that she would whip after the guests arrived.

It was June 27 and they were going to celebrate Serge's first birthday. He was fully recovered from his surgery and happy all of the time. Serge didn't walk yet and the doctor had told Suzanne not to worry because his illnesses had delayed his progress. Dr. Gilbert said the child would be walking before summer was over.

Suzanne had invited her dearest friend, Josette and her fiancé, Felix. Her mother and sister would be there and she hoped that Ivan might stop by for just a little while. Serge's godfather, Monsieur Sloma, felt it was too dangerous to leave his home to visit the little family. Everyone was being watched so carefully, and he did not want to bring attention to the Morgen home.

It was a warm summer day and Suzanne had prepared the outdoor table with a cloth she had embroidered and set seven places for coffee and dessert and a highchair for Serge. She placed a vase with daisies and nasturtiums from the garden at the front of the house in the center of the table. Suzanne glanced at her watch; it was nearly three o'clock. Everyone would arrive within a few minutes.

Serge was still taking his nap when Suzanne heard Josette's voice calling out to her as they came down the cement walk on the side of the house. Suzanne ran outside and greeted them in the garden. The two friends hadn't seen each other very much since the occupation and they embraced for a long time.

Josette and Suzanne had met in school shortly after Suzanne and her family had moved to Brussels when Suzanne was just eleven years old. In high school the girls studied an academic curriculum in the morning, and went to Ferdinand Coq School of Art in the afternoon. The school had a great reputation and Suzanne's hard work enabled her to enroll in the Academie des Beaux Art after graduating. Suzanne was hired by the House of Gion, a textile design firm on the Rue du Chatelain in the fashion district. Ultimately their lives took different paths, but their friendship was treasured by each young woman.

Within the next few minutes Eva and Francine came over through the gardens. Everyone spoke at once greeting each other and embracing. It was evident that coming together for a happy occasion was long overdue for all of them. Francine asked her sister if she should get Serge up from his nap.

"Only if he has awakened on his own. Otherwise let him sleep; he'll wake soon," Suzanne directed.

Francine skipped into the house and found her little nephew sitting up in his playpen in the salon. He smiled at the sight of her, and she reached down and picked him up. She felt his wet diaper and saw the supplies on the nearby table. Francine didn't like to change diapers, but figured she could help out since the company was there. Serge giggled as she tickled his belly while getting him cleaned up. Within a few minutes she was carrying him to the garden and the party being held in his honor.

"Look who's here," Francine announced coyly. "The birthday boy."

He was passed from woman to woman with kisses on his cheeks. Serge didn't mind it at all; he laughed and giggled in glee.

"I changed his diaper, Suzanne," Francine said proudly to her.

"Thank you very much. Now go and enjoy the party with everyone, Francine."

Suzanne stepped back and smiled. She had her camera in the kitchen and reached inside for it. "Turn and look at me and smile for the camera, everyone!" she exclaimed. Suzanne put the camera on the table and said, "We must save some pictures for the cake and the candle."

Suzanne slipped into the kitchen to finish the preparation. Within a minute Josette was at her side. "*Cherie*, let me help you."

"All right. Will you make the coffee while I whip the cream?" Suzanne asked her friend.

"Of course. You have cream, Suzanne?" Josette sounded incredulous.

"Yes, I bought it on the black market. For this occasion I thought I must!" Suzanne told her.

"*Cherie*, have you heard anything from Maurice?" Josette asked.

Suzanne had not received any more news since the letter and the arrival of Ivan. She did not even tell this to her dearest friend in fear that she would be putting someone in harm's way. "No, Josette, nothing. I know he is fine. I'm sure he is thinking about us all right now. He will remember it is Serge's birthday, and he will have us in his heart and in his prayers."

"Yes, of course, *cherie*," Josette replied. She was very worried for Suzanne. Maurice adored his wife and child and would do anything for them. Josette prayed he really was safe.

The women loaded up two trays with coffee, sugar and cream, cakes and strawberries and a mound of whipped cream and brought them out to the happy family and friends. Suzanne prepared the birthday candle and Felix handed Serge to her. Suzanne put him on her lap and Felix got the camera ready. They all began to sing Happy Birthday. Serge turned and looked inquisitively at his mother and then quickly looked back at everyone else singing loudly. As the song ended, Suzanne leaned forward with Serge and blew out the birthday candle. Felix was snapping away with the Brownie.

"Did you make a wish for him, darling?" Josette asked.

19

"Yes," Suzanne whispered. Everyone was silent for a few moments. They realized what she was wishing.

"*Maman*," Serge shrieked in joy.

They were startled and then everyone began to laugh and blow kisses to the one-year-old boy. Eva began serving the beautiful cake Suzanne had made for this day and Josette served the coffee. The plates were then loaded with the strawberries and a dollop of cream. Francine made sure they all knew that she had picked the berries with her older sister.

The afternoon went by quickly as family and friends enjoyed each other's company, and they intentionally avoided talking about the war to savor the celebration of Serge's birth and his recovery from serious illness. Josette had insisted on doing the dishes so that Suzanne could enjoy these moments of happiness. When they looked into Suzanne's eyes they knew there was a great deal of worry and sadness with which she was coping.

It was nearly seven when their friends departed. Eva asked Suzanne if she wanted to have supper with her and Francine.

"No, *Maman*, I had enough with all of the cake and everything. I think I'll go in and listen to the radio until Serge is tired and ready for bed. He needs to unwind from all of the excitement," Suzanne sounded tired.

"All right, Suzanne. Thank you, the party was lovely. I think we all needed a party," Eva said. She kissed her daughter and Serge one last time and went home just behind Francine.

Suzanne wiped Serge's face with a cool wash cloth in the kitchen and sat him on a blanket on the dining room carpet with a few of his toys. He had gotten new toys today and was having fun playing with a little teddy bear.

Suzanne turned on the radio, and after a few minutes she found a broadcast from England. They were playing tunes from the Benny Goodman Orchestra. She sat back in her easy chair and let the music envelop her.

Suzanne tapped her foot in time with *Stompin' at the Savoy*. After Louis Armstrong, she liked Benny Goodman the most of the American musicians.

Half an hour had passed when she was startled by a noise outside. The geese began to honk in warning from her mother's house, and she felt alarmed. She was going to pick up Serge and realized he had fallen asleep on the carpet. Suzanne sprang to the kitchen, all the while thinking about who could be coming. It must be Ivan, she decided. He probably wanted to come but knew it was dangerous during the day. She stepped outside and saw a man coming through the shadow of the hedge in Eva's garden. Eva was also alarmed and standing by the back door.

"Who is there?" Eva called out.

"Me," the man answered.

Just then Suzanne saw it was Maurice. She was on the verge of calling out his name and then clapped her hand over her mouth in fear of announcing to the whole of rue Virgile that her Jewish husband had returned and was ready for a Gestapo investigation. Suzanne ran through the yard past the honking geese and met her husband halfway through the yard in the intricate gardens they had planted.

They embraced immediately and she whispered, "*Cheri, cheri*, I can't believe you are here."

Maurice kissed her and felt her tears as he pressed his cheek against hers. "Oh my *bebe,* I promised you I would come home."

"Yes, darling, you did," she whispered and clung to him.

"Suzanne, I love you. I missed you so much," Maurice whispered back.

"*Cheri*, it is Serge's birthday!" Suzanne almost shouted.

"Come, you must kiss, *Maman*, and let her know you are all right," Suzanne said.

Maurice leaned down and picked up a very large bag. Suzanne hadn't notice it until just now. "Maurice, what is that?"

"It's a gift for our one-year-old son," he said as if he just came back from town after a shopping spree.

"Oh, my. Well, go talk to Mama and then we'll hurry inside," Suzanne was anxious to get Maurice inside their home. She was very aware that neighbors might be watching all of this.

Maurice approached Eva and embraced her. He turned to Francine and kissed her on the cheeks. "I am just fine. There is no need to worry. Tomorrow I will tell you everything. Now I am very tired and I want to see my son while it is still his birthday," Maurice said.

"Of course, Maurice. We are so happy you are here. Go home and we will see you tomorrow," Eva said.

Suzanne was waiting at the back door for him to walk the few meters between the homes. Maurice stepped over the threshold and walked quickly into the dining room where he put down his large parcel. He kept his distance and stared at his little boy curled up on his blanket on the floor. Suzanne moved close to her husband. She could see his shoulders relax and his tense stance was being replaced with a supple posture.

"Maurice, do you want to wake him?" Suzanne asked.

"Oh, no, *cherie*, let him sleep. Tomorrow I will spend the entire day playing with him. Why don't you carry him upstairs and put him in his crib, then we can sit and talk," Maurice asked his wife.

"Yes, darling, I will." She picked him up with the blanket hoping he wouldn't wake and started up the stairs. As she reached the landing, Toto came flying past her and leaped into the lap of Maurice who had just removed his jacket and settled into one of the easy chairs. Suzanne smiled to herself knowing what pleasure Toto would give her husband.

While Suzanne worked quickly to put Serge into his crib for the night, Toto was licking Maurice's face and bouncing on his lap. The little dog missed his master and was making sure he showed proper affection.

When she entered the room she saw Maurice stroking the dog. Toto had settled down in his lap and was perfectly content to receive the loving strokes from the master of the house who had been away for so long. Maurice looked up at Suzanne who smiled broadly at him. She took a chair and pulled it very close to his.

"Oh, Maurice, I was so worried that you would not get back," she said with a sense of relief going through her entire body.

"I know, *bebe*. Did you get my letter?" he asked.

"Yes, darling, and then Ivan and Amand came back, and they told me more details but I couldn't help worrying about you every day," Suzanne blurted out the words. Maurice understood the release of emotions she was going through.

"Suzanne, will you get me a cognac?" Maurice asked.

"Of course," she exclaimed. "How stupid of me. I haven't even asked you if you wanted anything to eat or drink," she was embarrassed.

Maurice watched as his wife glided gracefully to the armoire and took two glasses and a bottle of French cognac from it. Her motions brought back memories of the first time they met. It was the summer of 1936 at a Sunday afternoon tea in the ballroom of the Hotel Metropole. Maurice had watched as the maitre de hotel escorted two young women to a table for six. The taller of the women was strikingly beautiful with her blonde hair done up in a French twist. She wore beautiful pale blue linen dress with white trim that fit her perfectly and fell mid-calf on her long, lovely legs.

The orchestra was finishing a waltz and Maurice rose when they began a lively fox trot. He took long strides across the floor and leaned close to Suzanne's ear. "Pardon mademoiselle; may I invite you to dance?" Maurice asked. Suzanne turned quickly and was looking into the face of a very thin, dark complexioned man.

23

After just a moment, she instinctively said yes. He helped her with her chair and she placed her napkin on the table. Suzanne rose and took his arm as he led her to the dance floor.

In just a few beats the two newcomers fell into step with the other dancers. He addressed her by introducing himself. "My name is Maurice Morgen."

"I am Suzanne Duchesne," she replied.

"Do you come here often?" he asked.

She wondered about his accent. He made no mistakes in his French, but he definitely had a foreign accent. She wondered if he was Dutch or German with his last name. Either nationality would not be suitable for her mother, or for her. "Oh, I come here a couple of times a month with a few friends," Suzanne finished.

"This is my first time here," he said.

Suzanne was thinking that she was glad he had come here. Maurice Morgen was tall, probably a little more than 6 feet. He was not extremely handsome, but was good looking. His eyes were set wide set and dark and his brows were neat, thick, but not bushy. Maurice had a prominent nose and his mouth was broad but not very full. His hair was combed back and in style as were his well-tailored clothes.

Suzanne replied, "I hope you are happy that you came, then. The Metropole is a very nice hotel."

"Yes," he smiled, "I am glad because I have asked the loveliest young woman in the room for this dance."

Suzanne didn't answer and looked down with some embarrassment. At that moment the fox trot ended, but Maurice did not lead her off of the dance floor. After just a few moments another waltz began. "Will you give me the pleasure of another dance?" he asked with a smile.

Suzanne nodded her head and lifted her face as he put one arm around her waist and took her hand in the other. She smiled back and they fell in step with the beautiful music. He was an extremely elegant dancer and led her around the floor of the ballroom with skill and

24

ease. She felt a little chill down her spine as they whirled around while the strings gave substance to the Strauss waltz.

Maurice's memory of that beautiful afternoon was interrupted when Suzanne returned to his side with two glasses of cognac. "Please tell me everything, Maurice," she said.

Maurice recounted their journey as Ivan had not too long ago. Suzanne did not interrupt the tale in case Ivan had left out anything of importance. He told her about the textile factory he worked in Toulouse. He could have stayed but felt he would not be in grave danger here in Brussels.

"It is only a matter of time before France falls to German occupation, too. There is no real army and DeGaulle is in England to represent his country as an ally nation," Maurice said confidently. "What do you know about regulations that will affect me, *cherie?*"

"When we went to city hall to receive our ration identification and cards, *Maman* and I had to lie. I told them I lived with only my baby and *Maman* with only Francine," Suzanne told him.

"How did they react?" Maurice wanted to know.

"They wanted to know where my husband was and I said I didn't know, that he was worthless and left me and our sick baby behind because he was a coward. I'm sorry, Maurice, that I had to say those things that aren't true," Suzanne was almost in tears.

"No, *bebe,* don't be sorry. It was a wonderful story to tell and I bet you acted well and were indignant!" Maurice clapped his hands in joy.

The noise startled Toto and he leapt from Maurice's lap and scampered away to a soft cushion on the divan in the salon. Maurice and Suzanne looked at each other and burst out laughing. The little dog made them realize how happy they were to be together again.

"Enough recounting of stories for tonight, my darling," Maurice said. "Let's go up to bed. I want to hold you in my arms in our own bed and not think about this rotten war for a while."

"Yes, my darling. You go upstairs, and I'll make sure everything is locked," she told her husband.

Maurice was happy to oblige and took his jacket off the arm of the chair and walked upstairs. Suzanne followed him with her eyes and then quickly locked the doors, turned off the radio and picked up the toys that Serge had been playing with and tossed them in the playpen.

She moved up the stairs quickly and went into the bathroom to wash herself. Her dressing gown was hanging on the back of the door, and she slipped into the peach satin gown and tied it around her waist. She brushed her hair and dabbed just a bit of cologne on her neck.

As she walked into their bedroom the room was dimly lit by the small lamp on her dresser. She could see Maurice's naked chest and the sheet folded at his waist. He smiled at her and she shut the door. Suzanne moved to her side of the bed and her husband's eyes followed her every movement. She untied the sash on the gown and slipped it off and put it on the chair next to her bedside. Maurice's breath caught in his throat as he looked at her beautiful body, and knew that the next hour would be spent in pleasure for both of them.

Suzanne slid into the bed next to her waiting husband. They looked deeply into each other's eyes, and Maurice folded her into his arms as their lips met. The night was filled with passion, love and a deepening trust. Somehow they both understood that nights like this had to be treasured as their future together was totally obscured by the war forced upon them and their country.

Resistance

Three months had passed since Maurice's return, and Suzanne was happy to be busy with her household routine while her husband was often in the city to sell some diamonds. She had been worried for his safety, but Maurice had promised her that he knew his way around many back alleys and into the backrooms of cafes where diamonds and gold were bought and sold every day. He explained that this was the only way he could make money so that they would be able to survive the War.

As Suzanne washed the dishes, she remembered the time she learned that Maurice was in the jewelry business. She had been a bit forward after they had enjoyed several dances when they first met, and asked the tall, interesting man about his foreign accent.

Maurice had smiled and answered, "Oh, yes, my French is not very good."

"But it is!" she interrupted.

"I'm glad you think so. I am from Poland," he told her.

"Oh," she said and paused before continuing. "I wouldn't have guessed. Have you been here a long time?" she asked.

"Yes, I came here in 1932 with my aunt. She felt that Poland would be suffering, you know, politically with the new German government."

"I knew a few Polish girls in art school," Suzanne mentioned. "Your name doesn't sound Polish; it sounds German or Dutch, maybe."

"It's....," he hesitated just for a moment, "it's Jewish."

"Oh," she said, not knowing what to say next. In her opinion that was not a bad thing. Suzanne knew that Jews were having a bad time in Germany now, and had bad times in other countries for a long while. Here in Belgium, at least in the cities, there were always Jews. No one seemed to care one way or the other.

Suzanne continued to ask him questions. "What kind of work do you do?"

"I design jewelry and also make clasps for handbags," he said.

"That sounds wonderful," she said with a smile. "Do you work for a large design house or a small jeweler?"

I work for a small jeweler who wholesales the clasps to the manufacturers. You know, like Hermes and the others," he finished.

"Yes, I understand. I work for a design house."

"You do?" he was really surprised. "Please tell me about your job and your company."

"I work for *Gion*. We design textiles, mostly for carpets. I went to the Academie des Beaux Arts and got the job a few weeks after I graduated," Suzanne told him with her laughing voice.

Maurice had asked her to go to the cinema with him the following Saturday evening, and she accepted. The couple quickly discovered they had a passion for American jazz and spent many evenings at the clubs around the Grand Place in the center of Brussels. They also enjoyed long walks in the woods by the Chateau Dilbeek near Suzanne's home.

As she finished tidying the kitchen, her thoughts of the past were interrupted by knocking at the back door.

****

Amand Van Troch was sitting in the dining room as Suzanne entered with a tray of coffee. She placed a cup with steaming black coffee in front of him and offered condensed milk and apologized for not having sugar. "It's nothing," he said, "I prefer it black." Shortages were common place by autumn of 1940, and Suzanne was happy that she still had coffee to serve.

As they sipped their coffee, Suzanne studied the angular face of this long-time family friend. He was very handsome with his well-defined features and thick brown hair. Amand and her brother shared the same desire for adventure which cemented their friendship. Now she

28

was curious about the reason for his visit. She waited impatiently for him to come to the point rather than to chat about the neighborhood and weather.

"I suppose you wonder why I am here, Suzanne," he finally began.

"Why, of course, Amand. You are always with Ivan when you come to visit. I hope nothing is wrong," his best friend's sister replied.

"I won't waste time. Nothing is wrong presently, but of course everything is wrong. I don't have to tell you. Your brother and husband are in danger every day of being arrested," Amand said.

"Yes, of course. Please go on," she prompted.

"I've joined a group here in the city," Amand said. "It is a Resistance Group." The last words hung in the air, and Suzanne grasped the importance of them.

"We are doing things to protect people right now," Amand said. "Later we will decide ways we can harm the Germans."

Suzanne was staring intently at his face. She liked the way he spoke and the confidence that came from the words rushing past his wide lips and full mouth. It was a face she knew she could trust. "Go on, Amand."

"We need someone to do forgeries, Suzanne. To make false identity papers for some of our group members and for others that may come under suspicion by the Gestapo," Amand said.

"So why are you telling this to me, Amand?" Suzanne wanted to know.

"Because I think that forger could be you," he responded.

Suzanne stared at him incredulously, and took a minute before she responded. "Why would you think such a thing, Amand?"

"Because you are an artist and designer," he replied. "I've seen some of your work. It is meticulous and very detailed. I know you can learn to forge the papers and the signatures."

"But the papers .... how would I have the correct identity cards?" she wanted to know.

Amand put down his cup and looked deeply into Suzanne's eyes. "I already have the papers. I have many. You don't need to know how I got them, but they are invaluable to the cause."

Suzanne didn't reply and Amand continued. He could see that she was interested. "Suzanne, listen to me. Your brother needs a new identity card. If he has the same identity as me, he will be able to move about freely. I have permission to stay here and work without fear of being sent to work in a factory in Germany."

Her eyes widened and she asked Amand, "Isn't it dangerous for you both to have the same identity?"

Amand was glad to hear Suzanne getting curious and being less resistant. "Not really," he answered. "The Nazis are more interested in everyone having correct documents. They are so regulated that paperwork is more important than anything else. Ivan and I must not travel together, that's all," Amand finished with a small smile on his mouth.

"Oh, Amand, I just don't know what to say," Suzanne said. "What about the safety of my family? What if I am found out?"

Amand said in a low, serious voice, "Suzanne, we are all in jeopardy. We have to do something to protect ourselves. Our government didn't and now it can't. Only an underground movement can help. It will be up to all of the resistance groups and fighters across Europe to prepare for a counter attack by the British. Eventually the Americans will get in this war and we will be their allies. We need you, Suzanne." Amand's statement was so sincere that Suzanne nodded her head in agreement.

"Wonderful!" he exclaimed. I will come back tonight, after the baby is asleep for the night and no one will see me enter through the back garden. I'll have some papers. Please get something with Ivan's signature on it so you can practice. I have the appropriate seal and by tomorrow morning there will be two Amand Van Trochs."

As he stood to leave, Suzanne did also. Amand took her shoulders into his strong hands and kissed her on both cheeks. "Suzanne, I am not so much a patriot as I am an angry man. These *Boche* do not belong in our country threatening the wellbeing of our families and friends and we must work against them."

"Yes, Amand. I agree and I will do what I can," Suzanne answered. "I will see you tonight."

Suzanne sat back down and felt overwhelmed with emotion. An air of exhilaration coursed through her as she contemplated her role in the resistance against the German occupation. At the same time she was fearful of being caught, but she pushed away those thoughts. It was her nature to worry too much and it was time to be brave and to contribute something to protect her family and her country. Suzanne knew she was a patriot, and she believed Amand to be one also no matter what he had said.

Serge called for his mother from his crib on the second floor of the little house. As Suzanne went to get him, she thought about preparing dinner for the two of them. Maurice hadn't been home more than once or twice a week in September, and she never knew if he would come by. If he did tonight, she would tell him about Amand. She was sure her husband would agree, and she sensed he was involved in all sorts of underground political activity besides the diamond buying and trading.

As the young mother reached for her child, she understood that everything she and Maurice were doing in secret against the Germans was to protect the lives of their child and the lives of other children and their futures.

****

The autumn turned quickly into winter during the first year of the war. It was cold in the homes along Rue Virgile and everywhere else in Brussels. Suzanne and her mother had decided it was better for them to all stay in one house during the day and it was easier for Eva and Francine to stay at number 33 so that Serge had all of the baby necessities handy. The women tolerated the cold with layers of sweaters, warm socks and scarves wrapped around their necks. Eva cooked the midday meal with whatever they could find in the shops. They had quite a lot of jarred vegetables from the summer's garden, and everyone tried not to complain.

Suzanne had gotten very thin, and had to alter most of her skirts and dresses. Eva, a very good looking woman at age 57, had also lost weight and was pleased with her appearance. They both knew it was frivolous to consider making any new clothing for themselves at this time. Eva did make clothing for Francine who was still growing at the age of 13. It was important for the girl to have something new now and then.

Christmas was only two weeks away, and Suzanne had been busy making small gifts for her family. She liked to work on the loom her mother had given her a few years ago, and had made some very lovely scarves that were practical and the colors she used would make each person's gift distinctive. Of course, no one was expecting gifts this year, but Suzanne knew it would be good for their morale to have a little something for everyone. She was also trying to keep her ration card purchases to a minimum in order to buy more food for the holidays. Suzanne was praying that Maurice would be able to stay in the house for a few days and she wanted him to eat well. He was so very thin. She knew he was living on coffee, beer and cigarettes and very little else. Perhaps he would gain a kilo if she could feed him.

As Suzanne worked deftly weaving a beige, tan and black scarf, she let herself remember Maurice's last visit more than a week before. He had come to the house through the rear as he always did. It was nearly two o'clock in the morning and as she slept, she didn't hear him coming up the stairs. It was only when he slipped into the bed and pressed his naked chest and arms against her did she know he was there.

Immediately she knew it was Maurice. The smell of his soap and the tobacco smoke that lingered in his hair put Suzanne totally at ease, and she turned to face him. In the dim light that seeped through the cracks in the shutters, they could make out each other's faces and they both smiled.

"Oh, Maurice, darling, you've been gone for two weeks this time. What is happening?" she wanted to know everything that occupied her husband in the busy and dangerous city just beyond their neighborhood.

Maurice hesitated. He was going to avoid the question and tell her there would be time to talk about that later, but decided that his wife had every right to know. "My Aunt and Daniel are now in hiding, *cherie.* She has devised a very clever scheme to protect them from the Gestapo searches," Maurice said proudly. His uncle had died of a heart attack shortly after his factory had been seized by the *Boche,* leaving the aunt to make decisions to save her son and herself.

"Tell me what they have done. Where have they gone?" Suzanne was concerned and curious.

"Actually, nowhere," he replied.

"But, you just said....."

"I know I did. Let me tell you the tale. The aunt went on a shopping spree over the last few months buying religious icons for the house. Catholic, of course. She decorated the entire second floor with them and then the bedrooms on the third and fourth floors. She asked a very good Catholic friend to hire a carpenter to build a false ceiling in the salon and dining room. You know the ceilings are at least 5 meters high. Well now they are only 3 meters!" Maurice exclaimed with excitement.

The Ginsbourgs lived in a beautiful old stone row house located in a very nice neighborhood. The primary rooms all had high ceilings making them very lovely but very difficult to heat.

"I don't understand what purpose the ceilings have except to make it easier to heat," Suzanne was perplexed.

"That's it exactly, darling. If the Gestapo goes there they will think that a Catholic family is now in residence and that the ceilings were installed for warmth. The aunt and Daniel will hide between the false ceiling and the real one!" Maurice declared. "It's brilliant."

"How long will they stay in there?" Suzanne asked in a whisper still unsure of the plan.

"They will be there from sunrise until supper each day," Maurice said. "They will only eat and drink the bare minimum so they won't need the toilet. At night they will come down through a removable piece of the ceiling with a ladder, and have supper and use the house normally," he added. "They also asked the Catholic friend if their daughter and family would like to live in the main house, and they are. Aunt Rose wrote a lease for them. If the Gestapo arrives, they can show the lease to them proving they are there legally. The family will tell the Germans that Madame Ginsbourg and her family left Brussels and gave them the number of a bank account to deposit the monthly rent. Isn't it fantastic, *bebe?*" Maurice asked.

Suzanne was quite surprised, and she had to agree. It was a remarkable plan. "Yes, Maurice, it is wonderful, and they are safe. Such a plan wouldn't work for us, though, would it?" She sounded disheartened.

Maurice put his hand under her chin and lifted it towards him so he could see her better. "No, *bebe,* we don't have high ceilings. And, no, I couldn't stand the idea of hiding in a big closet for the rest of the war. I'll take my chances on the streets, in the cafes, and once in a while here at home."

"Oh, Maurice, I know it is dangerous for you every day. To know you could be safe would mean everything," Suzanne said wishfully.

"I know, I know," Maurice said. "But, it is an impossible idea. Listen, darling, I am a smart man and so is your brother. We are doing just fine dodging the authorities. The *Boche.* Brussels is a big city with hundreds of cafes and little streets and alleys. We will be safe, don't worry."

Suzanne embraced him with all her strength, and he responded with tender kisses. Their love making ended in a deep, restful sleep for the young couple.

When she heard Serge stir in his crib, Suzanne left the bed swiftly. It was half past six. Sunrise didn't come at this time of year until nearly 9 o'clock in the morning, and Suzanne would let her husband sleep until eight. She would fix him a good breakfast, and then he could vanish into the dark winter morning undetected.

"Suzanne. Suzanne," Eva's voice broke into her memories.

"Yes, *Maman*."

"It's time to get supper started, and put our sewing and work away," her mother looked at her curiously.

"All right, *Maman*," she sounded as though she had been awakened from a dream.

"Are you all right, Suzanne?" Eva wanted to know.

"Yes. I was just wondering when Maurice would be home again. It's been so long."

"You know, Suzanne, you probably shouldn't have married him. Why did you have to find someone different? A Pole and a Jew?" her mother asked callously.

"*Maman!*" she exclaimed. "How can you say such a thing? And if I remember correctly, you pushed me to get engaged. He was a good catch, you said." Suzanne was angry.

"Yes, yes, I did," Eva said. "Oh, Suzanne, I didn't mean anything by it. But Maurice has made your life more complicated."

"Yes, and he has complicated your life, too. But so has your son. He is just as much in hiding as my husband," Suzanne was indignant. "I don't want to hear you say such a thing again. Do you hear me?"

Eva knew she better back down. "Yes, Suzanne. Now let's stop arguing and get supper made."

Suzanne let the subject drop and started putting away her wools and the loom. Her mother always had an opinion about her eldest daughter's life. What she should and shouldn't do. But her remarks stung painfully, and she never wanted Maurice to hear them.

Francine had been sitting in the salon reading a book and had put it down when the argument began. "Francine," her sister called her now. "Will you please bring Serge downstairs from his nap? I think I heard him a moment ago."

The younger sister was glad for a diversion, and put her book away. Eva had retreated to the kitchen, and Suzanne moved next to Francine. "Forget you heard what just happened, Francine. *Maman* didn't know what she was talking about."

"I know that, Suzanne. Maurice is a wonderful man," Francine said.

"Yes, well remember that and don't ever tell him what *Maman* said, all right?" Suzanne asked.

"Of course. I'll never say anything," Francine said. She liked having a secret between them. "I'll go and get Serge."

Suzanne finished putting everything away, and felt confident no one would say anything out of line to her husband. Her brave husband, she thought. He's as much a patriot as anyone born here. She went to the kitchen to help prepare supper.

****

It was nearly midnight and Suzanne was still reading a fashion magazine, and listening to the radio playing soft classical music from the BBC. She was startled by a knock on the back door and quickly moved towards the kitchen. Moving the curtain, Suzanne could see it was Amand. She unlocked the door and stepped aside.

"Amand, it's so late."

"Yes, I know and I apologize but I have information for you," Amand said breathlessly. "Give me all of your forgery materials."

36

"What's wrong?" she wanted to know.

"We have information that the Gestapo may pay you a visit soon," Amand said.

"Why? How do you know?" Suzanne asked.

"Look, Suzanne, I'm not positive, but, one of our group members learned that anyone married to Jews would be questioned. We have to assume it could be any day," Amand said.

"They asked me where Maurice was after the occupation began in the spring," Suzanne said. She tried to dispel the fear that was growing inside of her.

"Whatever you told them then doesn't matter now. They want to know everyone's location, Suzanne, and you must be prepared," Amand told her.

"I told them he had left us stranded; that he was a coward. Shall I stay with that story?"

"You might as well, Suzanne. But, you don't want any kind of evidence showing your involvement in the underground in your house," Amand stressed.

"Yes, Amand. Thank you for coming to tell me. I'll go and get everything quickly." Suzanne left the room and went upstairs to gather the papers, inks and stamps that were supplied by the Resistance. She put everything in a small business portfolio so that Amand, if seen, would look like any other man going about his business.

Suzanne ran down the stairs and handed the portfolio to Amand. "Have you seen or heard from Maurice in the last week?" she asked.

"No. But I know he's all right. Ivan has been with him several times and has told me," Amand replied.

"He doesn't come home very often because it is too dangerous," Suzanne said.

"Suzanne, I know it is difficult for you to manage on your own with the baby, but Maurice must keep out of the reach of the Germans."

"I'm not complaining, Amand, I just miss Maurice and worry about him so much," she said.

"Of course you do. I will try to bring you news as often as I can," Amand said.

"Don't put yourself in harm's way, Amand."

"I can move about freely so far. Please, don't worry about me. I must go now," Amand said. "If the Gestapo does come, just answer their questions and stick with your story that your husband has abandoned you, all right?" Amand asked.

Suzanne nodded, and Amand told her he would check back with her in a couple of days. Amand took her by her shoulders with a reassuring grip and they exchanged brief kisses. Thank you for everything you are doing to help us," Suzanne said.

"I'll see you soon," Amand replied.

Gestapo

The three loud knocks on the front door of 31 rue Virgile on the morning of December 21st made the hair on Suzanne's neck stand up. She knew it was the Gestapo. It had been two days since Amand gave her the advanced warning, and Suzanne anticipated this moment with fear. She stood up, but didn't move towards the door. Suzanne was feeding Serge breakfast in his high chair, and now he looked up at his mother but didn't make a sound.

Three more knocks came. Suzanne walked into the salon. She could see the automobile parked in front of her house, and knew it was them. Suzanne reached for the knob and opened the door allowing the cold morning air to hit her in the face. The two men were dressed in civilian clothes with topcoats and hats. The man closest to her spoke almost immediately. "Frau Morgen? Frau Suzanne Morgen?" he asked.

"Yes."

"We are Gestapo agents," he stated. The agent opened his wallet showing identification.

Suzanne barely glanced at the wallet and said, "Yes. What is it?" her voice was remarkably steady.

"We have a few questions to ask you," he said. "Will you let us come in, this may take a little while?"

"Yes," she replied. Suzanne moved aside allowing them to enter.

"My name is Mueller and this is Herr Ronschadt."

Suzanne only looked at him but did not move.

Mueller began to speak rapidly. His French was quite good, and there was no hesitation. "Frau Morgen, we are looking for your husband. When was the last time you saw him?"

"In May when he ran away before the occupation," Suzanne answered quickly.

"And he did not come back?" Mueller said.

"No. He left me and my baby on our own. It has been terrible for us. I've been taking in sewing to make money to live on," Suzanne said.

Serge began to make noise from his high chair, and the Gestapo men turned their attention to him. Suzanne went to him, and lifted him out of the chair. She seated herself and held the toddler on her lap. Mueller smiled at the child briefly and turned back to his mother.

Ronschadt hadn't said a word, but his eyes kept roaming around the room. He would have little snapshots of the room, its furnishings and personal items. Ronschadt did not see any evidence of a man being in residence.

"Now, Frau Morgen, getting back to your husband's whereabouts; you must have an idea of where he went," Mueller said. His voice was condescending.

"No, I really don't. He went to France, but has no family there. I imagine he must have somewhere to live and work. I just don't know," she replied.

"Frau Morgen," Mueller's continued, "you are a beautiful woman and you expect us to believe your husband is such a coward that he would leave you alone?"

"If I had known my husband would abandon us, I would have never married him," Suzanne answered.

Mueller didn't speak for a several moments. Ronschadt looked at him, but did not speak. The interlude was unnerving, and fear began to creep into Suzanne's throat. She didn't know how she would be able to answer more questions. Finally the silence was broken.

Mueller stood up and his partner followed suit. "Frau Morgen, thank you for answering our questions. We have nothing further at this time. However, if you do hear from your husband or see him, you will do yourself and your family a service by contacting us and letting us know. Do you understand?"

Suzanne stayed seated holding on tightly to Serge. "Yes, I understand."

Mueller reached in his pocket and pulled out a card holder. He held out a card to Suzanne with his name, the Gestapo office address and phone number. Mueller saw her hands around the baby and laid the card on the table and said, "Cooperation, if you should receive news or information, will protect you and your family. Good bye, Frau Morgen."

Suzanne finally rose, and the men turned towards the front door and let themselves out. Mueller turned back to shut the door. "Go back inside Frau; the baby will be cold." The door was shut quickly.

Serge began to wiggle in his mother's arms, but she just stood there staring out of the window until their car pulled away. Suzanne felt as if she would collapse. She put Serge in his playpen, and sat heavily on the sofa.

She reflected on the interview and felt it had gone fairly well. Suzanne never wavered in her story, and her delivery had been sincere. Mueller seemed to believe her.

After several more minutes Suzanne got up and cleared away the baby's breakfast. Her mind raced with all sorts of possibilities. In just a few days the family and some friends would gather on Christmas Eve. She hoped desperately that Maurice would stay away. Suppose the Gestapo would watch for him to return? Suzanne decided she must see Amand, and give him a report of the interview so that he could get word to Maurice and Ivan not to come home.

****

The shutters were closed tightly on all of the houses along rue Virgil. Inside there were small gatherings of families and friends for the first Christmas under German occupation.

Suzanne had decorated the little pine tree on the buffet with the ornaments she bought for the first Christmas she and Maurice had spent together. Francine lit the candles on the tree, and Serge was surprised and delighted by the twinkling lights as they reflected on the glass ornaments.

Josette was pouring a dessert wine, and everyone's plates were loaded with wonderful cream puffs, chocolate mousse and marzipan fruits. Suzanne spent many of her rations on this evenings treats. Josette had helped by buying the marzipan with her rations.

The radio was tuned to the BBC, which was playing a fine assortment of Christmas carols in English and French. The announcer had said there would be a special address to the people of Britain and Europe by the king at ten o'clock.

Eva remarked how glad she was that they were able to have a traditional celebration, and no one commented on the absence of Ivan and Maurice. Suzanne had reached Amand the day after the Gestapo's visit. She often saw him when she ran her errands on bicycle at the small shops on the Chausee. Suzanne rode past Amand's house a few times before going to several shops. When she was in the drug store buying some hydrogen peroxide, Amand walked in the shop. The clerk said good morning to Monsieur Van Troch and Suzanne turned and saw him.

"Good morning, Amand," she said.

"Good morning, Suzanne," he replied. "How are things going?"

"Not badly. I've been busy lately with unexpected guests. They are gone now, but I have many things to take care of before Christmas."

"*Merci*, madam," the clerk said to Suzanne as he gave her change for the purchase.

"*Merci*," she answered quickly. She took her time putting her change away hoping Amand would go outside right after her.

Amand asked the clerk for a prescription the doctor was to call in for his mother.

"No, Monsieur, there is no prescription. Are you sure?" the clerk asked.

"Oh, don't bother. Perhaps I didn't listen to my mother well. Maybe she has yet to talk to the doctor. I'll find out and come back later. Good bye and thank you," Amand said. He was on the heels of Suzanne and they reached the outside together.

Suzanne walked over to the bicycle rack, and put the package in her basket. She walked the bike downhill and out of the sight of the drug store. Amand walked on the opposite side of the bike.

"Amand, you must tell Maurice and Ivan not to come home on Christmas. It is too risky," she declared.

"How did it go, Suzanne?"

"Not too badly. I think they believed me," Suzanne said. "They didn't stay too long, and I told them Maurice had gone to France and I haven't heard from him since. I was in a terrible situation, being alone with my child. The one agent, the only one who spoke, almost seemed sorry for me," Suzanne continued. "I don't trust them. He left his card and said if I get news, I should cooperate with the Gestapo and things will be better for me and my family."

"Of course," Amand replied. "Actually that is probably true, Suzanne."

"Well I don't give a damn about what will be better. I just don't want Maurice and Ivan getting caught. Perhaps the Gestapo will be watching on the holiday," Suzanne said.

"You're right, Suzanne. I'll get the news to them. Trust me," Amand said.

"Of course I do. Amand, when you think it is safe for me to do my work, please bring what I need," Suzanne reminded him.

"Yes, I will," Amand answered. He tipped his hat and said, "Merry Christmas, and give my regards to your family." Amand walked away quickly and turned the corner onto the Chausee.

Suzanne turned her attention to their guests seated around the dining table. Everyone had been

43

served, and she put Serge in his high chair where he could see the pretty little Christmas tree.

Felix Picavet lifted his wine glass and offered a toast. "Let us wish for the safety of all of those we love and that next year we will be liberated from this terrible occupation."

"Chin, Chin," was the echo.

They began eating the lovely desserts and everyone complimented Suzanne and Eva for the delicious treats. Serge enjoyed the whipped cream and Suzanne tried to keep his mouth clean between spoonfuls.

The evening passed by like many other social gatherings over the years. Secretly, Suzanne wished that Maurice were here. Her head told her that was unwise, but she yearned for her husband's company, his laughter and his gentle and caring ways. There was a small package with a beautiful scarf she made to match his top coat sitting on the buffet. Suzanne wished with all her might she would be able to give it to him by the New Year.

****

Maurice and Ivan were sitting with three other men at the kitchen table in a room behind the Café Cigale in St. Gilles section of Brussels. Maurice was thinking how funny it was that they were only a few blocks from the apartment of the Picavets. He didn't dare call on his friends and put them in danger.

The five of them were all staying very low. The owner of the Cigale lived upstairs and had closed the café for the evening. His wife was on her way to church, and he went downstairs to have a drink with his friends and compatriots. When Marius entered his own kitchen the group greeted him warmly. They had been drinking for a few hours and definitely had too much.

"Marius," Ivan belted, "thank you for your hospitality!

"Yes, Chin Chin," the others refrained. "Marius!"

44

"All right boys. I know it is tough to spend Christmas Even in this dingy kitchen and not in your homes, but I think you better slow down on the drinking," Marius advised.

"Sure, sure. Whatever you say," Maurice replied. "Being drunk has helped me forget that I want to be with my beautiful wife and son."

"Chin Chin," they replied.

"Listen fellows, I just want you to be alert enough to get out of here should the *Boche* come by," Marius said.

"Now why should *les sal Boche* want to come here?" Maurice asked.

"They don't," Marius answered, "but you never know."

"He's right, you know," a fellow named Pierre chimed in. "We should try to get some sleep and slip out of here tomorrow."

"Sleep is a good idea," Marius agreed, "but I don't advise you go anywhere until tomorrow evening. Except for church, everyone will be staying at home on Christmas until the evening. You'll be able to leave then, and blend into the crowds.

"All right, Marius," Ivan said. "How about some pillows and blankets to help us get through the night on the floor here."

"Right. I'll go get them and be right back." Marius climbed the stairs to his apartment.

Maurice leaned over to Ivan and whispered, "tomorrow night I am going home. I refuse not to see my family on the holiday."

"That may not be too smart, Maurice," his brother-in-law answered.

"I don't care. I know how to be careful. Besides if I see any German cars anywhere near Mortebeek, I will not continue."

"Suit yourself," Ivan muttered. "I can't tell you what to do."

45

The weather was very cold, but there wasn't any snow and Maurice was grateful for that. Snow could make tracking someone much easier. There were many people on all of the city streets and in the trams on Christmas night. Friends were going about visiting. Those with some money were having a meal in restaurants.

Marius had opened the café at five o'clock, and many neighbors were stopping in for a drink and to wish each other a merry Christmas. Maurice and the other men had come out and mingled in with the customers. One by one they all left going to various destinations; mostly to other cafes where they were known by the owner and where Germans seldom ventured.

Maurice reached Mortebeek around eight o'clock. He knew the streets and backyards by memory. With shutters closed and street lights out because of the blackout, there was only the light of the moon and stars and they were dim tonight. He was in the rear of his own yard, and made his way past the pen for the sheep without stirring her from her sleep. Maurice took the key to the door out of his coat pocket and fished around for the keyhole. He hated startling Suzanne like this, but knew it was better than a knock on the door.

He walked quietly into the dining room and saw his wife sitting alone in her favorite chair near the radio. Soft music was playing and her head was bent forward. Her hands were slack in her lap as she slept. He thought she must be very tired to have fallen asleep here.

Maurice walked over to her and knelt down beside her. He removed his hat and gloves, and touched her arm. Suzanne woke slowly and was not startled. She smiled at him realizing he was at her side or perhaps it was just a dream, but seemed very real.

"Merry Christmas, *cherie*," he said softly.

Suzanne smiled again. "Merry Christmas, Maurice, I knew you would come even though I said not to."

"I stayed away as long as I could," Maurice said. "There are a lot of people out and about visiting now. I checked the entire area for German cars and there aren't any. So, here I am."

Suzanne took his hand and then leaned forward and kissed him.

"How is the little boy?" asked Maurice.

"Serge is fine. He loved the tree when we lit it last night!" she told him. "Maurice you must be hungry. What can I get you?" asked Suzanne.

"Nothing, *bebe,* I ate earlier. I was with Ivan and some others, and we had plenty with our host," Maurice assured her.

"Will you stay all night, darling?" asked Suzanne.

"Yes. And I plan to stay for a while. I will be careful and won't go around during the day. There is no money to make right now during the holidays. I haven't even seen a diamond dealer for days. So, my sweet wife, you will have me under your feet for a few days!" Maurice exclaimed.

Suzanne put her arms around his neck and told him how happy that made her. As Maurice held her in his arms, he knew he put them all in danger, but he would be on the watch the entire time. He vowed to himself that harm would not come to his family.

******

The days following the new year of 1941 were dreary both in climate and in spirit around the homes on Rue Virgile, the city of Brussels and throughout Europe. The Blitz on London and many other towns in England, had commenced in September, and after day and night raids by the Germans, many lives and properties had been destroyed. Hitler's Luftwaffe attacks were relentless.

Suzanne could never get accustomed to the German bombers and fighters flying overhead on their way to Great Britain. When they flew at night to hit the targets that were still burning as a result of earlier daylight bombings, she would bolt upright in her bed and go to the front window pulling open the blackout curtain. She listened to the loud, thundering noise that awakened her.

England was warned about the strikes by the underground, and deployed fighter aircraft trying to destroy as many bombers and fighters as possible. Many of the brave men flying and fighting were killed. Some were able to return to England after making some successful strikes, and others had a precious few seconds to jump from their planes and parachute onto Belgian soil. After surviving the jump, the Resistance would go out looking for the fliers and bring them into the network of safe houses and businesses.

While she watched the planes grow smaller in the night sky, Suzanne knew she would have new identity cards to make to help the Resistance hide the pilots.

New Identities

Suzanne pushed Serge in his stroller on the shady foot path surrounding the Chateau de Dilbeek. The weather was warm this afternoon, and the young mother and son did not stand out. Other women and their children were walking on the path, while some sat on the park lawn and played with their babies or young children.

When they reached a fork in the path, Suzanne took the less traveled left trail. After several more meters, an elderly man came towards her, tipped his hat and dropped an envelope onto the top of the stroller. Suzanne nodded, and he walked on. She knew no one was behind her, or the man would not have made the drop. Suzanne quickly inserted the envelope inside her blouse and buttoned the jacket she wore. They proceeded another 100 meters and stopped next to a large tree stump along the path.

After taking a deep breath, Suzanne maneuvered the stroller to turn back towards the chateau and park. She was relieved to see that there was indeed no one there. Before continuing, she peered in at Serge, and saw that he had fallen asleep. She would now walk the last kilometer along the Chausse de Ninove to Rue Virgile and the privacy of her home.

When she arrived at her back door, Eva called over to her daughter and little grandson from the canvas chair in her garden. "Suzanne, come over and sit with me in the shade."

At first Suzanne was going to decline, saying that Serge was sleeping, but then the toddler called out, "*Mamie, Mamie*" he used the affectionate term for grandmother.

"All right, *Maman.*" Suzanne wheeled the stroller over to her mother's yard.

"Suzanne, it's so warm today, why are you wearing a jacket?"

"In the shade of the park, I needed a jacket, *Maman*," Suzanne said. Her mother never ceased to amaze her. Did she actually think her daughter couldn't dress properly? "*Maman*, I'll be right back. I want to take off my jacket and go to the bathroom."

She turned and left Serge in her mother's care while she took out her key and entered her home. Suzanne headed for the stairs. On the landing she removed the jacket and hung it on one of the coat hooks, and then entered the small bedroom at the rear of the house. In there, she had her art supplies and sewing items. Suzanne removed the envelope from inside her blouse and opened it.

There were instructions to make three sets of false identity papers along with photos of the young men. They were all British fliers who had been rescued by the Resistance somewhere in the countryside of Belgium. The men had most likely passed through a few safehouses by this time. She would complete the final pieces for their fake identities so they could make their way back to England through the *Comete*.

Suzanne thought about the men and women throughout the country who hid the fliers, and then moved them along a network of safehouses so they could eventually reach Gibraltar to get back to England. She felt they were risking their own safety much more than she. Suzanne opened a drawer containing water color paper and hid the envelope among the art supplies. She would begin working on them after dark when Serge was in his crib for the night.

In her dressing room she washed her face and neck to cool off a bit and paused to look at her image in the mirror. The face looking back was serious, but she thought, she hadn't changed too much since the war began. Her pale face was thinner and the features more pronounced. She was still young and attractive. Suzanne suddenly chided herself for worrying about her own looks. How foolish, she thought. Hurrying down the stairs, she stopped to pick up a few of Serge's favorite toys so he could play while she and her mother sat and enjoyed the beautiful July afternoon.

******

It was nearly two o'clock in the morning when Suzanne put down her sable brush. All of the identity cards were done and finished drying. She had inspected each one carefully and brushed off any finger prints she may have left anywhere on the papers. Suzanne put on a pair of white cotton gloves, and inserted each card into a separate envelope. She then placed the three into a slightly larger envelope and placed it inside of her water color papers.

After turning out the light, Suzanne pushed the blackout drape open, and let the warm summer breeze into the stuffy little bedroom. She looked out at the night sky and the stars that shone clearly, and then she saw the three faces of the British fliers. They had serious faces in their recently taken photos and tomorrow or the next day they would have French names, birthplaces, addresses and occupations as they traveled via the instructions of the Resistance.

Suzanne walked across the hall to check on Serge before she went to sleep in her own room. As she peered over the top of the crib, she could see her son sleeping peacefully. For a moment Suzanne thought about the danger she put them in every time she took a drop from other another Resistance member and worked on the identity cards. She was on a watch list of the Gestapo because of Maurice, yet they had not bothered her since she had told them her husband had left her. She didn't know if the agents would ever come back, and she really didn't care. Luckily, Brussels was a big city, and the Gestapo had many people they had to keep tabs upon. She hoped they would not come around again.

As she left the room, she reminded herself that all Belgians needed to contribute something to the resistance against the Germans. She had to continue to take risks until the occupation was over and the *Boche* were beaten. Everyone was anxiously waiting for the Americans to get into the war. The English couldn't do it alone, not even with the Resistance workers and fighters throughout occupied Europe.

******

Summer was coming to an end, and since the Blitz had ended in May, most nights were quiet and void of bombers and fighters flying over the city. Life in occupied Belgium went on not as before, but in a fashion they had become accustomed.

Suzanne was hanging the freshly laundered linens on the clothesline across her garden. There was never enough soap, and clothing had to be worn more times before going into the laundry. There was never enough of anything they used to take for granted. Suzanne would buy on the black market, but only for food she needed for Serge to make sure he would remain healthy. She had gotten use to going without butter and chocolate and many of the other foods she loved, but she would not let her son be poorly nourished.

The days seemed to drone on endlessly at the end of August. Before the war, the family would often go to the seashore for a week or two, but not now. The beaches were heavily fortified and guarded to thwart any type of invasion by the British. In the past, they would visit Eva's brother in the Ardennes Forest near the French border, but the rail service had been cut off after the city of Namur lying to the south of Brussels. There was no reliable transportation to allow them to visit each other as they once did.

Spirits were low, but they had gotten use to the way daily life had become. Seeing Nazi officers at the cafes in the Grand Place was no longer shocking; it was the way things were.

The English were recovering from all of the bombing and destruction in London. Radio broadcasts on the BBC kept telling Europeans that the Germans had not succeeded in destroying the courage of the British people, and they had not been able to invade the shores of Great Britain.

With the German Army and Luftwaffe concentrating on the assault on Russia, the Belgians could mostly focus on themselves and deal with the regulations forced upon them by the occupying troops. It was a relief to have the spotlight on the battles with Russia.

Maurice and Ivan were both spending a little more time at their homes, and Eva and Suzanne were very happy to know where their men were. Maurice did not jeopardize the safety of the family by attracting attention to himself during the day. If he needed to meet diamond buyers, he would leave the house at night and meet in obscure cafes or he'd travel in the predawn hours and business would be conducted in the backrooms of cafes and bars. Then Maurice would return to rue Virgile the next evening.

Suzanne worried more when her husband was home and coming and going from their house. She felt he exposed himself to the *Boche* each time. Maurice would always reassure her that nothing was going to happen to him and that soon, he was very sure; the Americans would be entering the war. He told his wife that once the Americans joined in the fight, the Germans would be destroyed.

She knew this was true, but it was already more than a year since they were living with the occupation. Suzanne often asked her husband how long it would take for the Allies to defeat Hitler. Maurice would tell her she worried too much, and that they just had to go about their lives. One day they would be celebrating and would be dancing in the streets.

Suzanne knew her husband was making everything much simpler than it truly was just to make her feel safe. She was happy and felt safe when he held her in his arms, but the uneasiness would always return as soon as he was out of sight. What Suzanne and Maurice didn't know yet was the master plan for eliminating

Europe of all the Jews that lived throughout the continent within the borders of each occupied country.

As the warm summer of 1941 drew to a close, German Jews were being forced to wear the Star of David on their clothing to identify them where ever they went, and Hermann Goering had already given orders to prepare for the Final Solution to the Jewish question throughout occupied Europe.

Unexpected News

The winter of 1942 was very cold. Citizens of Brussels coped with the temperature and lack of coal just as they did living under the thumb of the Third Reich. Maurice managed to spend a few days with his family in late February without being observed. The Germans were focused on the Russian front, but were not making headway. Hitler had not used history to his advantage. Napoleon's great army had been beaten by the Russians during the winter of 1812 and suffered thousands of casualties. The German Army in 1942 was not able to endure the freezing temperatures and deep snows. The soldiers did not have the equipment or the stamina to defeat the Soviet Army nor the Russian peasants.

Hatred of the Russians increased the atrocities perpetrated by the Germans. If they took prisoners, they were often slaughtered or sent to prison camps that did not even pretend to uphold the rules of the Geneva Convention as it applied to prisoners of war.

The BBC kept the Belgians informed of the bad news for Germany, yet it didn't do much to lift their spirits. The lack of fuel and food supplies added to their misery and fear. They were not starving, but they were almost always more than a little hungry. Everyone got thinner and some got ill more easily or didn't recover quickly from colds or other ordinary maladies.

When Maurice had returned to his home, he brought some canned meat and a little sugar he managed to buy on the black market. The family feasted on the canned ham accompanied by preserved vegetables from the summer's garden. Eva had used the sugar to make a cake with the flour, vanilla and an egg from her goose. It was such a simple cake but it was as delectable as if it had come from any one of the fabulous patisseries the family had once been able to patronize. The women all thanked Maurice for having found the sugar and spending many francs to buy it. While holding his young son in lap, he smiled with satisfaction for having the ability to give his family a little bit of pleasure.

Late at night Maurice and Suzanne kept warm by making love and holding each other closely each night during his return to their cold, small house. Suzanne was so happy to have him next to her, but at the very next moment she was engulfed with fear thinking about his imminent departure. She hadn't dared to ask how long he would stay because she knew she would hate the reply.

Maurice stayed close to his wife during the day or played with Serge, and Suzanne felt secure knowing that they were truly a married couple and that she was not alone. He often regretted marrying his lovely *bebe* because he put her in danger every day of this war. Maurice never expressed these emotions to his wife; he knew she would protest. He wanted all of their time together to be memorable and special so that she would always remember him even if he was gone. Maurice knew he was living precariously, and there wasn't much he could do about it wanting to make as much money as possible so that Suzanne and Serge would have something to live on if he were arrested. And so, Maurice continued to trade in gems and gold with men that were all under the watchful eye of the Gestapo. At the same time, he passed information along to aid in the Resistance efforts whenever possible.

Since the news had arrived that the Americans declared war on Japan and Germany after the attack on Pearl Harbor, the instant euphoria among the Belgians had evaporated. Everyone was questioning when the Allies would plan and carry out an invasion of Europe in order to battle the German Army. The impossible winter weather did not help the planning at all, but Churchill urged them to be patient while the Allies prepared their armies, navies and air forces to defeat the Third Reich. Maurice knew they had to be patient while the armies assembled and deliberated their attack. He wondered, only to himself, if he had enough time to see them become victorious.

****

Suzanne walked slowly from the tram stop on the chausee through the cobbled streets leading her home to rue Virgile. She walked past the familiar shops and houses not really seeing them. She was preoccupied with the news she received an hour before.

She arrived at her house and entered through the back door as she always did and went directly to her bedroom to change her clothes. She removed her hat and then the lovely, if slightly worn, beige woolen suit. While she dressed in the same white blouse and navy blue skirt she had worn the previous day, she suddenly burst into tears. Grabbing the edge of her bureau she lowered herself onto the upholstered seat and sobbed into her hands. After a minute she felt around the dresser for a handkerchief and blew her nose.

Suzanne was pregnant. Dr. Gerard told her there was no doubt about the diagnosis. Even though she was stunned by the announcement, she knew it was true. The morning sickness was the same as when she was in early pregnancy with Serge. It was now the beginning of April, and she had only seen Maurice briefly a few times since they had spent several wonderful, cold nights in their warm bed. Now she regretted not trying to prevent a pregnancy. How could they cope with a new baby? They? Her husband would not be by her side as he had been when she spent two weeks in the hospital and arranged for someone to help her at home.

She pulled herself together and went into the bathroom to wash her face. Suzanne smoothed out her clothing and looked at herself in the mirror. She would have to manage and rely on the help of her mother and younger sister. Francine had recently had her fifteenth birthday and would have to help take care of Serge when she couldn't. As she gave her image one final glance, she decided to go next door and tell her mother the

57

news. Francine would hear later when she returned from school.

As she entered her mother's kitchen, she called out to her.

"Suzanne, I'm with Serge in here," Eva replied.

"Hello, my little boy. Are you having a nice time with your grandmother?" Suzanne asked.

"Yes, *Maman*. We are drawing. Look," said Serge.

"Oh, my, how beautiful your drawing is. Tell me who is in the picture?" Suzanne asked.

Serge pointed to the simple figures he had drawn in a garden. "This is you, *Maman,* and here is Papa and me!" he exclaimed.

"Yes, I see that!" Suzanne replied with joy. After a pause she continued, "Soon you will have to add someone else to your picture."

"Who, *Maman*?"

"A baby brother or sister."

Serge looked confused, and Eva just stared at her incredulously.

"What are you saying, Suzanne?" Eva whispered the question.

"I am going to have a baby. I went to the doctor today and he told me he is very sure," Suzanne said.

"*Maman*," the little boy looked very perplexed, "do you mean like Madam Temperman's baby?"

"Yes, Serge. Your little friend Emil has a baby sister. Maybe you will have a sister like him. Would you like that?" asked Suzanne.

"No. I want a brother, *Maman*. Please," he said.

"Well we won't know if we will have a brother or sister until the baby is born and we have to wait until next autumn to find out. All right?" Suzanne asked.

"How long is that, *Maman*?"

"Right before Noel. You remember we had Noel and St. Nicholas day, don't you?" Suzanne asked.

Serge nodded.

"It takes a while for Noel to come again, and we all have to be patient. We will have a new baby for Noel," Suzanne reassured her son. She glanced at her mother.

"Suzanne, how could you let this happen?" Eva was still whispering.

"Because I love my husband, *Maman*. I'm not like you. I'm not filled with hatred for the man I married."

There was silence for a moment. Suzanne was surprised at her response. Eva was shocked.

"What do you mean? I have three children, and I had two baby sons that died. How can you say such a thing?" Eva sounded hurt.

"How, *Maman*?" Suzanne queried. "Every day after we moved to Brussels you told me how you were so happy that my father was dead. That he was a drunk and treated you like his servant. Did you think because I was only eleven years old that I didn't understand what you were telling me?"

Eva just looked at her for a few moments before answering. "I did hate him and when we left Villers, I was humiliated before our family and the neighbors. I couldn't help telling you because you are my oldest child and I had no one else to talk to. I know you love your husband, but, Suzanne the new baby will be so difficult for you and for us if the war is still on."

"I know, *Maman*. I'm sorry I said that to you about my father. I don't want to be pregnant, but I am, and I'm not going to do anything to get rid of it. After the war, Maurice and I will have plenty of good times to raise our children."

Eva nodded at her daughter. She did not expect or want her daughter to have an abortion.

"*Maman*, you and Francine will have to help me more with Serge as I get big and after the new baby is born."

"Of course we will, Suzanne. Of course," her mother answered. "You have plenty of room in your house, and Serge will have to be in a big bed before then."

"We will manage, *Maman*. Please don't worry. By November the Allies will surely be pushing the *Boche* out of Belgium. Out of Europe!" Suzanne exclaimed.

"Let's hope and pray that they will," Eva said. Come; let's make a few little sandwiches. Francine will be home from school soon and it will be time for coffee."

"Yes, *Maman*, let's do that." Suzanne was glad to get back to doing something routine. Funny, she thought, they still said they would prepare for the four o'clock coffee even though they hadn't had real coffee for over a year. The best they could get was a very bitter chicory, but the afternoon ritual remained intact and it was a time of day when each member of the family could talk about something that had happened that day. Sometimes they gossiped about families from their neighborhood. Often letters arrived from distant cousins or friends in the country, and they shared all of the news. But mostly Francine would talk about her day at school. She told them what she learned and would also share the gossip of the other girls and their families. Afternoon coffee was a time they could rest and put aside the war while they enjoyed small sandwiches filled with their own jam and the hot bitter, brown liquid they still called coffee.

Arrested

After Suzanne put the iron away and all of the neatly pressed clothing, she collapsed in a chair near the window of the dining room. New clothing was out of the question and so, she mended, washed and pressed their apparel as best she could to always look presentable. Of course she had saved her maternity clothing and it was not very worn. Suzanne saved her best suits and dresses for the days she went to town in Brussels.

The last time she had been to the city was over a month ago at the prodding of her dearest friend. Josette saw how much the strain of war and her pregnancy showed in all of Suzanne's actions and words. In mid-April the two long-time friends went to a movie. It was an Italian film and was preferable over a German made movie. The once loved American cinema had been off limits to all of Europe since the occupation. At least the Italian films were gayer, and the language behind the French subtitles was pleasant to their ears. Neither of them would go to German movies. Hearing the guttural tongue on the screen was like rubbing salt in all of their wounds.

As they enjoyed glasses of Dubonnet at a café on the Grand Place on this very pleasant spring day, Suzanne explained the wonderful time their family had had on Easter only a week before. It was the last time she had seen him. Maurice had arrived home after dark the evening before the holiday. Although he tried to be as light-hearted as he could, his wife could tell that Maurice was worried about his own safety.

Maurice feared for his wife's safety and asked her to stop forging documents for the Resistance, but she refused. Suzanne told him if he could continue to risk his life and her brother was always on missions with the Resistance and the *Maquis*, then she, too, must continue her small contribution to saving lives of the pilots and civilians who were under surveillance. Josette was uncomfortable talking, even though in whispers, about such matters in a public place.

Suzanne understood and continued to talk about the lovely Easter weekend. "You know what, Josette? Maurice brought home a few candies and we put them in the flower garden. He held Serge in his arms and pointed to the bells and told him that the bells had brought sweets to their house so that their little boy could have a wonderful Easter treat!"

Her eyes became damp as she spoke. "Isn't it something, Josette? My Jewish husband has kept all of the traditions of Catholics alive for his son and for me."

"Maurice is a wonderful husband and father, Suzanne," Josette almost choked on her own emotion as she whispered to her friend. "When the war is over, you two and your children will be able to live a great life. Just wait and see, dear."

"Yes, Josette. I'm sure you are right," Suzanne smiled. As she finished her drink, she knew she didn't believe a word of what she had just said. She only knew that she must continue to live one day at the time.

******

Maurice was walking quickly down a quiet street on the north side of the Grand Place. He had avoided the streets near the North Train Station since there were always German troops, officers and the Gestapo by all of the stations. He arrived at the little café where the diamond sellers and buyers often came. In the late afternoon a group of men of all ages would frequent this café on rue Grétry. The apartment upstairs was a safe house for the fliers that had been shot down and were awaiting transport that the Resistance provided to Paris and often to Spain to be able to get back to England.

A few men were already seated at two tables and Maurice strode to one and greeted everyone briefly with a handshake. The barman didn't move but was waiting for Maurice's order. "One beer, please," Maurice asked of the familiar and friendly face of the middle aged barman.

After he was seated, the beer was placed in front of him by the daughter of the owner of the café. Maurice thanked her and took a quick sip. The men began discussing the news of the war, in matter of fact tones. Hopes were higher now that the Americans began to arrive in England. They were all resigned to the fact that it would take months before the buildup of troops was great enough to invade Europe.

The friends and acquaintances spoke of the German U Boats attacking the merchant vessels and troop ships on the North Atlantic Ocean. News would come from the BBC whenever a U Boat was destroyed. Every strike against the Nazi war machine brought hope into their collective lives.

Suddenly the door burst open. Maurice had his back towards the door but in the next instant he saw the looks on the faces of his companions as they recognized those that entered. Before Maurice could turn around, the German voices shouted "Gestapo! Don't move!"

One agent repeated the command in French. "Gestapo! *Bougez pas!*"

No one moved as the footsteps of two Gestapo came into the room. They were soon followed by two more agents. All of the men wore raincoats over their civilian suits and wore hats. They all had pistols in their leather gloved hands.

The two teams of Gestapo moved to each table and demanded the men to take out their identity papers. When one agent reached Maurice and flipped open his card, he sneered as he looked from the photograph to the man. *"Juden,"* he announced.

Maurice did not have false papers. He had sincerely felt that he could continue to hide in alleys and safe houses throughout the large city. One of the Gestapo handed all of the papers of Maurice's table to the other agent as he told them to stand up.

The men's eyes darted from one to another. All accepted the fact that they dare not try to run. With four Gestapo inside armed with guns, they could only guess how many else were outside of the café. The barman was told to join the group while the girl was told she could remain, but must close and lock the door of the café.

"You are all political prisoners of the Third Reich," announced the agent who had only spoken in German. Again, the other agent translated into French. "You will get into the truck outside. We are taking you to the prison."

No one spoke as they were prodded with the gun barrels in their ribs. The weather was warm and the men were all wearing suits without topcoats. Cigarettes and lighters were left behind as they were hurried out the front door.

A small truck waited outside where four German soldiers, rifles ready, stood near the rear gate. Now the men were shouted at to get into the truck as the soldiers poked at them with their rifles. When they were all squeezed together, two of the soldiers leaped into the back with them, guns pointed at chests. The four Gestapo men climbed into their sedan parked behind the truck. Apparently the truck driver was already in his seat as the engine turned over immediately upon the one Gestapo turning on his car engine.

The truck lurched into second gear and the men were jostled but barely moved because they were crowded into the truck body. They bounced along the cobbled streets and made their way to the opposite side of the city in very little time. When the truck stopped, Maurice could hear a gate opening. He could see outside and the row of houses looked familiar. When they rolled through the gate he could see the words on a plaque mounted on the brick wall. *Prison de St. Gilles* it read. Of course it was familiar. He and Suzanne would often pass by on the tram whenever they would go to the apartment of their good friends, the Picavets.

This was no friendly house visit. This was a political round up. Several of his companions had false papers and might be released. Others were very active in the *Comete* movement of the Resistance, and he hoped they wouldn't search the apartment above the café where they had just been. Maurice knew for sure his luck was probably the worst. His identity card bore his true name, date and place of birth. Before he and the others were again prodded by the rifles to disembark the truck, he thought of Suzanne. He knew she would be devastated by the news of his arrest.

They jumped off the truck one at a time and were hurried through the massive front doors of the prison. Once inside, they were told to line up in two columns and were then marched to a large holding cell. When the cell door was locked, two soldiers turned their backs to the new prisoners and stood on each side of the door with rifles at the ready. The Gestapo agents walked away down a corridor.

At first no one dared to speak. They all wondered if the guards could understand French. After a few more minutes a fellow named Claude whispered to the others. "Who has diamonds?"

Three men nodded their heads. Maurice did not. He had planned on buying some today and thus, had quite a large amount of francs on him.

Jules whispered next, "Perhaps we can bribe our way out of this."

Claude shook his head. "No, having the diamonds makes us guilty of possessing contraband. They have reason to imprison those with diamonds."

Just when Jules was going to suggest they try to hide the precious stones, one of the Gestapo returned. He spoke in French. "Each of you will be questioned separately. There will be no talking in this cell, understood?" The Gestapo repeated the order of silence to the guards in German.

Henri was taken first. There was no reason for his selection as number one. He did not have diamonds nor did he have much money. Henri was only at the café today to pass some time with his compatriots.

The cell door was opened by a guard on command of the Gestapo agent. Henri moved along the hallway ahead of the agent who was now holding a pistol aimed at his back.

The men in the cell listened to their footsteps fade and then the loud bang as a door of the interrogation room shut behind them. All of the friends looked at each other in silence with worried and somber expressions on their faces. Long ago they had all pledged to keep their entire activities secret and to never give up any information. Some knew more than others, and they all feared they would be tortured and would give away information to their enemies.

Maurice did not know the names or addresses of many safe houses. Yet because he was a Jew, he would be treated more harshly than his companions. As the minutes dragged by slowly, Maurice could only think of his family. Would he be released? Would they break his willpower? Surely they knew he was married to a Belgian woman, and he wondered if they would go to their home again.

One by one, the men were taken down the corridor. None of them returned to the cell and each remaining man couldn't help the increasing fear each felt for his own survival. Finally, there were only two men left in the holding cell. Maurice was taken, and Claude was left to be last.

When Maurice entered the room he could smell the sweat of the men that had been here prior to him. He quickly scanned the room. It was rather large, and the thick, old prison block walls were painted gray. There were a couple of electric lights that hung down above a long wooden table. There was a short bench on one side and four wooden chairs on the opposite side of the table. Three Gestapo were seated there, while the agent that brought him into the room ordered him in French to sit down on the bench. He finished his evaluation noticing,

66

with a sense of relief; there was no blood anywhere in the room.

The questioning began in a non-hostile manner. All of the Gestapo in the room spoke French and they asked him basic questions while looking at his identity papers. Maurice answered yes to all of the obvious questions about his birthplace, when he had immigrated to Belgium, his work and his family.

"When was the last time you corresponded to your family in Poland," he was asked.

"I have written letters now and then, but I haven't had a reply in over a year," Maurice answered honestly.

"Do you wonder why?" one of the agents asked mockingly.

"Yes," Maurice hesitated but continued. "I believe they must have been sent to a work camp in Germany."

Maurice saw the smug looks on all of the Gestapo faces. His interrogator replied, "Yes, I believe you are correct, Herr Morgen. What do you think about the possibility of joining them?"

Maurice hesitated for only a moment and answered, "I never really thought about it. I've made my life here for the last ten years."

"Yes you have, Herr Morgen, and you have an Aryan wife and a son to look after, don't you?"

This was the worst question he could be given, Maurice thought. He had to respond quickly in hopes of not jeopardizing the welfare of his family. "My wife has her mother and other family members to look after her. I haven't seen her in a while." Maurice wanted to keep up the farce that began when he went to France with the impending occupation.

"Yes, yes. We know all about your cowardice and abandonment of your wife and child, Herr Morgen," he said with a thin smile. "We'll see if she comes to your rescue now since you obviously weren't man enough to stick around to watch the German Army march in and take over this pathetic little country."

Maurice didn't reply. He looked at the Gestapo agent as stoically as he could manage.

"Now, Herr Morgen, what is it you do to keep money in your pocket? How do you eat?"

"I …. I get by. I have a few colleagues who help me. I don't need much," Maurice said as calmly as he could.

"Yes, I see that you are a very lean man, Herr Morgen," the Gestapo agent was too polite as he continued to address him as Herr Morgen. Maurice was afraid of what was to come.

"Do you know that some of your, ah, colleagues were carrying diamonds, Herr Morgen?"

"No, sir. I didn't know that."

"Take off your jacket and empty your pockets," the Gestapo ordered.

Maurice stood and did as he was told. One of the other agents moved to his side of the table and patted him down. He was told to turn his pockets inside out. The only items that were now on the table was his wallet containing the francs he had, a handkerchief, and a cigarette case and lighter. The agents passed the items around and examined everything. Finally the interrogating agent remarked, "Quite a bit of money for a man with no job, don't you think, Herr Morgen?"

"Yes, well, it's all the money I have. When it is gone I will have nothing left to live on," Maurice said with as much honesty as he could muster.

The agent laughed. Then all of the Gestapo laughed. This was very unnerving to Maurice. More so than any of the questions he had been asked.

"Well, Herr Morgen, since you don't have diamonds, yet you were picked up with some men who had them, you must have another expertise, hmmm?"

"No, sir."

"Perhaps you are working against the German Occupation, eh? Perhaps you belong to a Resistance cell, do you think?"

"No, sir."

"Maybe you are a spy, Herr Morgen."

"No, sir."

"No, sir? Every answer is no? Then why were you with a group of men who have politics against the Third Reich, Herr Morgen?"

"I don't know, sir."

"Well, now, we are not going to waste our time right now, Morgen. We still have one of your colleagues to question. You will be put in a cell here in the prison and you will be told what crime you will be charged with when we are ready. Get him out of here, the agent barked."

Another Gestapo opened the door and ordered two guards to take Maurice to a cell. Maurice grabbed his jacket off of the bench and was shoved through the door by one of the guards.

As they wound their way through several corridors, he was put in a very small cell by himself. The heavy door was shut and locked from the outside. Maurice blinked several times as his eyes adjusted. There was a little light coming from the small window at the top of the rear cell wall. He turned and saw a crude iron bed with a thin mattress. A small blanket was folded at the bottom of the mattress and there was a bucket in the corner to relieve himself.

Maurice hadn't let himself think about the possibility of arrest. If he kept his hopes for the end of the war and a defeat of the Germans, he felt that he wouldn't be captured. Yet he had made no real attempt to hide. When Maurice felt he could safely maneuver his way in the darkness of night to be with his wife and son, he did. By continuing to deal in diamonds and gold he could provide his family a little more than they had without him. Maurice Morgen had often vowed to himself that he would not abandon his family in order to save his own skin. Even now, in the semidarkness of this prison cell, he held out hope that he might be let go if there was no proof of illegal business activity.

Maurice gave very little thought to the fact that he was a Jew. Perhaps he would be sent to a work camp in Germany, he thought. Many men from families in Brussels had been sent to work there, and they wrote their families every week. The war couldn't last too much longer after the Americans come over, he mused. These new ideas kept dancing in his head as he sat on the edge of the bed and finally lay down. He could see Suzanne's face when he closed his eyes and began to drift into sleep.

Prison

Suzanne walked out of the bakery, and placed the small loaf of bread in the basket of her bicycle. She was mounting it to ride to a butcher on the Chausee Ninove in hopes of finding a small piece of beef or bones to make a soup. She was almost under way when Amand pulled up beside her and told her to ride alongside of him. Suzanne didn't answer and pedaled to keep up with her long-time friend.

They rounded the corner, and when Amand could see no one near them, he slowed to a stop and Suzanne followed his lead. They pulled over to a side street and walked their bikes around the corner. Amand could see the anxiety in Suzanne's lovely face.

"I won't waste time, my friend. I learned late last night that Maurice was picked up by the Gestapo the day before yesterday," Amand said.

Suzanne drew in her breath and gasped just a little bit.

"Listen, Suzanne; he was picked up with seven others in a café. They were all listed as political detainees. That is not so bad, you know," Amand tried to give her hope.

"Where is he now?" Suzanne managed to ask.

"In St. Gilles. I don't know much else. If they don't have proof of any political activity, it's possible that he may be released," Amand said.

"All right," Suzanne croaked. "What should I do?"

"Nothing. You can do nothing. You will receive an official letter about his imprisonment. You mustn't let on that you already know or they will know he is involved in a network and the other men, too," Amand warned.

"I won't, Amand. I promise," Suzanne said.

"Go home. I wanted to tell you so that if the Gestapo comes in person, you won't have a shock. Are you all right, Suzanne?" asked Amand.

71

"Yes," she said hesitating. "I'm all right. I'll go home right now. Thank you, Amand. Thank you for telling me."

Suzanne turned her bicycle around and began to ride home. As she did the tears streamed down her face, but the wind blew them dry just as quickly as they fell.

****

Serge had been at his grandmother's house. Suzanne did not go over and get him, nor did she tell her mother the news. She went into the living room and sat down staring at nothing at all.

After nearly an hour she heard the footsteps of the postman. Suzanne flung the front door open before Monsieur DuBois reached it.

"Hello Madame," the postman said politely. He handed her an envelope. As he did, a compassionate look spread across his face. Suzanne took the envelope and could see clearly that it was from St. Gilles Prison.

She didn't say a word to the postman. She turned away from him and shut the door behind her. Suzanne walked into the dining room and picked up a knife to slit open the flap on the envelope. Her hands trembled and she managed to sit down before removing the letter within the envelope. As she opened the folded pages the large type in German assaulted her senses.

Wehrmachtuntersuchungsgefangnis. And then in the handwriting of her husband was his name: *Morgen, Moszek*. She saw the next sentences were in both German and French and she quickly read the rest.

I am here in the prison at St.-Gilles, and please send me as soon as possible, a package with clothes and toiletries, sealed and bound with twine, not in a suitcase: *1 shirt, 6 handkerchiefs, 2 hand towels, 2 pairs of socks, 1 shaving cream.* Also include these groceries: *bread, butter, sardines, jam and eggs.* Maximum weight of package, 6 kilos. This package can be delivered Monday, Tuesday, Thursday or Friday afternoon,

72

between 1500 – 1700 hours in prison, and it must have name and cell number.

Maurice signed his name: *M. Morgen.* It was counter signed by Abteilung *A. Schmide.*

Suzanne stared at the page. She felt totally numb. She knew his handwriting and was sure this form was filled out by Maurice, but she wished he could have written a few more words.

After a few more minutes, she realized how stupid she was. Obviously he wasn't allowed to write more and she should be happy to know that he was all right, and that he was permitted to receive clothing and food. She folded the page and put it safely in the drawer of the buffet thinking about the items she needed to get together to deliver the package tomorrow afternoon.

Suzanne ran out of the back door to her mother's and burst into the dining room. "*Maman,*" she said loudly, "Maurice is in St. Gilles prison."

Eva was seated at the table writing a letter. She dropped the pen and exclaimed, "What are you saying?"

"I found out this morning that he was arrested with some other men by the Gestapo as a political prisoner. Amand found me and told me. When I got home the postman brought a letter from the prison," Suzanne said.

"And, what did it say?" Eva demanded.

"Not much. Only a form that Maurice filled out and asked for some clothing and food. I can bring it there tomorrow between three and five o'clock," Suzanne said.

"Oh, Suzanne, this is so terrible. What will happen now?" asked Eva.

"I don't know, *Maman,* but at least I know he is alive and can receive food. Maybe they will release him. Please, *Maman,* don't say anything to make me lose hope. I have to believe that they will release him eventually," Suzanne said in desperation.

Eva looked at her daughter and responded, "Of course, Suzanne. They often pick up political suspects and then find no proof, and they release them. We know some of these people."

"Yes, we do, *Maman*. They will release him if they have no proof," Suzanne uttered.

She sat down and put her face into her hands and cried softly. Eva rose and put her arm around Suzanne's shoulders trying to comfort her. She spoke softly to her daughter, "We will get through this together. Somehow we will. Now you must prepare the things Maurice needs so that you can deliver the package as quickly as possible. I'll keep Serge here. He doesn't need to see you so upset. If you want to come and get him later, just come over for supper. All right, *cherie?*"

Suzanne nodded and pulled a handkerchief out of her pocket and dried her face. She left her mother's home, and set about the task of getting the items Maurice needed in prison.

****

A week had passed since Suzanne delivered the package addressed to her husband in St. Gilles prison. She had asked if she would be able to visit him and had been told not at this time. The desk clerk had stared at her for a long time before he told her she was dismissed and took the package.

When she left the prison she walked a few blocks to the apartment of Josette and Felix. They were both at home and invited her to stay for supper after she told them everything she knew about Maurice's arrest. Suzanne declined the invitation. She had needed to see her friends but didn't want to burden them with her terrible sadness.

As she walked to the tram stop, a man came along side of her and addressed her in French. "Madame Morgen," he said.

Suzanne was startled and looked at the man closely. He was in civilian clothes and did not look like a German but had an accent. "Yes," she finally replied.

74

"I saw that you were at the prison today, and I would like to help you," he spoke quietly.

"Help me?" she questioned. "How can you help me?" asked Suzanne.

"I am in and out of the prison on official business every day, and I have influence over the Gestapo," he explained matter of factly.

"I still don't understand," Suzanne whispered in fear someone walking past would hear her.

"I can see to it that your husband is released," he said. "They have no proof of any crime that he did. If you can get me some money, I believe I can have your husband released," he spoke in a self-assured manner.

Suzanne hesitated fearing for her own safety but finally she grasped at the hope of Maurice's freedom. "How much money do you want, Monsieur?"

"25,000 francs, Madame Morgen. That is not too much for one's freedom, is it?" he gave her a thin smile.

Suzanne nodded at him, and he quickly gave her instructions of where and when to deliver the money. As quickly as he had appeared at her side, he disappeared leaving a stunned young woman with yet another obstacle to conquer on her own.

****

Three days after she had been to the prison, Suzanne was walking briskly towards the Place du Grand Sablon. Although it was May 1, the sky was gray, and the threat of rain hung heavily in the air. If these were normal times, Suzanne thought, she would be hurrying to meet Josette in the park. Times hadn't been normal for nearly two years as the Germans occupied their city and country.

Suzanne had learned that the man who had approached her about freeing Maurice was an Italian named Contucci. He made contact with her on the Chausee Ninove while doing her shopping the next day, and was joined by a second Italian he called Nicolette. More detailed instructions were given to Suzanne, and the Italians told her that a Gestapo agent would meet her to pick up the money. They assured her that the German would take care of the release of her husband.

Most of the benches were empty, and she chose one that was far from another that was occupied. Suzanne had a shopping bag with her and she pulled out a magazine and began to leaf through it as though she had nothing better to do on this dreary spring day.

Nearly ten minutes passed, and Suzanne began to get very nervous. What if the Gestapo agent did not come to the park as the Italians had told her, she wondered. Thoughts of betrayal and punishment flashed through her mind as she continued to wait looking towards the street entrance of the park. After another five minutes, a man seated himself on the end of her bench. Suzanne was startled since he had come from behind her.

It had to be him. In that very instant Suzanne felt a wave of relief, and she looked at the man. The man tipped his hat. He had a newspaper under his arm, and he laid it next to her. Suzanne looked away and kept turning the pages of her magazine. The next five minutes seemed like an eternity as she tried to concentrate on her movements finally placing the magazine into the folded paper. The German stood up and smoothed out his trench coat. He leaned towards the center of the bench, and picked up his newspaper with an unnoticeable thick magazine in it.

Tucking the bundle under his arm, he moved away from the bench passing in front of Suzanne and headed toward the main entrance of the park. Suzanne stared at his back until she could no longer see him because of the hedges. She looked around at the mostly empty grounds, and felt assured that no one had paid any attention to the man or to her.

Moments later Suzanne was walking away heading for the tram stop so that she could get back to her house and her family. As she hurried, she prayed that these men would keep their promise to buy

Maurice's freedom. It had taken several pieces of jewelry for her to raise the 25,000 francs, and she hoped desperately that it was enough.

The Visit

Every two weeks Suzanne delivered packages to St. Gilles Prison, so that her beloved husband might have fresh clothing and something decent to eat while they awaited his fate. She had not been contacted by the German to whom she gave the money for her husband's freedom. Every day when Suzanne went about her errands, she prayed he would appear to tell her Maurice would be released.

Finally on May 24 she received a light brown envelope addressed to her in Maurice's handwriting. As she carefully opened it, her hands were shaking with anticipation.

Warden Schmide's name was at the top of the letter, and the first page was a printed form with instructions. Suzanne scanned the page for the French translation and read:

General Instructions: The prisoners must write on the lines. The prisoners must write legibly and strictly about family affairs. The prisoners must not reminisce about life in prison. No objects may be placed inside the correspondence.

Correspondence: In general each prisoner can write and receive one letter every two weeks. They cannot write letters to the German court. If they abuse this, all correspondence will be terminated. All letters are censored.

Visits: The visits (3 visitors maximum) will be admitted Monday, Tuesday, Thursday, and Friday in the afternoon between 2:30 and 5 o'clock. One visit every two weeks with written authorization from the police or the military tribunal. Condemned prisoners, after judgment, may have visitors every 8 weeks. Children between 3 and 16 will not be admitted for visits.

Packages: Packages with laundry and food are allowed every 2 weeks during the visitation hours.

Suzanne carefully opened the letter that was folded in half. There, clearly written on the lines, was Maurice's handwriting.

Very dear families,

I am doing well, and I received the package with great pleasure. Dear Suzanne, in the next package, send me 1pair of overalls to keep my trousers clean. 1 shirt and as much to eat as possible. 4 breads, 1 pack of tobacco, sardines and a few cubes of sugar.

I suppose you are continuing to go for massage. Write me anything of interest. Ask for money from the office to live on. I left my money, about 7,000 francs. When you go for the papers and for the package, ask at the same time to be able to visit me, that will give me great pleasure.

Kiss the little one for me and send me a few photos. I have nothing else to write other than I hope for the best. I kiss you tenderly. Best to all.

Mau

The tears started flowing down her face, and Suzanne quickly put the letter on the dining room table so that her tears would not blot out his beautifully written words. She was ecstatic to have this letter after nearly a month, and to know for a fact that he was still alive. Suddenly she bolted from her chair and grabbed the calendar that was on the table by the telephone. She counted the days since the last package was delivered and knew she could visit with a new package on Friday if she could get a letter of authorization.

Suzanne quickly wrote a letter to Maurice telling him they were all in good health and lied about having plenty to eat so that he wouldn't worry. She was careful to write only about family and not break any of the censor rules. After addressing the envelope and placing the postage on it, Suzanne dashed out of the house to the post office so that it would be delivered before her visit.

****

As Suzanne left the police station, she was totally despondent. The desk sergeant had told her she would have to come back in a week to pick up the authorized letter to visit her husband in prison. The thought of waiting another week seemed like an eternity. She was desperate to see her Maurice.

Although she was only 25-years-old, Suzanne's legs felt heavy and her mind and body were weary as she trudged to the tram stop. The package that she carried would have to be delivered to St. Gilles Prison, and left to the guards to deliver to her husband so that he might have better nourishment even though she couldn't see him. Suzanne went through the motions feeling so utterly alone in the world.

*****

The following Friday Suzanne received the same news at the police station; she would have to check again in a few days. This time, when she was sure she was totally alone on the street, she let her tears flow and choked back the sobs as she rode her bicycle through the streets towards home. There wasn't a package to deliver, and she decided to let her misery engulf her.

Suzanne was able to get through the afternoon by doing the routine work that was always a part of her life and the lives of all the wives she knew. She became absorbed in ironing their clothes, and was relieved when it was all neatly stacked and hung in their armoires.

Before she began preparing supper, Suzanne phoned her mother and told her to come over with Francine and Serge so they would eat together. She had made a soup the day before and she didn't want to spend the evening alone after her morning disappointment.

Just before they sat down for supper, someone knocked on her front door. Suzanne rushed toward the front hall and could see the postman through the window and quickly opened the door.

"Madame Morgen, I was at the office late, and had the mail that will be delivered tomorrow. When I saw the one from the prison, I thought it might give you pleasure to receive it right away," he said graciously as he handed it to Suzanne.

"Oh, my," Suzanne's face lit up as she reached for the envelope. "Thank you, Monsieur DuBois, you are too kind. Thank you."

The postman smiled, turned and walked away.

Suzanne couldn't help herself and smiled at his thoughtfulness. She opened the letter quickly as her mother and sister begged to know what it said. The young wife read aloud:

June 6, 1942
Very dear family,
I received the second package and it gave me great pleasure. I am doing well and my thoughts are with you. Dear, Suzanne, take the documents to be able to visit which will give me great pleasure. Write me a letter. You can write every 2 weeks. Send me if possible vitamins, a light weight trouser and. If you want to make a partial package, ask for a paper for an exception for the clothing.

I pass my time reading a book. Ask Maman to help you a little with your work at home. Send me by mail 200 francs because I don't have any more money for the canteen.

Try to find out the reason for my incarceration. Do everything possible to get me out of here.

I kiss you very tenderly and also my child and the family.
Bebe

Yes, it is wonderful to have news today after so many disappointments with the police, Suzanne thought. Then she realized that he hadn't received all of the packages she sent. He had only received two! At first she thought about making a complaint at the prison, and then she laughed at herself. What difference would it make to them? The dirty Germans. They did what they wanted. Rules were their rules, and they could break them but the Belgians had to obey.

Suzanne had risked everything to deliver the 25,000 francs to the German. The Italian assured her that her husband would be set free. How stupid she had been to believe him. At that moment she decided that she, a Belgian citizen and wife of a political prisoner, would go to the police station every day to ask for her letter of authorization to visit her husband. If she made a pest of herself, perhaps the *Boche* would give it to her just to be done with her.

******

On June 13th Suzanne walked away from the tram. The sun was bright, and it heartened her spirit. The letter with the printed rules for visitation was placed carefully in Suzanne's handbag. As she approached St. Gilles Prison, the guard recognized her and was prepared to receive the package.

"Just a minute," she said in a pleasant voice. "I have a printed letter explaining that family can visit a prisoner with proper authorization."

"Yes, Frau. Do you have written authorization?" the guard was matter of fact in his demeanor.

"Yes. Suzanne reached into her handbag and pulled out the second document that she had obtained at the police station, and showed it to the guard.

After a few moments, he threw open the gate, and told her that at the prison door another guard would look at the document and show her the way.

Suzanne tried not to think about something going wrong. She went through the process of having the document checked and rechecked. The package she carried was examined as was her handbag for any forbidden objects. Finally she was led to a room for visitation where she was told to be seated and wait for the prisoner. She could barely contain the excitement she felt.

While she waited Suzanne finally began to look around. The room was large with a very high ceiling and dull gray painted walls. There were narrow windows that you couldn't reach but they let in the daylight. She was seated at a long wooden table with a few chairs on each side. The air was damp and cool and she imagined it would be dreadfully cold in the winter.

Finally the door opposite her was flung open by a German guard, and a very thin man walked behind the guard while another guard followed him. She got to her feet and saw Maurice. Her heart sank for a moment until he smiled at her, and then she smiled back as tears welled in her eyes.

The guard ordered her to be seated, and she was. Maurice was ordered to sit across from her. They sat staring at each other for several moments, and then he reached for her hand. Suzanne tore the gloves from her hands and placed his hands in hers as if she were protecting him.

"Oh my darling *Bebe*," Maurice whispered hoarsely. His throat was thick with the emotion he felt at that moment. The prisoner was filled with more love for his wife than he had ever felt during their lives together.

"Maurice, *cheri*," she said with a longing that showed in her eyes. "I have missed you desperately. Are you really all right, my darling?"

"Yes, Suzanne, I am. Truly, I am," he tried to assure her.

"You have lost so much weight. Have they given you my packages?" asked Suzanne.

"Yes, and I thank you so much, darling. How is our little son? How is the family?"

"Everyone is fine, Maurice. Serge is growing like a weed now. He'll soon be three years old."

"I know it is almost his birthday. Are you planning a party?"

"I haven't thought about it, darling. I .... Well, it hasn't seemed very important," Suzanne said.

"But it is important," Maurice said. "Every child knows that his birthday is important. Please, *Bebe*, plan a party in the garden with the family and with the friends. Tell me you will."

Suzanne looked at her husband with wonder. He was so selfless. "Of course I will. It is nearly a month from now. Perhaps you will be home."

"Shhh," Maurice whispered even lower. "Don't talk about things that might be."

She understood that she might be breaking a rule. They talked for another five minutes about the family and Maurice tried to make a point, without saying names, that she should get help from his friends. Suzanne understood the men he meant that she could go to for money.

"Listen to me, Suzanne," Maurice said. "We may only have a few minutes left. I want you to do everything I told you so that you will be prepared for the future. The new baby will need milk and medicines. You must have enough money. Promise me you will do everything to claim all of my money," his voice had become barely audible.

Suzanne nodded slowly. She understood that he was owed money by several colleagues. Months before Maurice had told her to take several diamonds and rubies along with gold to their friend and jeweler who lived on a nearby street. Jean van Leda had designed and cast several rings, bracelets and brooches for her, but until now Suzanne had not needed to sell any. The value of the gems was worth more than francs and was the family's safety net for the duration of the war.

"I promise, Maurice, I promise to do everything. I just want you to come home," Suzanne croaked out the last words.

At just that moment, one of guards stepped forward and said loudly, "The visitation is over. The prisoner will be returned to his cell."

Maurice squeezed his wife's hand and got up immediately. There was no hesitation on his part. He knew he must obey orders instantly to avoid repercussions.

Suzanne stared at him as he turned and walked through the door with the guard who had remained stationed by it. The guard who spoke French announced, "Frau, you must leave this room and exit the prison." He strode to the door as Suzanne rose and picked up her gloves from the table. By the time she turned around, the door was open, and she almost ran out of the room. She was escorted to the outdoor courtyard where she finally took a few deep breaths, put on her gloves, and walked quickly to the gate where she was let out onto the street.

At that moment Suzanne wanted to sit down and cry. She wanted her husband to be there to hold her in his arms and soothe her fears. At the same time, she couldn't wait to get far away from the prison to the relative safety of her own home and family, and so she hurried down the street to await the tram.

The Accusation

Three of the men arrested with Maurice had been set free after about one week in jail. Amand had brought her that news, and had told her to keep up her hope. Suzanne had not told Amand that she had paid the German man, a Gestapo man she had figured, to get Maurice freed. She hadn't wanted Amand to be mixed up in this mess more than he was. As each day passed her hope diminished.

On June 17 Suzanne, her mother and little Serge were sitting in the sun drenched garden. Her son would soon be three years old, and she had endured his illnesses, her country's occupation and the imprisonment of her husband. In her current pregnant condition she often felt that she should give up hoping to ever have a happy life again.

Suzanne's reverie was interrupted by her mother. "Suzanne, I think the postman is approaching. I heard the bell on his bicycle."

"I'll walk around front," Suzanne offered lifting herself out of the garden chair.

My mother has good hearing, she thought as she watched the postman's arrival. He stopped at two other houses before he reached her.

"Anything for me or my mother, Monsieur DuBois?"

"Yes, Madame. For you. Nothing for your mother today. Good bye, Madame," he said after handing the mail to her.

Suzanne leafed through a few envelopes and then saw the German envelope. Fear gripped her instantly but she continued to the garden and took her chair quickly.

"What is it, Suzanne?"

Suzanne didn't answer, but her mother saw the fear in her eyes and waited for her daughter to open the envelope.

There was only one sheet of paper that was typed. It was all in German and then as she focused on the top of the page, her breath caught in her throat, and she gasped audibly.

"Suzanne!" her mother shouted.

"It is from Breendonk, *Maman*," she uttered.

"Oh, it can't be possible," Eva's voice trailed away with disbelief.

Suzanne nodded as she sat stunned by the realization that her husband was no longer in St. Gilles Prison. The letter was dated the 16th. Maurice was now in the Concentration Camp outside of Brussels.

Eva stood up, "Give me the letter, Suzanne. I'll go over to Madame Temperman and ask her to translate it for us."

Suzanne only looked at her mother with eyes that implored her to bring back news that she was wrong. She handed her the letter.

Eva walked over to her neighbor and knocked at the back door. It was opened quickly by Madame Temperman, and Eva disappeared into the house. As the long-time neighbor and friend read the brief letter, she shook her head with sad acknowledgement.

"Madame Duchesne, this is not good news."

"I know that. Please tell me what it says," Eva requested.

"Yes, of course I will." Madame Temperman translated quickly to Eva. "You are notified of the prisoner that is sitting in jail, to send the ration card, validated, no later than June 25, 1942, to this prison. This time frame is very important, and must be kept. The letter is signed, the Warden, *Sturbannfurhrer.*"

Madame Temperman handed back the letter. "I cannot read the warden's name, it isn't legible."

"What does it matter," Eva said in a low voice. "Thank you, Madame. I will have to tell Suzanne."

"Please tell Suzanne how terribly sorry I am, will you?" Madame Temperman said.

Eva nodded and walked out into the sunshine towards her daughter's garden. Serge was sitting on his mother's lap and Eva sat in her own chair.

"Well, *Maman*, what did it say?"

Eva told her daughter what Madame Temperman had said and emphasized the importance of returning the ration card very promptly.

Suzanne didn't answer. She was absorbed envisioning Maurice in that dreadful old fortress that had ceased to serve any purpose for hundreds of years until the Nazis came and made a concentration camp there. It was only 25 kilometers from the city, and when the newspapers had reported that prisoners were being kept there and forced to work like slaves, Belgians were horrified.

At that moment Suzanne gave up hope. She could no longer believe that the ransom she had paid for her husband's release would one day free him. Suzanne had clung to that tiny strand of hope for weeks and with the arrival of this letter with the name Breendonk at the top, her best expectation could only be that Maurice might survive the rest of this damn war imprisoned just outside of Brussels.

****

On the Saturday after she had received the news of Maurice's new imprisonment, Suzanne rested quietly on the sofa after dinner. Francine took Serge for a long walk to Dilbeek so that she could nap.

The expectant mother tried to think pleasant thoughts to lull her into a peaceful sleep, but she kept thinking about the conditions her husband must survive. As ordered, Suzanne had taken his ration card to the city hall and gotten it validated. She asked the clerk in charge how she could ensure its delivery to Breendonk within the time allowed. The clerk told her to mail it right away and there should be no problem.

Suzanne had never been to Breendonk. It was not open to visitors as a museum or a landmark. It was

88

just an old, dirty fortress that was surrounded by Flemish farms. Not far from its location was the small town of Malines, known as Mechelen in the Flemish language. She had heard some stories through her acquaintances in the Resistance, that Jews and political prisoners were transported from Malines by train to work camps and concentration camps in Germany. How convenient for them, Suzanne thought, to have a fortress as a holding spot before deporting Belgians to Germany.

She flung her arm across her eyes as she lay on the sofa trying to block these thoughts from her mind. Suzanne felt totally helpless and couldn't imagine how she could help Maurice now.

After about thirty minutes, Suzanne got up from the sofa. Although sleep evaded her, she had rested a bit and decided to get on with some of her daily housework before Francine came home with Serge.

As Suzanne sorted through a basket of clothes to be mended, she heard the bicycle bell of the postman. She arrived at the front door before he did and anxiously awaited the mail. She hoped for more news. Perhaps Maurice would be allowed to write to her and she could learn of his condition.

Moments later the postman handed her only one envelope. The imprinted name and address were in German. Just touching the letter made her fear the contents. The postman didn't say a word. He tipped his cap and turned away. Suzanne walked back inside and leaned against the front door as she shut it.

She didn't hesitate for another moment, and walked through the back and found her mother at her own back door. "*Maman*, please come with me to Madame Temperman. I have another letter in German."

Eva did as she was asked and the two women walked the few steps to their neighbor with dread in their hearts. Madame Temperman answered the door only a moment after Eva had knocked. She had been busy cleaning and was now drying her hands on her apron.

Suzanne began, "Madame Temperman, I need your help again to read this letter I've just received."

"Why of course, Suzanne," the small, wiry woman answered. "Come and sit at the table. The children are all at the park playing so we won't be disturbed."

Madame Temperman was in her mid-thirties and had three children. Serge would often play with little Emil in the garden or on the playground. Recently Madame Temperman had told them she had just learned she was pregnant again and that their unborn children would make good playmates in the future. Eva wondered why after having three healthy children she would allow herself to be pregnant again. It seemed like the Flemish were determined to have more babies just to outnumber the Walloons.

"Suzanne," Madame Temperman interrupted Eva's thoughts, "you haven't opened the letter." The neighbor handed her a knife she kept on the table for the mail.

Suzanne opened the end of the envelope carefully and withdrew two pieces of paper. It was an official document. She handed it quickly to Madame Temperman who scanned it briefly. Before even looking at the second page, she said, "Suzanne, this is very serious. I will translate it as accurately as I can."

"Is it about my husband," Suzanne interrupted her.

"No, it is written to you."

Suzanne's mouth opened as if the cry out, but she did not. Eva was stiff with fear and asked, "Please, Madame, please read it."

"It is from the Court of the General, 672, and dated yesterday, the 20th of June. This court is writing to: Suzanne Augustine Morgen Duchesne. She is a Belgian citizen born September 21, 1917, in Thisnes, living in Anderlecht – Brussels at 31 rue Virgile. The charges: She is accused on May 1, 1942 in Brussels of bribery. She offered a superior military official gifts or other bribes of 25,000 francs for her husband to be set free.

90

"The charges are paragraph 333 of RSTGB. The evidence is: she confessed. Your punishment is to sit in prison for three weeks. The 25,000 Belgian Francs was given to the military. After the punishment announcement has been made, you have 3 days to appeal, in writing or verbally, to the judge or by an officer, the one that charged you, to drop the charges. By written appeal, it must arrive within 3 days."

Madame Temperman paused and looked directly at Suzanne. Suzanne nodded indicating her to continue reading.

"In case of the involvement of the Rechtskraft, and interference, I order that these charges will apply until the end of the war.

"The judge in charge of this case has the ultimate power over this case."

"It is signed by *Feldjustizinspektor Reber*," Madame Temperman concluded. Now Madame Temperman looked directly into Eva's eyes as if for guidance.

"Suzanne," her mother said forcefully as if to awaken her daughter who sat limply at the table. "You must respond immediately to appeal. We must deliver the appeal on Monday in order to meet the three day allowance."

"Will it make any difference?" Suzanne asked weakly.

Her mother was even sterner now. "If you don't, you will be in jail for three weeks. How can you survive even three weeks in your condition? Suzanne, you must listen to me."

"All right, *Maman*." She began to rise and turned to Madame Temperman. "Thank you for helping us with this," her voice trailed away.

"Oh, Suzanne, don't thank me. I wish I could do something to help you. Good luck, my dear."

Mother and daughter left their neighbor and went to Eva's house. Francine was inside with Serge and they were at work coloring a drawing they had composed the day before.

"Look, *Maman*, at how pretty I'm making the picture," the little boy smiled at his mother.

"Yes, *cheri*, I see how beautiful it is," Suzanne said.

Francine was looking at her sister and knew something was terribly wrong. Eva spoke before her younger daughter had a chance. "I will tell you later, Francine. Suzanne and I are going to her house to work on a letter together. You stay here with Serge, all right."

"Yes, *Maman*," Francine obeyed but wanted to know what was going on.

Suzanne kissed the top of Serge's head and in those few minutes she knew she had to appeal. She couldn't risk being in jail and of harm coming to her. She had to be there for her son and for the new baby. The *Boche* might really hurt her in jail. She had heard stories about the abuses of women. She would write a letter of appeal to deny any guilt.

Breendonk

There was a cloud of fog lying over the fields as a troop truck approached the gate in front of the old fortress. A dozen prisoners were inside with two German soldiers as guards. Maurice could hear the exchange of orders and acknowledgement between the driver and the guard at the gate. He understood the German because of his knowledge of Yiddish.

It was dark inside of the truck except for the murky, gray light near the tailgate. They proceeded over a bumpy drive and then came to a stop and the engine was cut. One of the soldiers from the front came around and opened the tailgate and their guards jumped down and then order the prisoners to do the same. The guards had their rifles pointed at the prisoners.

Each of them had a small bag with a couple of changes of clothes, soap, razors and personal possessions. They had been told to bring them. The prisoners jumped off the tailgate with their bags and made room for the next and then the next man to jump down. They didn't speak and waited for a command.

Within a few minutes a military officer came around from the front of the truck and spoke to them in German. He shouted, "Jews line up on the left and others on the right." Maurice moved to the left side reluctantly since he considered himself a political prisoner but had no choice now. Two others were on the left side, also.

The military man, a captain, Maurice thought, walked over to the left. "So, no yellow stars on your coats, I see." He poked Maurice in the shoulder with his baton, "How long were you in St. Gilles prison?"

Maurice didn't hesitate, "Since April."

"No wonder," the captain snorted. "Now we make all the Jewish pigs where yellow stars on their coats." He gave a laugh to no one in particular. "It won't matter in here. All Jews are kept together to live like the swine they are."

Maurice heard the words and he was very afraid. When the captain turned his attention to the other prisoners, Maurice told himself to stand straight and not let this German bully make him feel less of a man. The captain didn't have anything kind to say to others either.

The captain backed away and addressed them all, "You are here to work. That is your punishment for the crimes you have committed. You will be taken inside now and put in your cells. You will receive regulations from the cell block leaders. They will tell you what you can and cannot do. If you break a rule, you will be severely punished. Remember that. Anything you remember about the trouble you were involved in that got you here will make it easier for you.

"Guards, take the men inside to their cells now," the captain ordered.

As Maurice followed the order he could see many prisoners at work in the yard around the big stone walls of the fortress. He could hear the sound of pick axes and stones hitting the shell of wheel barrels. This did not make him fearful. He would rather be outdoors working and getting to breathe clean air rather than staying in the dank, dark cell like he was at St. Giles.

They were ordered into an ante room to their right after passing through a gated corridor that was padlocked when they were all inside. After a few minutes an officer came in and spoke in German and then in French. He told them they had to leave their bags in this room. They were not to be trusted with razors and they would all be issued uniforms. Then they were ordered to only keep their identity cards. They would be interrogated soon and would need the cards. Maurice was happy he had placed a very small photo of Suzanne in the breast pocket of his shirt. He would make sure to remove it when he was given the uniform to put on. Her beautiful face kept his hope alive whenever he would look at it.

In short order they were shouted at to leave the room and their belongings and exit through a rear door and follow the guard. Soon the men were walking down a wide corridor with high, arched ceilings. The walls and ceilings were stone and were painted white. Single light bulbs hung down from above about every ten meters.

They were ordered to halt and a cell door was opened. There were many wooden bunk beds stack two high with lumpy mattresses in the cell. On the opposite wall in the hallway, there were several small sinks with hot and cold water taps. The political prisoners were ordered inside the cell and two guards stayed behind with them.

Two other guards escorted the Jews down the long corridor passing two more large cells and then a latrine at the end of the hall that was made out of yellow ceramic tiles. Maurice and his companions whom he had never met before were told to turn left.

The corridor looked the same and there were two large cells on the right. There were no wash basins or water taps across from the cells. There were even more bunks crammed into the cells and the stench was overwhelming. The wooden bunks had thin blankets on them with straw sticking out from underneath. There were two buckets standing in the far corner smelling of piss and shit. Maurice almost gagged. He thought briefly of his earlier reverie about breathing fresh air and working outside. The thought of returning to this hell hole almost made him cry out in anguish.

They were ordered inside the empty cell and told they would receive uniforms and orders soon. The guards locked them inside and left. After they could not hear the footsteps any longer, the three Jews looked at each other. They introduced themselves in whispers and shook hands. At that point, they didn't know what else to say. They just stood and stared out of the cell wondering what fate was in store for each man.

Maurice and the other men had been given blankets and uniforms to change into. They were told to leave their clothing in a pile by the door. The little photo was safely transferred to the striped uniform's breast pocket. He had only glanced quickly at his wife's face not wanting to bring any attention to him.

It was at least seven o'clock before the other Jewish prisoners were returned. They were men of all ages. All of them looked exhausted from the work they were forced to do. As they filed into the cell they took their places in the bunks. The new prisoners stood to the side allowing the men to take up their positions. Before the cell was locked, two other Jewish prisoners came down the hall with a cart and a barrel. One came into the cell and headed for the buckets. He looked old and very tired, but he tried not to spill the contents of the pails. They were dumped into the barrel and as he carried them back to their place the other prisoner put the lid back onto the barrel stopping some of the smell from permeating the area. Maurice saw that the other prisoners paid no attention to this routine and figured everyone must get used to it.

Again, before the cell door was shut and locked, two more prisoners came with another cart. Now the cellmates came to life. They grabbed for tin cups and spoons they had rolled into their blankets and got off their bunks. The big pot on the cart had a ladle. One man ladled the contents into a mug and the other gave a piece of bread that was buried in a big box to each prisoner. As they got their rations they retreated to their bunks or various walls and corners of the room to eat in silence. The cart men signaled to the three newcomers. They had tin cups and spoons for them and gave them each a ration.

Maurice walked back to the wall where he had been and ate in silence. The thin broth with a bit of vegetables and potatoes tasted awful, but he knew he had to eat it. He dunked his bread in the liquid so that it would soften a bit and make it edible.

After a while Maurice heard footsteps. It was the captain they had seen earlier in the day. He hollered out a couple of names and two men got off the bunks and were lead away by a guard. Suddenly the captain looked in his direction and yelled, "Morgen, Moses."

Maurice felt his strength drain away, but answered, *"Oui."*

"Come with me, Morgen," the captain said.

Maurice wrapped his cup inside his blanket and left it on the floor. He walked to the open cell door and waited for someone to lead him. The captain said, "Follow me Morgen," with a wicked smirk on his lips.

He heard the cell door lock behind him. Maurice was only led a short distance down the corridor and made a left turn into a room. The room had a table and a few wooden chairs. A lone, bright light bulb hung over the table. The captain ordered him to sit down.

Presently a man in a very impressive German uniform entered. The captain saluted the officer and then stood near the door. The commander sat across the table from Maurice. "I am Commander Schmitt. I am responsible for the operation of this camp and to make certain that we have all of the information about the prisoners' treason against Germany. Now, give me your papers."

Maurice reached in his pocket and produced his identity card. Schmitt examined it and spoke in a normal tone, "I'm amazed that you use your real identity and do not try to hide that you are a Jew."

"I have nothing to hide. I am a citizen of Belgium and have been for many years," Maurice said.

"Yes, well now that Belgium is occupied by Germany your so-called citizenship is void. You are a Polish Jew, and you will end up like your Polack brothers," he sneered. "But you and I have more important things to discuss tonight, Morgen.

"You were seen selling jewelry to a variety of people. You know that is against the law, do you not?" Schmitt asked with a little smile on his face.

"I used to be a jeweler. I haven't had gems in a long time, Commander," Maurice tried to sound matter of fact.

"It is no good for you to lie, Morgen. We know you sold a brooch to a fellow named Picavet. And you associate with a Jew named Titz who we haven't found yet, but we will."

Commander Schmitt asked Maurice several more questions that seemed fairly unimportant to him so he kept his answers short and wasn't too afraid. Suddenly Schmitt turned around and barked an order to the guard at the door. After a few minutes a blond, muscular German came into the interrogation room. He was dressed in military pants and had a sweater pulled over an athletic shirt.

"Now let's try getting to the bottom of your trafficking in jewels again, Morgen," the commander said in a tone that brought instant fear to Maurice.

"I've told you everything, Commander," Maurice said.

The muscular German grabbed Maurice by the collar on his striped uniform and punched him in the stomach. The breath was taken away from Maurice but before he could even gasp, he was struck by a fist on the right jaw. This made his body fall backwards and he struck the stone wall with his back and his head bounced back and forth a couple of times hitting the same wall. Maurice was then able to take a breath because there was no follow up punch. He began to look across the room at Schmitt and the boot of the blond man hit him squarely on the left side of his ribcage.

The pain from this blow was excruciating. Maurice had never been hit like this at any time in his life. Even in St. Gilles prison, the most he had received were a few slaps to the face to find out about his jewelry deals. Now he huddled down where he had fallen and tried to protect his body with his arms.

Commander Schmitt told the young blond enforcer to wait outside the door. Then he told Maurice to get seated at the table again.

It took Maurice a minute or so to pull himself up and get into the chair. He knew he better act quickly to the orders.

"Now, Morgen, how about telling me about the men you do business with," Schmitt said. "If you do so, you can go back to your cell and we will let you go about your daily work schedule with the other prisoners."

As the interrogation went on, Maurice only told Schmitt about a couple of men he was sure were already under suspicion like Titz was. He didn't think he was giving information that was new. If he didn't tell him something, he would be beaten to death, and he had to try to survive for the sake of his family.

Maurice told Schmitt about Adrien Lamantier. When he did, Schmitt went berserk. Apparently he wanted to capture Adrien for a long time and this news was tantalizing to him. It also made Schmitt feel that Maurice had cooperated with him, and he let him go back to the cell.

The battered prisoner entered the cell and went over to gather his blanket and cup. All he wanted to do was to lie down and sleep. The two men from the train looked at him in horror but the others barely noticed his bloody and puffy jaw.

Maurice saw that there was some room on the second tier of the bunks and decided to take a spot. He felt he had earned it. At least he wouldn't have to sleep on the cold cement floor. No one stopped him from claiming this spot on the bunk. Maurice was new here and they had once been, too. He may live for a while or he might die. This was true of each and every one of the Jews at Breendonk.

It was not yet 5 o'clock in the morning and the sun had already risen when banging and shouting awoke Maurice and his cellmates instantly. Maurice had been in a deep sleep despite the pain in his jaw and his ribs. He could barely climb down from the bunk. The moist air in the cell and the stiffening of his muscles left him hunched over. As the men took turns relieving themselves in the two buckets, Maurice made this his opportunity to massage his side a bit and to try some stretches in order to stand erect. He knew it would be important to look fit to work outdoors.

After about 10 minutes the cart with the food came by and everyone scrambled to retrieve their tin cups and spoons. Maurice, like all of the others, received a ladle filled with some kind of thin porridge and a piece of bread. He observed the long-time prisoners eat very quickly; not like the evening meal that they seemed to savor. When Maurice heard the boots hitting the floor and echoing in the corridor he understood the necessity to eat quickly. Ready or not, they would soon be ordered to leave the cell to work outside.

Reaching the outdoors seemed like heaven for just a moment as Maurice tried to breathe the warm spring air deeply into his lungs. The natural instinct was interrupted by severe pain from his ribs. He thought that they must be broken! He breathed more normally and was glad to be in the yard. Moments later a new officer came out of the old fortress and began giving orders to the guards.

The guards shouted at them in German and while others shouted in French to march to the stone yard on the east side of the building. They were told to hurry. Why were they such lazy Jew swine? There was work to be done. Hurry! Hurry!

Maurice kept up and actually felt better exercising his legs and muscles. He could see some of the old men falling behind. Soon he heard the crack of the guards' night sticks on the backs of those that fell behind. Maurice hoped the guards would not beat the men to death.

When they reached the stone yard, Maurice saw other prisoners coming to work from the cellblock of the political prisoners. He wondered if he knew some of these men from St. Gilles or from his old life in the city.

The prisoner in front of him turned and spoke softly to him.

"Let's work as a team," the prisoner said. "One with the pick axe, the other with the wheelbarrow. My partner is an old man, and he is one that was beaten just a few minutes ago."

Maurice hesitated and then spoke, "Yes, I'd be glad to work with you. I don't want to make mistakes here and stand out."

"You are a smart man. Standing out here is very bad for your future. Now, quiet. We will get our orders," the seasoned prisoner whispered.

As the day progressed, so did the work. They were digging out stones and moving them to another part of the yard. Maurice couldn't imagine the reasons for doing so as the prison camp had been well fortified by many prisoners that came before him. There were barbed wire fences, a moat and thick fortress walls. The Nazis didn't need a reason to work the prisoners to near or real death.

He learned that his work partner's name was Samuel Levine. He had been in Belgium for his entire life after his parents had left Poland right after they married. Throughout the day the two men exchanged a few bits of information about themselves. The work gangs had gotten three breaks for water and only a small chunk of bread at noon. Maurice now knew what the cycle of an entire day was to be. In his heart he prayed that his Suzanne was trying to figure out a way to get him out of here. He was not ready to admit that this would be his plight until the war ended.

Finally, after working for 14 hours, the prisoners were told to stop and line up to return to their cells. Although Maurice was still glad he was outdoors with clean air, he looked forward to lying on his straw mattress to welcome sleep. He prayed that during his sleep he would see the face of his Suzy and his little boy. A faint smile came to his lips with these thoughts. Sleep. Yes, sleep and his dreams would help him keep his hope alive.

The Appeal

Suzanne had written a brief letter of appeal and delivered it to German Headquarters in Anderlecht early on Monday morning. Since receiving the charges against her on Saturday, she had thought about every possible outcome that could become her fate. Now sitting in the waiting area for the clerk to come back with a reply felt like an eternity. She wondered how the Germans had gotten so good at fear they imparted to the citizens of the country they occupied.

After nearly two hours, a clerk came from a doorway on her left and walked towards her. Suzanne stood to receive his message.

In a polite tone the clerk spoke in French. "Frau Morgen, here is the reply to your letter of appeal from the court commander."

Suzanne gave her best effort to receive the sealed envelope with dignity and then asked, "Is it written in German?"

"Yes."

"Will you please translate it for me?" Suzanne asked the clerk not able to think about waiting till she arrived home and sought out Madame Temperman again.

The clerk looked at her and was about to send her away when he had second thoughts. He turned and took a letter opener off of the desk and cut open the envelope. As he did so, Suzanne wondered if he was doing so out of kindness or to see her reaction to the probable bad news inside the envelope.

"Please sit down, Madame," the clerk said.

The clerk knew she was pregnant and perhaps was not as bad as his superiors, Suzanne thought as she took the chair behind her.

He removed the letter and read it to her:

"Frau Suzanne Stephanie Augustine Morgen Duchesne

In Brussels – Anderlecht
Rue Virgile No. 31

She is ordered to appear on Friday 26 June 1942, at 1600 in the building of the address above, Rue des quatre bras 13, Room 2.

If you do not appear, we will come and bring you here by force. This notice is to be brought with you."

The clerk added that it was signed by the 'Sonderfuhrer.'

Suzanne remained expressionless and then stood and asked him to give her the letter. As the clerk handed it to her, he gave her a piece of advice.
"Frau, when you come to the court. Bring your reasons for the appeal in writing and in German. Some of the court does not have a good understanding of French and you will not want them to misunderstand you."
Suzanne hesitated and then thanked the clerk for his advice. He turned quickly and left the room. She put the letter in her purse and left the waiting room.
When she reached the sidewalk, Suzanne took a deep breath of the summer air trying to cleanse the last hours out of her body. As she walked to the tram stop, Suzanne decided how she was going to deal with this. She was determined that she would win her appeal.

"*Maman*, where are you?" Suzanne called out as she reached her mother's home.
"I'll be a moment, Suzanne," her mother called from the second floor.
Suzanne removed her hat and gloves and took a seat at the table as her mother hurried into the dining room.
"Yes, Suzanne, what is the news?" Eva asked.

"I have to appear in court on Friday at four o'clock to give my appeal to them in person. The clerk handed me a letter after I had waited for two hours. I asked him if he would translate it, and he did. He also advised me to bring a written letter of appeal in German so that there won't be any misunderstandings if some of the court officials aren't fluent in French."

Eva nodded slowly, "I see. At least they did not deny you an appeal and that is good news. Now we must make them see that they cannot imprison a Belgian woman who is going to have a baby."

"Let's hope I can convince them of that," Suzanne said with determination. "*Maman*, we can't count on Madame Temperman to write this letter. She is not fluent in writing German. I will ask Amand if there is someone in our Resistance who can do the task."

"I agree, Suzanne," her mother said. "Yes, Amand should know who can help us. But before we get to work on that, let me give you something to eat. You haven't eaten much for days."

"I know, *Maman*. I had no appetite, but I know I must eat. Thank you, *Maman*," Suzanne appreciated how strong her mother had been to help her get through this ordeal.

Amand Von Troch did know a man who could write Suzanne's appeal in German and would be willing to do so. When Eva and she completed their final draft of the appeal, they were both relieved. They had decided to be factual and to ask the court not to be harsh. Amand read the letter and agreed that it was a good plan and promised to have the German version to her by Thursday night.

Suzanne filled the next few days by preparing a birthday party for Serge. He would be three on Saturday and the young mother wanted him to have his family and friends around him no matter what happened. If his mother was taken to prison, the rest of the family and good friends would celebrate with him and assure him his mother would be back soon. No one dared to speak about the child's father.

Francine sat on her sister's bed in the early afternoon of June 26, as Suzanne carefully applied her makeup and fixed her long blond hair with flattering waves. She put on one of the last pair of silk stockings and wore her best maternity suit made out of soft beige polished cotton. The outfit was trimmed with a cocoa brown appliqué around the edges and button holes. Her pumps were of pale ecru leather and she carried a matching purse. She finished the look with a lovely brown, wide brimmed summer hat on which she placed a wide ecru ribbon tied into a simple bow that was seen from the back of her head. Eva had made the maternity outfit for her when she was carrying Serge and the Germans had not yet invaded Europe.

She stood back from the mirror and assessed her appearance. "You look beautiful," Francine told her. "I haven't seen you look this beautiful since Easter when Maurice was here."

Suzanne was startled by her comment, but realized it was true and that her appearance since Maurice's arrest must be dreadful. "Thank you, Francine. I do think I look fine, and I hope that I will impress the court."

"Oh, you will; you will," Francine wanted to reassure her sister. She understood how brave her older sister had to be to go through this. "Come downstairs so that *Maman* can see you."

"I will be there in a moment," Suzanne said. "Go ahead of me, all right?"

Francine hopped off the bed and ran down the stairs to wait with their mother in the dining room. Serge had been put into his crib for his afternoon nap and would be asleep for another hour.

Suzanne looked at herself in the mirror again and took a deep breath. She knew she had to appear in control of herself and her emotions. She would let the court read the letter and ask her questions. Her

106

pregnancy was evident, but her beauty was even more so. As she put a hatpin in place, she would say and do everything necessary to stay out of prison not to jeopardize her family and the new baby.

At 3:30 on the afternoon of June 26, 1942, Suzanne Duchesne Morgen, entered the Palace of Justice. Many people looked at her as she made her entrance. She was stunning. She had passed some of her neighbors on her walk to the tram and they had greeted her and Suzanne returned the pleasantries. Everyone wondered why she was dressed so beautifully on a Friday afternoon and wondered where she was headed. If only they knew, she thought as she walked with her head held high and her back erect.

She crossed the room to the information desk of a clerk and handed him her summons letter. He addressed her in French and told her to have a seat in a waiting area to one side of the large room.

Twenty-five minutes later a German in military uniform came from behind closed doors and walked towards her. Suzanne figured he was a lieutenant. "Are you Frau Morgen?" he asked in a business-like tone.

"Yes," she answered and stood.

"Follow me," he said.

The lieutenant turned, and she followed through the same door he had entered the room. It was a large courtroom with high ceilings and the grandeur was overwhelming. Suzanne took a deep breath and followed the young man towards the front of the room. He stopped and indicated a bench for her to be seated. There were no other officials in the room.

Before the lieutenant turned away, she spoke out. "Lieutenant, I have my appeal written in German to give to the magistrate. Shall I give it to you?"

"No, Frau Morgen. You will have the opportunity when the court is seated." The young German then turned and entered a back room door.

Only a few minutes passed and then two doors opened and five Germans entered and took seats behind large, elaborate judge's bench. The lieutenant followed them and approached Suzanne. He asked her to come forward and take a seat at a table across from the trial court.

Suzanne rose gracefully and strode elegantly to the chair she was shown. She was fully aware that each of the members of the court was staring at her.

A court stenographer entered from the rear and set his machine on a pedestal and prepared himself to begin typing.

After Suzanne was seated, the lieutenant went to the side of the room and stood silently. The official seated in the middle of the court began.

"Do you speak German, Frau Morgen?"

"No, sir."

"I am told that you have a written appeal in German that you would like to present to the court," he said in French.

"Yes, sir."

"Do you understand the charges that have been brought against you, Frau?"

"Yes, I do."

"All right. Lieutenant, bring the letter of appeal to me."

The lieutenant came over to Suzanne as she reached in her purse and withdrew her statement. She handed it to him with a slight smile on her lips.

The official removed it from the envelope and scanned it quickly. "I will read your appeal written in German to the court.

"To the General:

Concerning the accusation against me, here is my response.

You are trying to tell me that I offered a member of the Secret Service 25,000 BRFs so he would try to help to set my husband free from prison in St. Gilles.

This accusation against me is not true at all. What actually happened is the following:

From the other side, someone offered to me, that they could help set my husband free. They know a top official in the security department that would help. I had no grounds not to trust him, I believed him, and met with a top official of the Secret Service, to meet in a café to talk about this matter. There they demanded, in order to free my husband, the sum of 25,000 BRFS. What they offered to do for this money, I believed them, but I did not know that this money was a bribe. In my mind, I thought that this was for the freedom of my husband.

I had no idea that this bribe would injure or interfere with the duties of this official. If the accusation, the bribery stays, I want you to know that it was not me, the accused, that made this offer. On the contrary, they made this offer to me, so I would be involved.

Also, I beg you to not be so harsh on me, because I am expecting a child and that is the reason I fell for this. To set my husband free, I wasn't thinking this was wrong, I believed them and because of these grounds, this appeal is given, I ask for you to not be so harsh. I ask that you lift the 3 weeks in prison time and to return the money that was taken by the military."

The four court officials had listened intently as the appeal was read by the fifth magistrate. Suzanne looked at each of them and rested her eyes on the man in the middle.

"Frau Morgen," he began in French as he put down the letter. "We understand your appeal and thank you for having it written in German to make your case clear. Do you have anything to add?"

"No, sir," Suzanne said.

"Gentlemen, do you have anything you wish to ask Frau Morgen?" asked the magistrate.

One of the others spoke. "Frau Morgen," he began, as he puffed out his chest appearing more threatening. "You are a beautiful Aryan woman. Please tell me and the court why you would marry so beneath yourself."

Suzanne hesitated and her mind raced for the right words. "Sir, before the German occupation, Belgium was a country where all races of people were accepted as citizens. As Belgians. When I met my husband, I met an educated and refined gentleman. I never considered him beneath me."

There were snickers from the magistrates and Suzanne was trembling in her core, fearful that she had been too bold.

The magistrate in charge finally said, "Seeing that there are no further questions, we will dismiss Frau Morgen. You will receive our decision regarding your appeal in a few days.

"Bring in the next person charged, lieutenant," the magistrate said.

Suzanne rose quickly and walked to the back of the room. She could feel all of their eyes watching her exit. Oh, how she hated these men and every stinking *Boche* in the world.

The lieutenant held the door for her, and she nearly ran out of the next room anticipating the soft June air to wash away the filth of the courtroom.

******

Anxiety was with Suzanne and every member of her household except for her little son. They celebrated his birthday in the garden with the neighbors, Madame Temperman and her children and with the Picavets. Her friends did not have children and insisted on bringing the cakes. They managed to buy some that were quite good on the black market trying to ease the stress in Suzanne's life.

Then on July 2 the Gestapo had come to question her at her house and wanted the names of the men she said talked her into giving them money. There had been two with Italian names that she remembered; Contucci and Nicolette. She did not know the German's name,

110

she had told them. Suzanne didn't know and also deemed it safer to involve only the Italians. Her plan seemed to work, and she was called as a witness twice in July.

These times she was summoned to the Palace of Justice by the top military inspector. Each time she went to court she dressed in her most stylish clothes and best hats. Suzanne did not want to appear weak or demoralized.

The visits by Gestapo agents on their little street made everyone afraid. They didn't want harm to come to the Duchesne family, and they didn't want prying eyes to notice any of them.

At last after her third court appearance and the second time as a witness against the Italians to extort money from a Belgian for their own personal gain, Suzanne received a brief letter letting her know that she had been found guilty, but because she had helped them with the trials of Contucci and Nicolette and due to the fact that she was with child, she could serve her three week prison sentence when the war was over.

When Madame Temperman finished reading this judgment to the three Duchesne women, a wave of relief enveloped all of them. "They really think they are going to win the war, Francine remarked smugly."

"Well, Francine, what makes you so sure they are not?" her mother asked.

"Because Churchill tells us they and the Americans will not let that happen!" Francine exclaimed happily.

The women all laughed, and Suzanne said very softly, "Let's pray that Monsieur Churchill is correct."

Survival

The rain pelted the windows of Suzanne's house on this dreary Monday morning in early November. Her mother was in the kitchen preparing dinner with a small piece of beef she had gotten from the butcher, potatoes and some vegetables they had canned during the summer. The house was damp and chilly but the smells from the little kitchen gave warmth to Suzanne's spirit.

Her pregnant belly made it difficult for her to get comfortable, and the young mother to be paced slowly from the salon to the dining room. She hoped the postman would arrive before dinner. On Mondays he often arrived later due to the extra mail in his pouch. Suzanne had not heard a word from her husband nor had any of her friends gotten any secret information about Maurice in several weeks.

In August after her ordeal with the German court was finally over, Suzanne had gotten a verbal message about Maurice's condition through Adrien who was very active in the underground. The message was that he was doing well and she shouldn't worry about him. The daily work was hard, but he would be fine and wanted to reassure her. Suzanne's heart immediately filled with happiness and moments later her common sense told her that there was constant danger for Maurice to survive in that vile concentration camp.

More than two months had passed without news. Suzanne slept poorly, her mind filled with terrible scenarios about her husband. The constant anxiety about his safety made her nervous and jumpy. Eva tried to get her daughter to relax thinking that her state of mind would continue to make her pregnancy more difficult and would lead to a difficult delivery.

As Suzanne set the table for the four of them, the doorbell rang. She jumped not really expecting anyone. Rushing to the front door she prayed for news about Maurice. Suzanne flung open the door and looked at the postman.

"*Bonjour, Madame,*" he said with a little smile. "I wanted to deliver to you before I go home for dinner. There is an official letter for you."

Taking the packet of mail, Suzanne saw the envelope with the German return stamped on the back flap and the camp name *Breendonk*. She looked up at the postman and softly said, "*Merci, Monsieur DuBois.*"

The postman understood that the envelope might hold good or bad news as he answered, "*bon chance, Madame,*" and turned to go.

Suzanne shut the door and leaned against it with her back. Taking a deep breath she went to the dining table and grabbed a knife to open the envelope carefully. Still alone in the room, she took a seat and slid a paper folded into quarters from the pale blue envelope.

Staring at it for a full minute she was sadden to discover that it was not from her husband. It was addressed to her and it was from the camp commandant, Schmitt. There was only one paragraph and as usual it was in German only.

Quickly Suzanne got up, rushed to the coat hooks by the front door and grabbed her rain coat. As she entered the kitchen, her mother looked startled. "*Maman*, I have a letter from Breendonk and must know what it says. I'm going to Madame Temperman now."

Eva nodded, "All right, *cherie*. Be careful not to slip and fall with all of this rain....."

Her mother's words trailed off as Suzanne was hurrying out to cross the yards to their neighbor. In a moment she rapped on the kitchen door knowing Madame Temperman would be busy cooking for her large family.

The door opened immediately. "Suzanne, what is wrong?" Madame Temperman asked.

These days everyone assumed the worst. "I'm not sure, but I have a very brief letter here from Breendonk. I haven't had news about Maurice since August, Madame. Please, can you take a minute to read it for me?"

"Of course, dear. Let me turn off the gas."

"I'm so sorry, Madame, to barge in, but I must know," Suzanne exclaimed. "Don't be silly, Suzanne. Please come in and I will read it right away," Madame Temperman led her to the dining room and made Suzanne sit down fearing the news might be bad.

The neighbor read it quickly and looked at Suzanne. "Everything is fine."

Suzanne sighed deeply, "Please read it to me."

Notice from the top official of the Secret Service, October 31, to Frau Morgen. In reference to your letter on the 25th of October, we are notifying you that your husband is alive and in the best of health. Packages cannot be sent because of embargo on packages that is still in effect. From the Prison Commander, SS Sturbannfurhrer Schmitt.

"It is good news, Suzanne. Maurice is all right, dear," Madame Temperman patted her on the shoulder.

"Yes, he is," Suzanne took a deep breath and exhaled slowly. She looked up and smiled at her neighbor. "Thank you so much. I'm sorry to be such a pest whenever I get a letter."

"That is ridiculous, dear. I'm glad that I can be of help. I'm very happy that you have some good news. When this filthy war is over, Maurice will come back to you and your children," Madame Temperman smiled broadly.

"Yes, you are right." Suzanne stood up to go. "Thank you again. The children will be home from school any minute and you have to get their dinner on the table. Thank you, thank you."

Suzanne was out of the back door in a hurry and made her way back to her home. Eva sat in the dining room awaiting her return.

"Maurice is fine, *Maman*. The letter is from the commandant and he is replying to the letter I wrote last week asking about Maurice and asking permission to send him a package. The response says that Maurice is alive and in the best of health, but no packages can be

114

sent. It's against their rules," Suzanne finished telling the news while shedding her wet rain coat and hanging it on the hook by the door. "Oh, *Maman,* I feel so relieved. No news for so long and finally this. I'm glad I wrote that letter."

Eva smiled at her daughter and said, "It is wonderful news. Now let's get dinner on the table. Francine should be home from school any minute.

"Yes, *Maman.* I'll go upstairs and get Serge from his room," Suzanne said.

****

There was barely any light that filtered in to the large cell. The windows were painted with dark blue paint, and only a glimmer came under the wooden door from the few lights in the corridor. Maurice looked up at the ceiling lying on the straw among a row of men whose shoulders almost touched in the wooden bunks. After coming to Breendonk in the early summer he had managed to claim the top bunk by September. The smell was less dreadful on the top row. If you had the misfortune of being in the first or second tier of bunks you learned quickly that you needed to get out. Prisoners with dysentery were often too weak to get out of the bunk and make it to the slop bucket. Just thinking about the conditions under which they lived revolted Maurice.

His youth and agility made him capable of climbing to the top, and he intended to stay there. When he closed his eyes he imagined the face of his beautiful wife. Sometimes Maurice would let his mind wander to the faces of his son and his mother-in-law and the rest of the family. One of his favorite daydreams took him back to the summer of 1938 before the war. Before Serge was born. He, Suzanne and Eva had taken a train to Bruges. They had even brought their little black terrier, Toto. After dining at a wonderful café along a scenic canal, they took a long walk to the outskirts of town. There were fields of hay waiting to be harvested and an old windmill. The family rested in the shade of the windmill and Toto ran with great energy several meters into the hay, stopped abruptly to take stock of his location and ran back to them. Maurice had his little Brownie camera and took pictures of the women and with their beloved dog. Eva took the camera from her son-in-law and took several photos of the young married couple on that idyllic day.

Thoughts of these happy times helped him to fall asleep and to rest without the fear he felt from sunrise to sunset as he and the other prisoners toiled in the yard of the old fortress, Breendonk. There had been little change on a daily basis for the inmates in the Jewish cells until mid-October. Occasionally a few new prisoners would be brought to their cell. By nightfall several of the prisoners would gather around the newcomers to get news of the war and to ask questions. Each of them hoped that the new prisoners might know someone from his family or perhaps a friend. From time to time that was the case. The bit of news about the war was seldom hopeful. There had been no major defeats of the Third Reich. The Americans were in it all the way in the Pacific with Japan, but there was no sign of them in northern Europe although Churchill kept telling them that there would be an allied invasion in the future.

During the middle of the night on October 22, the guards opened the doors to the cell. The white glare of several flashlights along with the shouting to get out of bed and assemble in the yard made the prisoners scramble. Most of the men slept with their shoes on or under their heads. Maurice quickly climbed down and got into his shoes effortlessly. They were loose because he had lost at least ten kilos since his arrest.

When Maurice reached the open door he saw that the Jews from the cell next to his were also filing into the hallway. They all trotted down the hall towards the exit located across from the toilets and showers for the gentile prisoners. Outside huge floodlights were shining upon them. The camp commandant Sturbannfurhrer Schmitt was there along with several other prison guards.

The prisoners stood in the damp night air for at least 30 minutes before Schmitt finally addressed them. "Some of you will be leaving our prison today," he began in a loud voice that they could all hear. "You will be taken to the nearby city of Mechelen. From there you will be sent to work in camps that need more laborers. With your departure from Breendonk, we will have more room to accommodate new prisoners here."

Schmitt spoke only in German. The commandant of Breendonk knew that most of the Jews understood him because they spoke that dreadful dialect of Yiddish that bastardized the purity of the German language.

"The lieutenant will read the list of those going to Mechelen. Come forward when you hear your name." Schmitt turned to his lieutenant and handed him a folio with the names. Schmitt moved to the side and stood with his aids as the lieutenant began reading the names.

Maurice felt the fear grip the pit of his stomach. Usually the pain in his and every other prisoner's stomach was hunger. This was far worse. He remembered that in August there were Jews removed from the quarry yard and they did not return. Sometimes they would hear the sound of gunfire from the firing squad when prisoners were executed. Those were mostly the gentile prisoners. The political prisoners as he had once thought he would be.

About a dozen names had been called out and the men shuffled to the front of the lineup. "Popovsky, Steinberg, Stern," the lieutenant called out and Maurice realized that there hadn't been any names with M's called. He was safe!

When the officer was finished with the names, another man in uniform came to lead the group of twenty away. The Jews from the two cells let their eyes follow the column of their fellow prisoners until they went around a corner and they stared ahead. They were not dismissed. So they stood in their rows until daylight made the autumn sky turn a murky gray. The prisoners stood for another hour.

Finally two guards came to the front of their lines. The guards were familiar. They were the Flemish SS who usually roused them from sleep by opening the big, wooden door to their cells and allowed the prisoners who tended to the kitchen and the pick-up of the slop buckets to enter and do their work. After drinking their thin porridge and eating a hard piece of bread, the Flemish SS lead them outside to work. Since they were already outside, they were lead to the quarry yard to begin working without being able to relieve their bladders or feel the stingy porridge hit the bottom of their stomachs.

Maurice decided to be grateful. His name had not been called. He was alive.

Only a week later, the Jews of Breendonk were again rousted from their beds in the middle of the night. Again they waited for the names to be called. Maurice thought about the words from the commandant. Schmitt had been truthful the week before. New men arrived to replace the Jews who had been deported. There was no one that Maurice knew but he was anxious for information about the war.

Some of the new arrivals had already been in the torture room. They had burns on their hands and arms and bruises on their faces. Others had somehow avoided interrogation but that didn't mean they wouldn't be called out later.

The men talked about Jews being picked up in Brussels by the hundreds and that they were sent to Mechelen to be deported to the labor camps in the east. All Jews in Belgium had to wear the yellow star, Maurice learned. That must have happened after his arrest in May.

Again the names were called and his was not. About forty men were marched away this time. Every man left behind wondered if they were lucky or might it be better to be done with the waiting and welcome the final relocation and probably death.

When Maurice let himself think about the future, he wondered how long he could really survive. He had to keep working hard and try not to get noticed by the guards. With his weight loss and with the damp, cold weather of November upon them, Maurice knew it would be hard to get through the winter without getting pneumonia or some terrible disease that might be the end of him. He had the will to live because of his adored wife and baby and a new baby that would soon be born.

Maurice became anxious wondering how Suzanne would manage with a baby and their little son. He would convince himself that she would be fine with the help of her mother and sister. Maurice knew that Ivan was in hiding and would be sent to a labor camp in Germany if he were ever caught.

When he thought about his own family, the welfare of his aunt who had brought him to Belgium came first. Maurice hoped they would continue to hide and not be found. Finally he allowed his mind to wander to his parents and siblings in Poland. Were they alive? He knew that many Polish Jews were the first to be rounded up and imprisoned in ghettos or executed in villages. Perhaps his brothers had escaped into the countryside to save themselves. After these thoughts came the guilt he felt for having left all of them years ago in their primitive village that seemed to be a part of the last century. Maurice had found Brussels to be so exciting and sophisticated that he immediately had felt that he was meant to live in society that appreciated beauty. The beauty of music and art and culture. The society where he had met his beautiful *bebe*, Suzanne. Maurice was determined to stay alive; his family needed him. He was committed to do everything possible to keep attention away from him and to survive.

Providence

The nurse came into Suzanne's room in the hospital in Anderlecht. She walked over to the window and opened the drapes. The morning sky was dreary but Suzanne smiled with anticipation at the nurse.

"Are you ready to see your little girl, Madame?" the nurse asked.

"Oh, yes. Is she pretty? Is she all right?" Suzanne asked.

"Yes. Yes to both questions," the nurse said. "The doctor will give you details when he comes in later, but she is very healthy. I'll bring you some breakfast first and then the baby, all right?"

Suzanne sat up in bed. "Yes, I'm very hungry all of a sudden."

"Remember, there's a war on. But we do have coffee and plenty of toast and jam," the nurse smiled at her.

Suzanne nodded as the nurse left the room. She had seen the baby girl right after her birth, but they took her away to clean her and test her and Suzanne had been exhausted. The delivery was more difficult than with Serge and had taken almost ten hours. When the nurses brought Suzanne to her bed, she fell instantly asleep.

Now after eating her breakfast quickly and using the bathroom, she was helped back into bed. The door opened and a different nurse brought the baby to Suzanne. She took her in her arms and looked at her. The baby had blonde hair and plenty of it with little curls around her forehead. She was long and thin and so much like Serge when he was born.

"You see how pretty she is? I think she might be hungry, too," said the first nurse.

"Yes, of course. I'll nurse her. Suzanne arranged her nightgown and after a bit of fidgeting, the baby began to suck. "I tried to nurse my first child, but didn't have enough milk. I hope I do this time."

120

"What will you name her?" the second nurse asked.

"Michele Nadine," Suzanne replied with certainty.

"Lovely," both nurses replied. "We'll leave you alone and come back for the baby in a half an hour."

Suzanne kept examining the child. She unwrapped the blankets and saw that everything about her was perfect. Hopefully there was no illness that would cause pain as Serge had had. As Michele nursed, Suzanne thought about her husband. How different it all was now. He was not there to fuss over her and the baby. How would he even know that he has a daughter, Suzanne thought with alarm? She would have to try to get a message to Maurice through her friends in the underground. She wanted him to know that he had a beautiful, perfect daughter, Michele Nadine!

Suzanne arrived home in a taxi accompanied by her mother two weeks later on December 7. Eva gave her a hand out of the taxi to steady her as she was holding the little bundle. The driver got her valise from the trunk and brought it to the door that was flung open by Francine. Standing next to his young aunt, Serge cried out, "*Maman* you're here with my sister!"

There was a great deal of jostling as everyone moved forward into the house. "Let me see her," Francine was shouting.

"I want to see her," Serge shouted more loudly.

"Move out of the way and let us take off our coats," Eva commanded. She turned to the taxi driver, paid him and thanked him for his service.

There was quiet and the children did as they were told. Suzanne put the baby on the sofa as she got out of her coat. She sat next to the bundle and began to undo the layers of blankets and finally was able to show the little girl to her son and her sister. Serge inched forward and looked at her. A big smile crept upon his face and then he looked up at his mother.

"Oh, *Maman,* she is so small. Like a doll. How will I play with her?" Serge asked.

"You can't play with her yet, silly," Francine scolded him. "We have to take care of her."

Suzanne laughed and asked, "Do you like her?"

Serge nodded and Francine said, "Oh, yes, very much."

"I'm glad. We're going to call her Nadine," Suzanne informed them.

"Oh, how come?" her younger sister asked.

"I named her Michele Nadine, but Michele is so ordinary. I want to call her Nadine.

"I like it just fine," Francine replied.

"Me, too," the three-and-a-half-year old brother answered.

****

Adrien had managed to arrange for a message to reach his old friend, Maurice Morgen, inside Breendonk prison camp. Through members of the underground, they had connections with a civilian who made food deliveries to the prison once a week. The civilian, Josef van der Witt, had been able to deliver messages and to get some out of the prison periodically over the last year. He was able to give the receiving clerk some extra provisions or a bit of money to secure this thin line of communication. Food, even with ration cards, had become increasingly scarce for civilians and military. Guards and clerks could be bribed easily to better feed their own families.

About one week after Suzanne's arrival home with Nadine, Adrien got the message on a tiny piece of paper to van der Witt. After another day passed, van der Witt passed the message to the guard who opened the doors for supper to be dished out to the prisoners. That night while the men held up their mugs for some hot, thin cabbage soup, the guard called out quietly, "Morgen."

Maurice was near the front of the line at the moment and he nodded and said, "Yes."

As the soup was being ladled into Maurice's mug, the guard motioned with his head to move to the right. Maurice did so with hardly anyone even looking at him. All the men wanted was their pitiful little supper that would leave them just as hungry when they finished as when they began.

The guard looked into Maurice's dark eyes as he pressed a tiny piece of paper into his free hand. Maurice clasped the paper in silence and nodded slightly. The guard moved a few steps backward as Maurice quickly made his way to empty space near the stone wall of the cell. He was in the shadows of the room as he opened the paper carefully. If he didn't read it right away, the thick wooden door of the cell would shut and there wouldn't be enough light to read. There were only a few words written.

Baby girl, Nov 23, Michele Nadine. Wife, children and family are all well.

Tears came into his eyes and flowed very slowly down his cheeks. He read the words again and then folded the paper and placed it into the breast pocket on his striped uniform.

The door remained open for a few more minutes and Maurice drank has soup and moved to the rear of the room to climb up to his space in the bunk. As he reclined, his surroundings seemed to vanish from sight and smell. He shut his eyes and pictured the faces of his family and of his new little girl. How perfect, he thought. A boy and a girl. I am truly a lucky man. He thought of the Hebrew prayer that men said for the blessing of a child born to him. The Hebrew words that he hadn't heard since his little son was born came to him so clearly, and he mouthed them in silence. He reminded himself to tell no one. Word might get out that he had gotten a message and perhaps no other messages would ever come. Perhaps someone else in the cell would be jealous and turn him in thinking he would receive a reward of extra bread. Yes, Maurice thought, he would keep this good news to himself.

He let himself drift away to sleep thinking about his family sitting in the garden in the summer with Serge playing and Suzanne holding the baby on her knee.

****

The early winter months had been cold and made the suffering of the war more miserable. Suzanne constantly tried to keep little Nadine as warm as possible keeping her near the little stove in the dining room. Her breast milk had dried up as it had with Serge, and she had to buy evaporated milk to feed the baby. Suzanne would sell a diamond or piece of gold to buy the food she needed for the family on the black market. Coal was almost impossible to get to make a good fire. Francine would gather sticks in the big field at the top of the hill above their houses or pick them up along the path in Dilbeek. The sticks burned faster than the coal so they would go to bed earlier to try and keep warm.

Nadine was a healthy baby, but she cried a great deal. She was content when being held by her mother, aunt or grandmother and began to cry the moment she was put into her cradle. She only slept a few hours each night and wouldn't fall back to sleep after Suzanne fed her in the middle of the night. She brought Nadine into her bed, but as soon as Suzanne fell asleep the baby began to cry again. Suzanne would have to walk with her in her arms trying not to let her cries awaken Serge.

During the afternoon when they were through with dinner, Eva would sometimes tell Suzanne to go to her room and nap and she would hold the child in her arms.

This had been going on for three weeks and it was almost the New Year. Eva and Suzanne had decided to invite a few friends for New Year's Eve. They couldn't go out because of the baby and Eva knew that her daughter needed to be with some friends and family. They invited the Picavets and Fred Caron who lived nearby. The guests insisted that they would bring some cakes and champagne to celebrate the arrival of 1943.

When the evening arrived, everyone was well dressed and the women added shawls to their dresses to try and be warm in the once cozy dining room. Serge was allowed to stay up until ten o'clock and nearly fell asleep in a chair before being put to bed. Nadine, on the other hand was wide awake and being passed from one person to another which kept her quiet as the adults enjoyed each other's company and talked of past celebrations and looked forward to the end of the war.

When the radio announced the arrival of 1943, Fred Caron popped the cork on the cold bottle of champagne he had saved and the family and friends toasted to a better year. They all wished for the invasion of Europe and liberation. Felix added a toast to Maurice and for the end of the war to bring about his release. Suzanne smiled at her good friends and said a little prayer for Maurice's safety. She had not heard another word about him since the commandant had replied to her letter.

****

Breendonk had been quiet during the weeks around the holidays. The commandant had had a leave and went to Germany to be with his family. There had been no other deportees since October 29 of 1942 and the Jewish prisoners hoped that they would be left alone to try and stay alive until the end of the war. There were always stories of Jews being rounded up in the city and in nearby Antwerp. The Germans did not make the Belgians confine their Jews in ghettos as they did in Eastern Europe; there just weren't that many of them in the country. The Jews were arrested, usually on false charges or in general round ups. Maurice knew that the synagogue in Brussels had burned all of the conversion papers, and he thought his wonderful wife, his Suzanne, would be safe from any kind of persecution by the Gestapo.

125

Maurice and his fellow cellmates were able to rest for 10 minutes during the midday and take a drink of water. There was always plenty of work although it seemed pointless and just a way to sap the strength they had. Luckily the short daylight of winter days did allow them to go inside earlier in the evening and not suffer the bone chilling cold in the quarry yard.

As their break had just begun and Maurice had sat down on a rock he observed a guard talking to a few of the prisoners. He couldn't hear the conversation but recognized the guard as the one who had slipped him the message about the birth of his daughter. Within a few minutes all of the men were whispering to each other and he finally heard the news. There was going to be a transport to Mechelen in about a week. No one knew how many it would be.

A deep fear tore into Maurice's heart. Something made him feel that danger was imminent. There hadn't been a transport for more than two months so why now, he wondered. Why had the guard started this rumor? Was the guard more humane than others? Was he trying to prepare the men to brace themselves?

Maurice could think of nothing else the rest of the day while they continued their drudgery. He was sure that deportation meant death for them. He decided he must get a message to his wife and thought about the guard who had brought him news. Maurice decided to try to get the guard's attention when they got their supper that night.

The door to the cell opened and Maurice had placed himself in the first group to get supper. He took his mug and walked toward the right near the guard. Maurice stared at the man until the guard finally looked back at him. The guard moved slightly to the right and checked the hallway assuring him that no other authorities were there. Maurice stepped closer and whispered to the guard, "Is it true?"

The guard nodded.

126

"Are we all being deported?" Maurice had a feeling about this.

The guard shook his head.

"Will you take a message back for me if I go?"

The guard shrugged slightly.

"I still have something of value I will give you."

The guard nodded.

"When?"

"I will let you know," the guard whispered.

Maurice moved away and drank his tepid soup. He knew there were some men with paper and pens, and he let it be known that he would trade two rations of bread for paper and a pen. By the time they were going to sleep, word came back to him that a deal was made and he would get what he asked for in an exchange.

A man named Berger approached Maurice in the morning holding a pen, ink and paper. Maurice handed him his bread and promised his evening bread later. Berger nodded as Maurice climbed to his bunk and stashed the items in his extra pair of socks he had managed to keep and bury in the straw. He went out into the cold morning air and looked forward to writing his letter that evening if he could find enough light.

As the day dragged on, Maurice felt the anxiety grow inside of him. Finally as the sun began its decent, the lieutenant told the men to quit and to line up in the yard. Maurice saw his guard was out in front of the men. Several minutes went by and the commandant came into view.

"I have received orders for a transport tomorrow. It will be good to get rid of some of you. I don't know why they don't take all of you stinking Jews at one time!" Schmitt laughed. The officers around him joined in the laughter.

"All right," Schmitt was serious again. He began to call the names. It didn't take long before he called out "Morgen."

Maurice immediately moved forward. He was not surprised. He had known in his heart that this was his time.

The guard watched him. Maurice stopped in the front line and looked back at the guard. The guard nodded ever so slightly, and Maurice knew he would be able to give him the letter.

There was not a long wait this time. The men were all told they could go back to their cells. Maurice scrambled to his bunk and got out the supplies. The door was left open, and he wrote quickly. He knew exactly what he wanted to say. Maurice wrote quickly and then folded the paper and returned the pen and ink to Berger.

They heard the wagon with the rations coming down the hall and Maurice rushed to the front. Berger was nearby and Maurice tossed him his bread as he moved swiftly to the right with the mug of soup in his hand. He didn't see the guard!

Maurice wanted to act normally and so he began to drink his soup looking for the guard so that he could press the letter into his palm along with a small diamond he had kept in his pocket. At last the guard came from the other end of the hallway and moved to the right side of the cell near Maurice. The last prisoners were still getting their soup ladled into their mugs.

Maurice let his right hand hang down and it was obvious to the guard that there was something in it. The guard moved forward as if to look deeper into the cell. His back was towards Maurice and Maurice deftly pressed the letter and diamond into the German's hand. The German felt the point of the little diamond and moved away from Maurice. His hand went into his pocket casually and then came out as he moved to shut the door of the cell.

Maurice went back to his bunk and fell back in exhaustion. The adrenaline had kept him going and his mission was now accomplished. He would face deportation tomorrow and whatever would lie ahead. Maurice could no longer pretend that he would be released from prison one day. He knew no one was coming back from the east. The end of the war was nowhere in sight. He had done as much as he could to provide for his family before his arrest. There was nothing left to do but pray for his journey.

Suzanne's face was there smiling at him as he closed his eyes for the last time in Breendonk. Breendonk, a place that disgusted his sensibilities. A place where he had been tortured and forced to work like a slave. It was a place that tried to dehumanize him, and it had failed. Whenever he saw the faces of his beloved family, knowing they were safe, he felt the German beasts had not won. The family of Maurice (Moses) Morgen would go on with his son and his daughter.

Deportation

Suzanne sat up in bed, her heart pounding rapidly. Something was wrong. She knew that Maurice was in danger. As she sat motionless for a few moments, her racing heart began to slow. Instinctively she reached out for little Nadine and fixed the blanket covering her. For once the baby was sleeping soundly.

As she slipped quietly out of bed, Suzanne grabbed for her robe and wrapped it around herself and put her feet into the slippers at the side of the bed. She walked out of the room and went across the hall to the little bedroom in the back of the house. Serge was fast asleep and Suzanne moved to the window that overlooked the garden. The glass was so very cold from the January night air. There was a large moon that was just beginning to wane and the young mother stared at it for a long time as she wondered what had awakened her so suddenly.

Although her heart was beating normally now, she felt that Maurice was in danger. Of course he's always in danger, she thought, but something is happening to him. Suzanne tried to remember if she had dreamt about danger. No, she hadn't dreamt at all. Looking at the moon she thought she could feel Maurice standing beside her. There was something very wrong.

A cloud passed in front of the moon, and it seemed to break her fixed stare. Suzanne shuddered, suddenly very cold. She turned and took another blanket from the dresser and placed it on Serge and left the room. Nadine was still asleep and Suzanne decided she must try to get back to sleep. As she was lying on her back staring at the dark ceiling Suzanne thought about many of the actions she had been forced to take since this war had begun. She never imagined living in danger just because of the man she had loved and married. Her forgeries for the underground made her a target if her cell were discovered. Her bold actions when charged by the Secret Service made her shiver in fear and also to beam with pride. What a crazy time it is she thought as she closed her eyes and slept.

****

Oh my God, Maurice prayed, "I'm so cold. How will I make it through this day?" Commandant Schmitt had not been mistaken. Early on the morning of January 13, the men were awakened with loud banging on the door and shouts from the guards. There was no clattering sound of the breakfast wagon and the order came to line up in the yard immediately. All of the Jews marched out into the piercing winter wind and stood in their usual lines. Thirty minutes later Schmitt came out dressed in his army overcoat, hat and gloves and barked the orders to the guards on each side of him. A lieutenant stepped forward and called out the names of the nine men being deported.

Each of them stepped forward and lined up in front of their cellmates whom they would never see again. The lieutenant moved to the head of their line and another guard came up behind them. Quickly they were marched out of the yard.

Maurice couldn't see much in the darkness. Each man was straining to see where they were headed. After a few more minutes they could see the gate through which they had once entered Breendonk. Now they were marched out and joined by more guards with guns to make sure there would not be an attempted escape. Maurice had dreamt of the day he could walk out of this hell hole. Now he wished he could remain.

On the other side of the gate, they were told to halt. A truck with headlights blazing came towards them and stopped a few yards away. The guards began to shout at the prisoners to hurry and get into the back of the truck. They followed the orders and climbed into the vehicle. It was a German troop truck and had room for more than the nine of them. Two guards jumped up and told them to slide forward on the benches. The guards sat opposite each other on the ends of the benches.

The driver went into reverse and rapidly turned the truck around, and soon they were headed away from Breendonk towards the highway. For about thirty minutes, they bounced along the road. They hadn't passed any other vehicles, and Maurice wondered what time it was.

The men arrived with their guards into a small city, and Maurice assumed it was Malines better known as Mechelen to the Germans and the Flemings. The Jews had heard rumors that the Jews were brought here for deportation by train to concentration camps in Poland or Germany.

It didn't take much longer to arrive at a railway yard. Maurice saw the train tracks because the moonlight was being reflected on the iron rails. The truck stopped suddenly giving everyone in the rear a jolt including the guards. They quickly recovered and began shouting at the prisoners to get down from the truck. The Jews did so following their guards. There were more Germans in military uniform waiting for them. They were shouted at and prodded with rifle butts to move forward. Soon they saw other trucks unloading people into the rail yard.

They were civilians. Men, women and even children. The children were crying, and the mothers tried to comfort them. Guards were shouting at them and telling them to stop the children from crying and screaming. The scene was chaotic only a hundred meters away from him. Maurice and all of his fellow prisoners were shocked by the families that were being herded by the guards. Suddenly Maurice wondered if he might know any of these people. They might be from Brussels having been picked up in a raid. Maurice felt helpless and totally deflated as the deportation unfolded before him.

Minutes later they were moved into a wooden shed of some type. He had observed that there were no railcars in the yard. Maurice guessed that this would be their waiting place until the train pulled in. Once inside there was immediate relief from the howling January wind. There was no coal stove or heat of any kind in the little building. The prisoners instinctively huddled close to each other to benefit from body heat.

Hours passed and daylight arrived, but no food. It must have been noon when two guards came in. One held a bucket and ladle. The second guard kept his gun poised and also held a tin mug. Without saying anything he ladled water into the cup and it was passed among a few men. Another two times the ladle was dipped and each man took two or three pulls on the mug of water.

When darkness came after the sun went down, no guards arrived with any kind of food. Maurice knew he could go without food for a day or two, and then he said a prayer to God to let him survive the cold.

The men were weak and so they slept a great deal. No food was delivered the next morning either. The guards only brought water. After sundown there was a lot of noise outside of their door. Maurice was alert and thought that perhaps the train had arrived.

It had not, but the door swung open and two additional guards carried a pot that had steam coming off the top. There were several mugs and each man received soup. It was heaven! There were tiny pieces of potatoes in the soup and it was hot. Another guard doled out old stale bread and each Jew took it as if it were the Sabbath challah. They ignored the mold on the crust and tore pieces from the rolls and dipped each piece into the mugs of soup.

Maurice had been ecstatic to get his portion, but he was also entranced at the civility among the prisoners and the guards. It was surreal and Maurice wondered if a better place awaited them at the end of their upcoming journey.

The next morning they were awakened by the guards and told to make sure they relieved themselves. They were given water and a roll. Shortly after the men were told that the train would arrive within the hour. No more information was given. The prisoners began to talk quietly. They had a bit more strength since they had received some food and had been able to stay inside the shed out of the winter air. The Jews' spirits had risen. Apparently they were all thinking of similar possibilities as Maurice. Yes, they all knew the stories about the trains going to the east and never coming back, but perhaps they were going to work camps and would try to survive until the war was over.

Soon they heard the whistle of the train in the distance and then the slow turning of the wheels as the train arrived and came to a stop. When their door opened, several guards were lined up outside and they shouted for the men to move outside quickly. Maurice looked up and down at the train. All he could see were cattle cars. Was that their mode of transport? Maurice almost laughed out loud. What had he thought? Did he think they would be riding in second class carriages?

After the reality of the train transportation sunk in, Maurice began to look at the families that had been rousted from other wooden sheds in the rail yard. Families with suitcases. Men and women wearing heavy winter coats. Some women had fur coats. If he and the prisoners were being transported to work in a labor camp, where were these families going, Maurice pondered? They were all going to the same place. He knew it. They were going to Poland to one of the hideous concentration camps they had heard about in rumors. They were never coming back. Never.

****

On January 15, Suzanne was busy polishing her silverware. She was seated in the dining room with Serge playing with his dominos and some toy soldiers. It looked as if he had built a little fort and was lining up the little metal soldiers. Eva held Nadine in her arms trying to rock her to sleep after her midday bottle. The radio was on and they listened to a Mozart concerto that was abruptly interrupted by the doorbell.

134

Eva looked up and Suzanne said, "It must be the postman. I'll get it"

Suzanne saw the postman through the window and she opened the door widely. "Hello, Monsieur, how are you?"

"Fine, Madame Morgen. I have mail I think you will find important," the mailman said.

He was already turning to go as Suzanne thanked him. She looked at the envelope on top. It was in a blue envelope, and she turned it over. On the flap she saw the name Breendonk handwritten. Then she saw Maurice's name at the top. It wasn't his handwriting, but she knew it wasn't an official letter.

Suzanne hurried to the table and reached for the knife and carefully opened the flap. Eva did not speak. She knew that it was something serious. Her daughter pulled out a small square paper that had been folded many times.

As she unfolded it, Suzanne felt her breath catch in her throat.

Jan 12, 1943
Dear Suzanne and Toto,
I just this instant received the order that we are leaving. I don't know when or to where. Nine of us are going. They always are making the necessary steps to follow the law. I always have hope of leaving here. I repeat, give no one the money. Guard it well and take care of yourself. Nothing is more important than taking care of the children. Don't be afraid, it will all end well. Help Maman however you can. My morale is high. I kiss you deeply, you my good love, and also my son, Maman, Francine, Ivan.
Bebe
My regards to everyone at Sloma. Ask Jean and he will give you instructions on how to get the most for everything. Aurevoir.

****

Suzanne went through the motions of life. She took care of her children and took in more requests for false documents than before. She vowed not to think about the future. She couldn't control her destiny. Her husband was sent away from Belgium, and she knew it must be to a labor camp or a concentration camp. In her heart she felt as though he would certainly die.

After receiving Maurice's letter she felt totally alone. He had said goodbye as if he knew it were forever. Suzanne decided to write to the commandant of Breendonk as she had once before and ask about his wellbeing. One little shred of hope was left that perhaps Maurice wasn't deported and that he remained in Breendonk.

On February 5 she received an official letter. Madame Temperman, always so kind, translated for her.

Notice from the Top Official of the Secret Service

February 4, 1943

To: Suzanne Morgen-Duchesne
In reply to your writing, January 28, 1943, we are letting you know that Mosek Morgen, by his own will, volunteered for the workforce.

From the Prison Commandant
Schmitt, SS

Suzanne took the notice from Madame Temperman and went home. She pulled out a little box she had used to put all of the correspondence from Maurice and from the SS and placed the notice in it. Suzanne put the box away in a cabinet in the dining room.

It was over. Her life as she and her darling Maurice had planned together was never going to happen. She would have to go forward without him and make it through this Goddamn war so that her children could grow and have lives without the *Boche*.

PART II

Ft. Bragg

The oppressive heat of the summer had made the men more anxious than ever to get news of being shipped overseas. Jack Kaplan had been working on base at Ft. Bragg after his basic training. Several engineer battalions were stationed at this gigantic facility known as the home of the 82nd Airborne Division. The bulk of the barracks to accommodate over 150,000 troops had been built before Jack's arrival. The engineers were kept on to build hangars and technical services buildings.

A few months after Jack's arrival to the base, the 82nd was divided in half and became the new 101st Airborne. The paratroopers stuck together and didn't have much in common with the infantry or the engineers, and all of the men seemed to prefer it to remain that way.

It was early August when Jack arrived at Ft. Bragg. During the second week of boot camp, the temperature was well over 90 degrees and very steamy making the daily training tough. None of the men in his platoon had been given a weekend pass, and there was no indication that there would be any in the near future. The hard work he had been doing as a civilian for the Bermuda Base Contractors to set up a defense post in the Atlantic had toughened Jack and his deep tan saved him from the North Carolina sun on their long marches. He felt sorry for the guys who were getting burned by the sun's rays. You could hear them groan as they tried to sleep in the stifling night air at Ft. Bragg.

His new friend, Phil Dupell, was holding up pretty well. He was used to hard work having come from a very poor family in a little paper mill town. Phil's small, wiry body lent itself to many of the agility skills they had to perfect. The two men had stuck together and wound up in the same barracks. Phil volunteered to take the upper bunk leaving Jack the lower which he liked. The other men in the bunks around them were from all over the country, but they didn't have much time to get to know each other the first week. By the time they were dismissed, got cleaned up and ate in the mess hall, they were too tired to do much more than lay down on their cots. Usually they drifted off to sleep before 'lights out.'

Jack had crossed the yard and entered the equipment depot. Several men from his platoon and others he had never seen were lining up. The sergeant talked loudly, but not in the usual harsh tone of their drill sergeant.

"Men, you've gotten your drivers' permits for a variety of vehicles," the sergeant said. "Now you're gonna take turns drivin' the trucks. Everybody line up single file. Three-quarter ton in the first line, one-and-one-and-a-half in the second and deuce-and-a-half in the third."

The recruits shifted their positions to line up correctly. Jack had never driven anything bigger than a limousine, but figured it wouldn't be too difficult. It wasn't an armored truck or a tank, he thought to himself. While he was standing in line waiting, he thought about his pal, Phil. He really liked him. He liked him as much as any of the fellows he grew up with in Coney Island. Phil had requested kitchen duty because he liked to cook, and his sergeant had given it to him. Jack had been surprised by Phil, but he explained that he had helped his mother in the kitchen being one of the older kids. Having a friend who was in the kitchen a lot might be a real asset, Jack figured.

After about half-an-hour, it was Jack's turn to get behind the wheel of troop truck.

"How long you been drivin'?" his instructor asked as he slid into the passenger side.

"About seven years, Sergeant."

"You old enough to say that, son?" the sergeant asked.

"Yes, sir. I'm 24 and driving since I was 17," Jack replied.

"Where y'all from, private?" the instructor sounded friendly and had a slight southern accent.

"New York, Sergeant."

"New York. They got any trucks like this in New York, soldier?"

"Not like this, Sergeant. But there are plenty of trucks. Delivery trucks, Sergeant," Jack sounded confident.

"Well the only thing you're gonna deliver is other meat heads like you! Now if you can figure how to turn this baby on and put her into gear, I want you to drive it down this road. Try not to kill anybody or I'll have to slide right over and push you out the door and take it over. You got it straight, soldier?" the instructor was barking now.

"Yes, Sergeant," Jack replied.

Jack pulled the choke, turned the ignition on and hit the starter. She came to life, and he put the truck into first gear easily. He gave a quick glance in his side mirrors and eased the truck onto the dirt roadway as he shifted effortlessly into second gear. After several more moments he had her in 4th gear as they were cruising down the road. He took a chance and looked quickly to his right to see the reaction of the instructor.

"Think you're pretty slick, hey soldier?" asked the sergeant. "Well, gotta admit you know how to drive. At the end of the road, I want you to turn right, go over to the yard down there. Then I want you to back it into the yard and get turned around. Think you can do that?"

"Yes, Sergeant," Jack was quick to reply. Jack did what was asked of him and did it well. When they returned to the starting point, he put her into first gear and turned off the engine.

"Okay, soldier, I like the way you handle the vehicle," the sergeant said. "You're good to keep on with the engineer training. You'll be learning a lot of other vehicles and heavy equipment during basic. If you're good at it, we'll send you to engineer school. What's your name and serial number?"

Jack gave him the information and the instructor wrote it on the paper attached to his clipboard.

"All right, get out of the truck and rejoin your platoon," the sergeant said.

"Yes, Sergeant. Thank you, Sergeant." Jack climbed down and jogged out of the equipment depot to find his platoon cleaning equipment under the blazing sun.

That evening when Jack and Phil were lined up for supper, Jack told his buddy about the truck performance and that he had been told he might be eligible for engineer training.

"Wow, Jack, that's good news. If I get kitchen duty after this, I might wind up anywhere," Phil mused.

"Yeah, but engineers need cooks, too," Jack patted Phil on the back.

"Sounds like the engineers might have good duty, Jack. What do you think?" Phil asked.

"I think that it sounds a lot better than being in a tank or having artillery training," Jack said. "Engineers think. They figure stuff out, right?"

"Yeah. What're you getting at, Jack?"

"If you're planning stuff and making things work, then you're not on the front line with a rifle and a bayonet looking for Krauts to kill," Jack said. "I think we need to find a way to stay with this engineer training."

"Sure, Jack. I'm with you. Just keep telling me what to do and I'll do it. I'd like to stick with you the rest of this war, buddy," Phil said with a smile.

"You got that right. Now let's eat," Jack said as they finally got their trays and were going through the food line.

*****

Training went on into September, and the bodies of the men got stronger and their reactions quicker. The extreme heat made it difficult for many of the young men, but their sergeants kept pressing them to go further on their marches and their runs. Jack had always liked the summer, but the stifling conditions in which they drilled and lived were almost too much. They were all bone-tired at the end of each day, and fell asleep despite the intense heat and humidity.

When the first phase of training came to an end in early September, it was time to celebrate. The young soldiers were finally given weekend passes and told to be back on Sunday night. Their company commander said they would be told on Monday where they were to report.

At 4:30 they were dismissed, and every man ran to the barracks to get cleaned up and put on their crisp khakis, and figure out how to hitch some rides into town. Every one of them planned to drink plenty of beer and dance with lots of girls. There was a big USO dance set up in the town's community center, and they were told that the bars were ready for them.

During the past month, Jack and Phil had made good friends with Carl Bare and Steve Curlovich. They had found a lot in common with Carl, who came from a small town in Ohio, and Steve, who had worked in a steel factory in Pittsburgh. They played cards when they weren't too tired, and talked about growing up and what they hoped the future would hold for each of them.

The four pals made their way into town and wound up celebrating in every bar and café. They danced with as many girls as they could, and Jack got three of them to promise to see him the next time he got a pass. He tucked their telephone numbers into his wallet after jotting down a brief description about them and their names on the slips of paper. Jack figured if he didn't screw up during training, he'd get a pass at least every two weeks, and wanted to know he would find at least one of the girls free and willing to go out with him.

Jack, Carl and Steve found themselves in engineering classes each morning, and out in the field learning how to use the equipment they needed to master. Besides driving a variety of vehicles, they learned how to erect Bailey and pontoon bridges. Instruction included explosives in order to clear away obstructions for the advancing troops some day and possibly blowing up railroad and vehicle bridges. The classroom instruction prepared the men in understanding the physics and mathematics of demolition and construction. Jack found the studies and instruction rewarding, and was glad that he had been placed in this platoon.

His buddy, Phil, was busy learning everything he needed to set up a field kitchen. Phil's tutoring included requisitioning food, calculation of quantities to prepare for an entire company of soldiers and learning the recipes for the large numbers a kitchen would be feeding. He, too, enjoyed his instruction, and hoped his superiors would keep him attached to the engineers so he could be with his good friends.

They finally started getting relief from the heat by early October, and were enjoying time outdoors for their field training. The soldiers were still fairly new, but they were treated better by the noncommissioned officers, and received their weekend passes as long as they kept up with their work and education assignments.

The cooler temperatures and shorter training days left the men ready for more recreation in the evenings. Exhaustion didn't dog them every day, and friendships became deeper as they played cards or pool after supper and talked about their home and lives when they were in their bunks at night. Jack played poker and shot craps a few nights a week, and managed to win enough money to keep sending some home where his father would put it into his savings account. He liked to play with fellas in other barracks to keep any resentment about his frequent winning out of the social network of his own platoon.

Now and then one or two of the soldiers would ask their sergeant if he knew where they would be headed after they completed training. The answer was always the same, "What are you worried about? You'll be killing Japs or Krauts soon enough."

The fact of the matter was that the sergeant didn't know any more than the men did. Everyone knew that there would be a build-up of troops to pull off the invasion of Europe. Would it be in 1943? The marines were fighting in the Pacific so the odds were that they would be going over to Europe. Since May, the United States had been giving military support to the operations in North Africa to help out the British who had been fighting Field Marshall Rommel since 1940. Would the desert of the North Africa campaign be their fate?

These speculative thoughts were the subject of many conversations around the tables of the mess hall and in their bunks at night. Every man wondering what was in store for him, and many wanting to take part of the adventure that was to be their fate. Almost every man prayed that God would keep him safe.

*****

As the engineers continued to build at a fast pace, they sometimes wondered if they were ever going to see action in the war. The soldiers watched the news in the Pacific carefully, and knew what their Marine and Navy brothers were going through fighting for bits and pieces of land against the Japs. Jack and his pals would talk about it at night and thank their lucky stars that they were still on good old American soil, but they knew it couldn't be for much longer.

Jack was in the barracks changing from his work clothes into a fresh pair of khakis after he had washed up in the latrine. Phil came in and immediately took off his shirt. Excitedly he told Jack he had heard some scuttlebutt in the mess hall.

"Jack, I heard some of the men talking about word that we were going to get orders to ship out really soon," Phil said.

Jack finished tucking his shirttails into the waistband of his uniform pants and replied, "You don't say? Did they say where?"

"Nah, just over there," Phil wished he knew more details.

"It's about time, don't you think, Phil?"

"Sure, but I didn't think you wanted to go over and fight, buddy," Phil said.

"You got that right. Listen, we're probably going to England and prepare for the invasion. Remember, Phil, we're engineers. We build stuff," Jack said laughing.

"Yeah, and we blow it up, too. That can get pretty dangerous, Jack."

"You're right, Phil, but I'm sick and tired of this base. The summer wore me out. It had to be worse for you, coming from Massachusetts, right?" Jack questioned his friend.

"Sure, I hated the summer. It was no picnic in the kitchen and mess hall either, you know," Phil said.

"I know, I know. It was damn hard work," Jack agreed. "Look, we're Yankees and that's that. Even the girls are different down here."

Jack mocked in a southern drawl, "We're ladies!"

Phil laughed knowing his ladies' man buddy had been thwarted by many southern belles who were brought up to do nothing more than dance with the boys and maybe give them a goodnight kiss.

Carl and Steve came in from their shifts and had their shirts pulled off their sweaty torsos before they reached the bunks.

"Oh, man, I thought we we're in the beginning of autumn. It's too damn hot!" Steve protested.

"Hey guys, get cleaned up and let's get our chow and find a card game tonight," Jack encouraged them to keep moving and not flop down on their bunks.

"I don't think so," Carl replied. "There's a new movie playing tonight."

Jack was slightly disappointed and said, "Okay. Let's get chow, see the movie and then get in a card game."

"You're in an energetic mood, Jack," his pal, Steve, stated.

"Yeah, I am. Let's get going!" Jack said.

"Okay, okay," it was Carl. "Let's go get cleaned up. We'll be right back, Jack. Wait for us, all right?"

"Sure, I got a letter I want to write anyhow. See you back here," Jack said.

Jack was happy they had decided to go to the movie. The film, "Coney Island," starred Betty Grable and George Montgomery. His pals kidded him that the movie would be about his own life on the famous Coney Island Boardwalk. It was instead a musical set in the Gay Nineties and managed to show off Miss Grable's fantastic legs! The cinema was packed with GI's all having a good time listening to the music and laughing along with the jokes. When the titles started on the screen at the end of the film, the house lights came on immediately and the over the microphone the men were told to keep their seats.

"Men," a sergeant was speaking, "If anyone has a pass for tomorrow, it is revoked."

Instantly there was some grumbling. Although it was the middle of the week, passes were issued on a rotation throughout the week due to the huge number of troops stationed at Ft. Bragg.

The sergeant continued, "Tomorrow during formation many of you will be issued orders. There is going to be a large movement of men. That's all we have for now. Go about your business. Dismissed."

Jack and his friends looked at each other. Phil spoke up first, "Here it comes. We're going to war."

"Don't get worked up about it," Jack reassured Phil knowing his pal needed the calming words.

"Hey, we want to get out of this damn place, right?" Carl asked.

"You're damn right, Carl," Steve spoke up cheerfully.

"Yeah, I agree," said Jack. "Now boys, let's not get down about this. Let's go and find us a nice poker game and some beers."

They headed out of the movies and walked down to the Enlisted Men's Club to enjoy some cards and a great deal of speculation about where and when they were headed.

Flight

Someone was knocking on the back door of Suzanne's kitchen. She looked up at the clock over the fireplace and saw that it was nine o'clock. It must be Adrien, she thought as she went to the door and opened it.

Adrien smiled at her and stepped inside. He kissed her cheek in greeting and walked into the dining room. The radio was playing softly and Suzanne moved across the room to turn it off. Facing her friend she asked, "What can I offer you to drink, Adrien?"

"Nothing. I've just come from a café and already had a couple of beers," Adrien smiled at her.

"Well, then, are you here to pick up?" she asked.

Adrien nodded.

"Good. I have quite a few documents for the flyers. Please watch the street from the front door while I get them," Suzanne said.

Suzanne felt this was the most dangerous moment, the exchange. You never knew when the Gestapo might come to your door. They hadn't been here since Maurice was deported but Suzanne was always afraid they would come to arrest her again and when they did, they would find her forgeries.

In her bedroom she moved the table next to her bed and lifted the corner of the carpet. Suzanne pulled out the large folder, pulled the rug back and tugged at the table to put everything back in place. She rushed down the stairs and saw Adrien move out of the doorway. He latched the front door and went with her into the dining room. All of the house's shutters were closed at sundown in compliance with the blackout law. There hadn't been any air raids for quite some time, but the Germans didn't want bombs from the allies hitting any of their buildings or lodgings.

Hidden behind the darkened windows Suzanne handed the folder to Adrien. He looked at the variety of false identity cards and smiled as he looked at her. "Your work is flawless, my friend. This will save the necks of many Americans and English fliers."

Suzanne nodded and then asked her friend "Is there any word, Adrien?"

"About Maurice?" he replied.

"Yes."

"No, my dear Suzanne. It's been seven months. You know all of the trains go to Poland from Malines," Adrien said.

"Yes, Poland. Funny, isn't it, Adrien? Poland, where Maurice was born and raised. He told me many times that he never wanted to see Poland again. He despised the way they lived. Everything was so primitive and the Jews had to fear pogroms. Now he's in Poland in some awful prison camp," Suzanne said with despair and sadness.

"Oh, my dear, dear friend, you mustn't think of this," Adrien said. "You have so much to live for right here. Your children and family," Adrien tried to boost her spirit.

"I know you're right. Please, Adrien, I must know if he's alive or not. You know so many people in the Resistance; please try to find out for me," Suzanne said.

Adrien looked deep into her clear blue eyes and he knew that she sincerely wanted to know her husband's fate. "I will try, Suzanne. I promise."

Suzanne nodded again.

"I have to go, Suzanne. I'll see you soon. All right?"

"Yes. I'll be fine. Go now and be safe," Suzanne said.

****

Only a week had passed since Adrien's last visit when he returned again in the late evening. Suzanne was reading a magazine to keep her mind off the worries that consumed her when the knocking came. She quickly let her friend in and walked into the dining room behind him. Although it was a warm August evening,

Adrien was wearing a jacket. He kept it on as he took a seat.

"I don't have any new documents, Adrien," Suzanne said.

"I still haven't finished delivering all of them from last week," Adrien replied and kept his eyes downcast.

"Something is wrong. I can see it in your face, Adrien."

"Suzanne, I have several things to tell you but, please, may I have something to drink?" Adrien asked.

"Of course. I have some cognac," Suzanne replied.

"Yes, please. Take one for yourself, Suzanne."

Oh God, she thought, he's going to tell me that Maurice is dead. Suzanne took two glasses from the buffet and found the cognac. She poured a generous portion for each of them and sat down across from Adrien.

"Tell me," she spoke quietly.

"Gaston was arrested today," Adrien said.

Suzanne was shocked. She looked up and her expression begged for more information.

"The Gestapo raided one of the cafes and found Gaston and two other men in our cell," Adrien said taking a long drink from his glass.

"Oh, Adrien, we are all in danger!" Suzanne's mind raced as she thought of the situation.

Gaston, the leader of their underground cell, had avoided arrest since 1940. She knew that the Gestapo would question him and torture him to find out who the other members of their cell are.

"You must leave Brussels, Suzanne," Adrien said.

"Yes, I know and I have had a plan in case this happened. I'll take my family with me to....."

Adrien cut her off in mid-sentence. "Don't tell me where you are going. If I am picked up, I don't want to talk. If I don't know where you are, it can't be revealed."

Suzanne nodded in agreement and then asked, "Aren't you going to leave, too?"

150

"No. I'll live on the streets and in the network of houses," Adrien said. "If I keep moving around like your brother and Amand, they won't find me."

"You sound very sure, Adrien. I hope you are right. Now, you said you had a few things to tell me; what else?" asked Suzanne.

Adrien looked directly into her eyes and his gaze lingered for several moments.

"Adrien, I'm prepared for whatever you tell me," Suzanne spoke bravely.

"All right, Suzanne. It's about Maurice. I know a man who does a lot of work in Malines and I found him. He knows for a fact that Maurice was on a train for Poland. The trains only go to a place called Auschwitz. It is a concentration camp that is primarily for extermination. My contact told me that almost all of the transports are going there for that purpose." Adrien took a deep breath and continued. "He saw Maurice being put on the train in January, and he said that his physical condition was terrible. He was extremely thin. My contact said that men held in prisons for months like Maurice, didn't have a chance. Only a few escaped execution if they were in very good health and strong. I'm sorry, Suzanne," Adrien's voice trailed away.

Suzanne had held Adrien's eyes as silent tears fell upon her beautiful high cheekbones. She wasn't surprised by anything he told her. She had told herself that he was dead after the letter he wrote saying goodbye. Instinctively she had known her precious *bebe* had been killed by the *Boche.*

Adrien reached for one of Suzanne hands and took it into his squeezing it ever so slightly.

"Adrien, thank you for telling me. I knew in my heart. Now I have to tell *Maman* what's happened to Gaston and I'll get ready to leave in the morning."

Adrien was amazed at how composed she was. She is surely brave and understands that it's up to her to keep her family safe, he thought. "I better leave," he replied.

They both stood and Adrien took her into his arms. He embraced her briefly and told her not to come back until the war is over.

Suzanne stepped back and said, "We won't. Be well, dear Adrien. I'll see you when the war is over," she managed a small smile.

Adrien left quickly through the rear garden gate. When he had reached the rear of the long yard and was about to go over the hedge, he stopped. Adrien put his face into his hands to muffle the sound of a few deep sobs. He had barely contained his grief while he was with his best friend's wife. No, his widow, Adrien thought. Her composure made him more emotional than he could bear.

He pulled a handkerchief from his pocket after a few moments and mopped up his tears. Adrien straightened his back and breathed deeply. He put the handkerchief away and checked the breast pocket of his jacket to make sure the folder Suzanne had given him earlier was secure. Adrien got over the hedge and zigzagged through several gardens making his way to a back street that would lead him to a safe house on a neighborhood street in Dilbeek. The forged identity cards would be welcomed by the leaders of the *Comete*.

****

Suzanne finished feeding the children breakfast. Serge kept asking where they were going and how long would they be gone. He wanted to know why his grandmother wasn't going with them. Finally Suzanne beseeched him to stop asking questions until they were out of the city. Francine was taking care of Nadine and finished changing her diaper. Eva was clearing the table and talking non-stop to both of her daughters.

After Adrien had left, Suzanne went next door to her mother's house. She let herself in the back door and found Eva reading in an armchair. Eva was startled by Suzanne's entrance.

"What's wrong?" she asked her daughter.

152

"Adrien came to see me, *Maman*. The leader of our cell has been arrested by the Gestapo."

"Oh, no," her mother gasped.

"I must leave the city with the children as we've talked about in the past," Suzanne said.

Eva regained her composure and answered, "Yes, you must. You need to take Francine with you to help you take care of Nadine. It is too much for you to go alone with two children."

"Yes, I agree, *Maman*, but I thought you will go, also," Suzanne said.

"No. I will stay here. I'll be perfectly safe. It will be too suspicious if both our houses are empty."

"Oh, *Maman*, what if the Gestapo comes and asks where I am. They'll surely come and question you."

"Suzanne, I've dealt with them before, remember?"

Suzanne nodded her head remembering the time that they had clipped the wool from their sheep so they could make yarn. The Gestapo had come asking all of the households to give them their wool. Not everyone had sheep, but there were a dozen or so in the neighborhood. Eva had planned well for that moment. She sent Francine to the attic telling the *Boche* her daughter would fetch the wool. Francine did, but it was old wool they had found from a discarded mattress and the moths had been feasting on it for a long time. Francine handed over a big sack of wool and the Gestapo left peacefully. Later that evening the women had laughed wondering if the *Boche* had discovered that not all of their wool was usable.

Suzanne smiled at the memory and at her mother. "I guess you are right, *Maman*. What will you tell them if they ask for me?"

"I'll tell them you went to Paris to try to find work in order to feed your family. I'll tell them I haven't received a letter from you and don't know where you are."

"You know, *Maman*, they are starting to arrest wives of Jews and children."

153

"I know. When you are in Felenne, Please get the children christened. They can't arrest them as Jews if they have christening documents."

"I'll think about it, *Maman*. That would dishonor Maurice."

"Maurice would do it himself if he were here, Suzanne."

Suzanne had decided not to tell her mother what Adrien had told her about her husband's deportation. She knew he was dead, but if she didn't tell anyone, maybe it wasn't true. She would tell her later when the war was over.

"You better hurry and be on your way, Suzanne," her mother broke her reverie.

"Yes. I'm so afraid we won't find transportation along the way," Suzanne said.

"Stick with the old roads. The Germans don't use them as much. You'll find farmers going back to their villages, and they'll give you rides. For now, get out of the city with the tram," Eva reminded her daughter of the plan.

"*Maman*, I won't write to you," Suzanne said. "I'll ask Uncle George to write but he will have to let you know by coding a message. I'll tell Uncle George to tell you that 'the deer are hiding in the forest knowing we, the hunters, are hungry for their food.'"

"Yes, Suzanne. When I know the 'deer are hiding,' I'll know that you are safe in the village."

"All right, it's time to go." Suzanne put her purse across her shoulder and chest. She had money, gold and diamonds hidden in various garments. They were on her and the entire traveling party. Her mother knew where the rest of it was should anything happen to her before the war ended.

The two women embraced and kissed on the cheeks. Eva embraced her other daughter and her little grandson. She kissed the cheek of the ten month old Nadine and helped them out of the house. "I'll lock up, Suzanne. *Bon chance, cherie.*"

"We'll see you soon, *Maman. Aurevoir.*"

Eva watched the family that meant everything in the world to her walk away with only one little suitcase so they wouldn't draw suspicion. She knew her brother, George, would help them once they arrived in Felenne. This damn war is destroying our entire family, Eva thought. If only the Americans would get here, the war will be won. It took the Americans in the last war and she knew it would take them again to kick out the *Boche.*

Arrival in the Ardennes

George Dejardin held Suzanne in his arms for at least a minute. He had kissed and embraced Francine and Serge and fawned over the new baby, little Nadine. When he took his eldest niece into his arms to kiss her on the cheeks, she fell against his warm torso. George stroked her back for a few moments and after hugging her he put her at arms' length to see how she looked.

"Suzanne, *cherie*, you look wonderful even after all this time in this dreadful war," George wanted to boost her spirits. "Come now, children, let's all go into the dining room for something to eat and drink.

"Gabrielle," he called for his wife, "Suzanne and the children are here!"

They followed their Uncle George into the large dining room and Aunt Gaby appeared from the kitchen. "Suzanne, Francine, oh my, and the two little ones." Gaby rushed to the women and kissed each three times on the cheeks. She leaned down and kissed her great nephew and pinched the cheek of Nadine who seemed too afraid of the new surroundings to protest.

"Come dears, come sit, I have some wonderful refreshments in the kitchen. Take off your coats and put everything down. You know where the WC is and it'll only take a few minutes to make some coffee," she was talking very rapidly. "What will the boy have to drink, hmmm?"

"I would like milk please," Serge answered politely.

Gaby clapped her hands together, "Then milk it is!"

As she rushed to the kitchen, Suzanne thought she had never seen her aunt so glad to see them. They had visited each other often before the war. George and Gaby's son, Andre, was the same age as Suzanne, and their younger son, Stephan, was only a year older than Francine. Suzanne remembered playing for hours in the stream that ran near their house. The boys would fish with their father and the girls would sunbathe and pick wildflowers to take back to their mother.

156

Eva didn't care for her sister-in-law, Gaby, very much but they managed to be amicable. George and his family enjoyed coming to Brussels for some city entertainment when he had holidays from the school where he was both teacher and principal. Eva was delighted to go to their house in the Ardennes to enjoy the fresh, clean summer air.

Suzanne took Nadine onto her lap as Francine went to the WC and then to the bathroom to wash up. She called for Serge to come and get washed up and he grudgingly left the dining room where he anticipated a cold glass of milk and perhaps some bread with jam.

Alone with her uncle, Suzanne let out a deep long breath. "Thank you for receiving us, Uncle George. I'm so glad we finally made it here."

"Oh, Suzanne, when we got Eva's letter telling us to expect you because you had no alternative, I worried so much. What happened my dear?" George asked.

Suzanne recounted the most recent details that occurred when Adrien had told her of the danger she, and possibly the children, were in. Then she explained what had happened to Maurice.

"Oh, my dear Suzanne, I don't know what to say. You have been so brave and risked so much," George said. "Here we have felt nothing from the war. We even have plenty of food because of all of the farms."

"Well, that's wonderful news," Suzanne said as her stomach growled. "We haven't had much to eat since we left home. We had some bread, dried sausage and water and we picked apples along the road."

Her uncle got up and went to the kitchen for a moment. When he returned he said, "I told Gaby to make sure there are plenty of sandwiches!"

"You're very kind; thank you," Suzanne said.

"We are family, Suzanne, don't be ridiculous," her uncle replied. "Go wash up now, I think I hear Francine and Serge coming down."

Suzanne left with Nadine and relished the water and soap as she cleansed her face and her daughter's. Soon they rejoined the family in the dining room.

Gaby had laid out the china and a huge platter of ham and paté with pickles. There was large tub of butter and a basket of bread. She had baked an apple tart and a bowl of whipped cream sat next to it. It was almost too much for any of them to comprehend. They hadn't seen this amount of rich, delicious food in years.

Serge looked at his mother and said, "*Maman* may I start eating?"

Uncle George looked at his niece and saw the emotion on her face and answered for her, "Of course, Serge, please take some sandwiches."

The family began to take sandwiches and Gaby poured coffee. Real coffee! It seemed unbelievable.

"I know what you're thinking," the aunt spoke understanding their astonishment. "We don't have coffee all of the time. We had quite a bit of it stored and we rationed it for special occasions and for Sundays!"

"Thank you for sharing it with us," Francine was truly grateful.

The family ate and drank and the Duchesne sisters and the little children couldn't believe the tastes in their mouths and the fullness in their bellies. It made them forget about the war for the time being.

"Tell us about your journey here, Suzanne. How did you manage?" George wanted to know.

Suzanne took a cigarette that her uncle offered. She hadn't had one for a long time, and it tasted very good although it caused her to cough a bit. She had put Nadine down on the carpet and Serge was playing with her.

"We left right after breakfast five days ago. First we took the tram as far south as we could on the Chausee Waterloo," Suzanne said.

She continued, "On the chausee a truck stopped and the driver asked how far we were going. I told him we were going to the French border. He was only going

158

to Nivelles to pick up a load of coal but we could get in the back of the truck."

"How did you know you could trust him?" George interrupted.

"His accent was pure *Bruxelloise*! Unless he was a collaborator, I knew he was fine. I had to take the chance," Suzanne said.

"Yes, of course, go on Suzanne," George replied.

"We got out just before Nivelles and stayed on the N5 going south," Suzanne continued. "We walked a few more kilometers and then looked for a place to spend the night. There wasn't any place that I could see, but Francine spotted a farmhouse. We went there and asked if we could rest for the night in their barn. They asked if the police were looking for us and I told them no, we just wanted to get out of occupied Brussels. We had had enough."

"And they let you?" Gaby asked. "Yes, and they gave us fresh milk and some cheese to go with the bread we had," Suzanne said. "We were fine there. The next morning we kept on walking along the national road for at least 20 kilometers. We had almost arrived in Charleroi. Finally, a truck stopped again. The driver was with his wife and they were headed to Philipeville. That saved us about 30 more kilometers. When we got there they invited us to stay in their house. We were exhausted from walking all morning and into the early afternoon. We were grateful that we had shelter and they shared soup with us that evening."

George was shaking his head almost in disbelief. How could his nieces do this grand feat with the little children?

"In the morning we headed east on the N40," Suzanne said. I knew we had to keep away from the French border in case there were guards. Germans. We walked and walked all day stopping only to rest and eat what we had. I think we walked about 30 kilometers, and then we saw an abandoned house on an overgrown farm. We were careful when we approached it. When we saw it was empty, we collapsed inside. There was no furniture, but we fell asleep on an old carpet.

"We slept too long this morning, but it was good that we did. After only a couple of kilometers a truck stopped along the road outside of Hastiere. The mountains get quite high there and it was going to be difficult. The driver took a long look at us and asked where we were headed. I told him the truth. I told him we were coming here. Something in his face told me he was with the Resistance and I trusted him. He drove us around the border and left us only two kilometers from Felenne. And here we are! Exhausted but very lucky."

Gaby stood up and declared, "I know it is early, but I have your bedrooms prepared if you want to go sleep early."

"Aunt Gaby, I think that is a wonderful idea," Suzanne said. "This is the first time I have felt relaxed in months. If Nadine doesn't cry, I will sleep for hours!" Suzanne declared.

"Let me show you the two rooms. I made a little bed for Serge to sleep in the same room as Francine. Is that all right dear?" Gaby asked.

"Yes, Aunt Gaby. We often sleep together," Francine was happy that they would all have beds again.

"In the morning, Uncle George, I'd like to find an apartment to rent. I hope you have some ideas," Suzanne said.

"Yes, dear. That is all for tomorrow. Now, go with your aunt and have a good rest. I'll see you at breakfast," George said.

****

The house was right in the center of the village of Felenne. It was a three- story, extremely large house built of dark red brick. The color and size of the house distinguished it from all of the gray stone homes along the street. The Eloy family owned it and had divided it into three apartments. Their hope had been that their two children would continue to live there with their families, but that didn't happened. Eloy's son had joined the Free French Army in 1940 and was still somewhere in France or perhaps in England. Monsieur and Madame Eloy didn't know for sure. Their daughter did remain in the Ardennes but moved into the home of her husband's parents after their marriage a year ago.

Monsieur Eloy was happy to help his friend, George Dejardin, with housing for his nieces and the children. There was a huge apartment with three bedrooms, a bathroom and W.C., and a kitchen. At the back door of the kitchen was a large garden and Eloy told them they could plant a garden in the spring. Meanwhile there were plenty of canned vegetables and fruits they could share. Uncle George added that he and Gaby had more than they would need for the winter.

Suzanne looked around the apartment and liked everything. "How much will the rent be Monsieur?" she questioned.

"200 francs a month, Madame," he answered. "Will that be agreeable?"

Suzanne was thrilled with the price. "Yes, monsieur, that will be fine. Please let me pay you now for the first month."

She reached into her handbag and Eloy replied, "Oh, don't worry about that now, Madame, please."

Suzanne brought out the francs. "Please take it now, Monsieur Eloy. I have set aside enough to pay for a year, but I hope the war is over before then!"

Eloy took the money. "Let's have a toast for our new agreement. Please come into the dining room."

Madame Eloy brought over a bottle of white wine and some glasses. Monsieur uncorked the French wine and poured each of them a glass. "To our new neighbors," he said lifting his glass.

"To the end of the war," Uncle George added. "*Vive la Belgique!*"

They each drank and said in unison, "*Vive la Belgique!*"

Suzanne finished her glass and shook hands with her new landlords. "Thank you very much. Now I'll go get the children and my sister and we will begin to set up the household. I couldn't bring more than one change of clothes and will need to sew some new outfits. Do you think I'll find what I need here, Madame Eloy?"

"Hmmm, if you don't find it here, we can go to Beauring and buy material. I'll talk to the women in the village and see if we can find some coats for winter. You'll need heavier coats than what you are wearing."

"Thank you again, Madame. If we can get to Beauring tomorrow, I can begin sewing. My aunt will let me use her machine."

"I have a good machine, also. Gilbert will take us to Beauring tomorrow," Madame Eloy said.

"Of course," Eloy replied.

Suzanne took the key offered by Monsieur Eloy and thanked them both again. She and her uncle left and walked the five blocks to the Dejardin home.

"Are you sure you want to rent the apartment, niece?" he asked.

"Yes, Uncle George. I don't want to be a burden on you and Aunt Gaby. The children get fairly noisy, and I don't want to disturb you. Your house was meant for you two and your sons, not an extra four people. In this apartment Francine can have her privacy which she really needs at this age. We will all see each other often," Suzanne offered a very reassuring smile to her only uncle.

Uncle George nodded as they walked side by side to his home. Before entering the house he turned to face his niece, "You will be safe here. I promise you."

Suzanne was moved by his concern and reached out and took his hand. "Yes, Uncle George, we will be safe here."

On the Town

Winter came soon after the men of the 347th and thousands of others had settled into the barracks at Radstock, England. Jack had made the right move in claiming the bunks near the little stove. There was enough coal to keep it going most of the day and all night. The men had taken it upon themselves to make up a schedule of soldiers in charge of stoking the fire and retrieving coal from the central bin. No one minded the task because without the fire burning they would be subject to freezing temperatures in the barracks.

Training during the day had been varied. The engineers had continuous combat training. Many of them would be going in at the same time of the infantry during the invasion in France. Many companies would be needed to off load the supplies and to set up the supply lines. After the invasion began, more engineers would be needed to clear out obstacles or to rebuild as the Allies moved deeply into France.

None of them knew what part of the French coast they would invade, but they knew that all of the beaches were well fortified by the Germans. There was no doubt that it would be difficult, and getting the supplies to the front would be of utmost urgency. The engineers trained continuously in building supply lines. They knew how to build bridges and how to blow them up. There would only be one chance to get it right, and all of their lives depended on getting it right.

Weekends came and went with most of the soldiers getting passes. Many of the GI's would visit the village taprooms and occasionally a dance that was organized by churches or the USO. They had plenty of good times, but the monotony was making Jack edgy.

Jack had been happy to get out of Ft. Bragg but the damp, cold winter in southern England was just as bad. Though Jack wanted the warm air of spring, he also dreaded it. Everyone talked about the invasion happening as soon as spring arrived. It made sense to him.

Hitler had taken some heavy losses dealt mostly by the Russians, but the Germans were still strongly entrenched throughout Western Europe. The allied countries were waiting for them to kill the Hun and drive them back across the Rhine and to destroy them. It weighed heavily on the minds of many of the soldiers. Jack knew the Americans were building an incredible military presence. The amount of artillery, vehicles, planes and ships couldn't really be fathomed. He was no general, but Jack had a lot of faith in Generals Bradley, Eisenhower and Patton.

Jack's company was attached to the First Army and Bradley since Ft. Bragg. There was always speculation about Patton's next command, and the possibility of reassignment of the engineers. The men had heard many stories about the General, and knew he was ruthless and hungry for battle. Jack tried not to dwell on his company's role for the invasion and made sure he understood his training. He and his buddies would all watch out for each other and planned on coming out of it alive.

Right before Christmas, Carl, Steve, Phil and Jack took a three day pass and went into London. They were able to take a train and were excited about seeing the famous old city.

The first day there, they took a sightseeing tour around all the famous places. Seeing Westminster Abbey and Big Ben along with Tower Bridge made history, learned back at Lincoln High School, come to life for Jack. Nothing was better than the real life experience, he thought. The friends found that Piccadilly Circus was the best place for American soldiers on leave. It was filled with locals and a horde of GI's, British and French soldiers. It was also a gathering place for very lovely young women.

The area reminded Jack of Times Square in New York. None of his friends had ever been to New York and Jack told them he'd take them around his hometown when they got back there.

There were dozens of pubs in the many buildings at Piccadilly. Jack and the fellas went from one to the next and to the next again. On their first night they all got drunk on the bitter, dark beer and wandered back to their hotel on Coventry Street singing. The four of them had gotten two rooms at the Royal Ivy Hotel and fell into their beds laughing. In no time, the laughs were replaced by the heavy snoring of inebriated men.

After sleeping late, the four Yanks enjoyed a breakfast of eggs and bangers and toast. They decided to take the drinking a bit easier on this night and to start looking for a night of romance. Phil told them he didn't mind if they wanted to leave him behind when they found dates.

"Whadya mean?" asked Steve. "Look Phil, I know you're from Massachusetts, but that doesn't mean you have to act like a Puritan, buddy."

Phil's face reddened with embarrassment. "I'm not a Puritan. I've got my gal back home."

"Yeah, yeah," it was Carl's turn, "We know you've got Marilyn at home. Don't you think she's still going to marry you, Phil, if you find a little friendship tonight?"

"We promised to be true to each other," Phil spoke quietly hanging his head down.

Jack spoke up, "Look, Phil, it's real nice and all that you love a girl back home, but you gotta think about your options now that we're not in the States anymore."

Phil looked at his best friend. "What do you mean?"

"I mean, none of us knows what's going to happen to them in the next few months. England might be the last time we see women. You don't want to die without getting a little foreign ass, do you, pal?" asked Jack.

Steve looked surprised. "Last time we see women? Hey, I plan to see and sleep with plenty of women in gay Paree, buddy!"

They all laughed, even Phil.

165

"Listen fellas," Phil felt a little more comfortable now, "I'll play it as it comes. Okay?"

"That-a-boy!" Carl cheered.

With the ground rules for the evening set, the friends decided to take in more of the sights around London town. They were amazed at the destruction of many buildings by all of the German bombing raids during the Blitz. There were old men, women and some youngsters working at those sites. They were loading up wheelbarrows with whole bricks and piling them in a storage area. Other laborers were picking up broken debris and taking it to a different area.

Carl let out a low whistle. "They'll have plenty of work to do here when the war is over."

That evening they found a terrific nightclub. The jazz band was fantastic, and it was playing all of the latest tunes from the States. Jack was sipping on his beer when he spotted a table of four lovely girls. He elbowed Steve and cocked his head in the direction of the women. A smile spread across Steve's handsome face softening the square jaw he had.

"Good eye, Jack. Don't know why I was dozing off," Steve chuckled. "Hey Carl," he poked him in the ribs.

Carl had been talking to the barman about Ohio. He was trying to explain to the limey that there was something other than New York in America. Carl was glad for Steve's interruption. "Yeah, buddy?"

"Over there at 11 o'clock, my friend. A group of four lovelies," Steve was trying to fake an English accent and not being very successful.

"They want Americans. Yanks," Jack reminded him.

"Yep, you're right and here we are. What are we waiting for?" Steve finished his beer and put the glass on the bar.

"Phil, you in?" Carl asked.

After a moment of silence, Jack said, "Yes, Phil's in for now. No harm in going over and talking with the girls, is there, Phil?"

Phil shook his head and moved along with his three pals not knowing what he would do. He doubted he would even be able to speak. He had only ever dated Marilyn and hadn't ever done more than kiss her. Even his last night at home before going to Ft. Bragg, they had only hugged and kissed each other. She promised to wait for him and to write him often. He promised to be true to her and to write as much as he could. They had both kept their promises thus far. Phil knew there was nothing wrong with going over to sit with the girls.

As they reached the table, Jack notice the girls seemed to anticipate their arrival. He spoke first, "Hi ladies. My name is Jack and these are my buddies. Carl, Steve and Phil." The guys all nodded slightly.

The medium height brunette with long flowing curls spoke for the table in a distinctly London accent. "Gentlemen, I'm Maureen and my friends are Alice, Mary, and Lenore," Maureen smiled back directly at Jack.

Jack was pleased to see that Maureen had a terrific smile and good teeth. All of the jokes that went around the barracks were about how pretty the girls were until they opened their mouths filled with crooked or sometimes missing teeth. The other girls smiled and they all had teeth that weren't bad.

Carl asked if they could pull over some chairs and join them. The girls nodded. As they got situated, Jack made sure he was close to the brunette, Maureen.

"How about some beers, girls?" Steve spoke up.

"Sure, we'd love some," Alice said as she moved a bit closer to Steve.

Steve signaled the waitress and they ordered 8 pints of bitter. The friends pulled cigarettes from their breast pockets and offered them to the girls who took them eagerly. Jack thought for a moment that the girls might not have enough money to buy their own cigarettes and beers.

The band was on break and it gave the guys the time to work up a little conversation. Lenore had moved over to Carl and that left Mary to converse with Phil. She was a slight young woman and fit in with Phil.

They spent some time getting to know each other and when the band came back, they danced together until they were so hot from the jitterbug that they decided to put their coats on and go outside. The girls told them they knew other clubs if they wanted to go elsewhere. Little by little they were definitely walking in pairs. Lenore and Carl went on to a club, and he let Steve know that he'd hopefully be bringing the girl back with him to the hotel in a couple of hours. Steve promised to vacate.

Phil told his pals that he and Mary were going to walk along the Thames for a while. Jack knew that meant he had the entire evening to entertain Maureen at the hotel. Steve and Alice walked several yards behind Jack and his girl as they walked to the Royal Ivy. They said goodnight to each other in the hallway on the third floor and went into their rooms.

Jack helped Maureen out of her coat and hung it on the hook behind the door. He put his own jacket on the back of a chair. Maureen sat on the edge of the bed and looked up at the handsome Yank she would spend the next few hours with. He looked American, she thought. He looks as good as any of the movie stars she had seen at the cinema. Finally she spoke, "You're not my first Yank, you know. But I don't do this all of the time."

Jack sat down next to her. "I'm sure you don't, but I bet you get lonely. All of the men are gone."

"You better believe it, Jack," she wasn't kidding. "This damn war has been going on for four years. We don't have enough to eat, we don't have cigarettes, and we don't have our men. I decided after you Yanks started coming over that I wasn't going to be lonely anymore."

168

"I'm glad you did," Jack said as he stroked her beautiful brown locks. "The W.C. is at the end of the hall if you need it."

"Yes. I have my diaphragm to put in. You needn't worry about doing anything on your end," Maureen gave a little laugh as she picked up her handbag and went out of the room.

Jack undressed and got under the covers. He plumped up the pillow for Maureen. The door opened and she looked over at him and smiled. "Comfy?"

"Uh-huh. I'll be more comfy when you join me."

Jack watched Maureen undress. She did so in a very natural way not trying to be seductive but his anticipation was heightened. Maureen slipped under the covers and Jack pulled her close and kissed her deeply. They made love hurriedly. They were both eager and satisfied each other quickly.

Jack reached for his cigarettes and Zippo. He lit two and handed one to Maureen. They smoked quietly for a few minutes and then talked about each other's lives. She was a lovely woman and they would never see each other again. For a moment Jack felt emptiness. That was not usual for him.

Maureen stubbed out her cigarette and reached over to play with Jack. "So you are an American Jew, I see," she stated.

"Anything wrong with that?"

"No, not a thing," all the while stroking him. "I'm just making conversation."

Jack responded, "Let's make this time a lot slower and see where it takes us."

Maureen only responded with a groan as Jack began to explore her body with his mouth.

The last day of the four friends' three-day pass dawned late. It was past 10 o'clock when they began to stir. Jack looked over at the second bed in the room and saw that Phil was asleep. He hadn't heard him come in,

169

but knew it must have been very late. Maureen had stayed until about two in the morning.

He smiled thinking about her. She was quite a young woman. Lovely and experienced. They had enjoyed each other's love making skills three times. Maureen wished him goodnight and good luck when she slipped out of bed to dress. As she pulled the door shut, Jack fell soundly asleep.

In the morning light, Jack pictured her face. He wondered if he might remember her face when he would be alone at night in the battlefield. That's what had made him feel empty last night. Phil always had Marilyn's face to remember and his relationship to comfort him whenever he needed it. Jack had no one.

He got out of bed, pulled on his pants, grabbed a towel and went down the hall for a shower. On the way back he knocked on Steve and Carl's door. "Rise and shine, fellas. This is our last day in London!"

Jack could hear growling. They were still alive. He pounded once more before entering his room. Phil was up and getting his stuff ready for the shower.

"Hey, Phil. Have a nice time last night?"

"Yeah, Jack, I did. Mary was a real nice girl. We talked a lot and I think we had a lot in common. We found a place that served fish 'n' chips late at night and we pigged out. Poor kid, I don't think she had much money to get a good meal very often. We had fun."

"Good, Phil, good." Jack started dressing.

"I'm going to the shower. The other guys up?" Phil asked.

"Yeah, pal, they're starting to move. Bang on their door again," Jack said.

The American friends spent their last afternoon in London, window shopping and looking at the Christmas stuff. Phil bought a nice scarf for Marilyn to send home as a gift. None of the other friends bought anything. They didn't have sweethearts. Later they found a really nice restaurant that served a good pot roast with mashed potatoes and carrots. They had chocolate cake for dessert. They enjoyed a place away from the damp and cold mess hall at the base.

None of them talked about the girls from last night. Carl, Steve and Jack had all smiled at each other, and because they had a lot of respect for Phil they didn't talk about the details of the previous evening. They walked a few blocks to Victoria Station and waited for their train back to Radstock.

On the ride back into the southern countryside, Jack thought he'd like to visit London again before winter was over. During the next few months they would all hone their skills until they could assemble explosives with their eyes shut, build a bridge in a matter of a day or two and get the supplies to the frontlines in their mock battlefields. The men in the 347th and all of the advanced section engineers would be ready for the spring of 1945.

Waiting for the Allies

The Dejardin family and their cousins from Brussels were spread out along the stream. George and his son Andre were quite away downstream fishing for trout while Stephan helped Serge put his fly on the lure on his pole. Serge had thrived since their arrival in Felenne. They had enjoyed some warm days in the autumn, and they had plenty of wood to keep their fire going throughout the winter.

Suzanne and her sister were sitting on a blanket in the warm May sunshine watching the men and keeping their eyes on Nadine who was running in the grass and picking flowers that bloomed wildly. At two-and-a-half, the little girl had boundless energy. Here in the calm and quiet life of the Ardennes, Nadine had calmed quite a bit. There were still nights with little sleep, but they were not constant as they had been in Brussels. The safe atmosphere had allowed them all to relax.

No one in this little village had ever seen a German soldier or official of the occupation. The mayor had been given papers that pronounced the laws of occupied Belgium in June 1940. Everyone was issued a ration card and told that gasoline was limited by ration also. After a few months, the mayor had called a town meeting and everyone agreed that there was no reason to ration food since they grew and raised their own. Gasoline would be used sparingly since delivery was not on any kind of regular schedule. The mayor, priest and school principal would keep records to show that rationing was carried out should an official of the Third Reich decide to make an appearance.

In this peaceful environment the Duchesne – Morgen household learned to resume living without fear. Serge went to school where his great uncle taught the older boys and his teacher, Monsieur LeClaire, taught him the rudimentary beginnings of language and mathematics. Serge was younger than most of the other boys, but Uncle George thought it would be good for him to get an introduction to education and would keep the boy engaged in structured activity.

Francine had finished school in the summer of 1943 and would have been in college if they had stayed in Brussels. Uncle George loaned his niece books from his time at the university. Weekly they would have discussions on literature, history and philosophy. Francine was content with advancing her knowledge realizing what an outstanding tutor she had in her uncle.

Now in early May 1944 they were all enjoying a Sunday picnic in the beautiful, warm sunshine. Family discussions revolved around the potentially imminent invasion by the allied armies. Churchill gave them hope as he spoke to them weekly in his French radio broadcasts.

Francine was off the blanket running along the edge of the stream with Nadine and Suzanne lay back on the blanket and closed her eyes against the sun. How wonderful this feels, she thought. The feeling brought her back in time when she and Maurice had been at the beach at Knocke sur Mer the summer after they had married. They were lying on a blanket in the warm sand with their arms entwined. Maurice was whispering in her ear telling her how much he loved and adored her and that they would spend their entire lives drenched in the warmth of the sun or in their own love when the sun was blotted out by dark rain clouds. A light breeze passed her cheek as Suzanne was seeing Maurice's face in the depth of her mind. The breeze felt like the warmth of her husband's breath against her cheek as it had that day on the beach so long ago.

Suzanne put her hand on her cheek and felt the warmth intensify. She did not want to open her eyes and break this wonderful spell. Or was it truly a visit from her beloved Maurice. She felt as though he was telling her everything would be all right. She was safe. The family was safe and no harm would come to them.

The spell was broken as Nadine ran onto the blanket and threw herself against her mother's body.

Suzanne shielded her eyes from the sun with her left hand and tussled her daughter's blond, curly hair with the other. Nadine gave a laugh then wiggled free from her mother's reach.

"Nadine, are you having a nice time?" asked Suzanne.

"Yes, *Maman*. Can we come here again tomorrow?"

"No. Not for the whole afternoon. It's Sunday and Uncle George doesn't have to work today."

"Why do we have to come here with him?" Nadine was beginning to pout.

"We don't have to, but it is more fun with the whole family. We can come here again soon. I promise," Suzanne said.

"Good," the little girl said as she sprang to her feet and ran away to play with her aunt.

Suzanne leaned back on her elbows and watched her children and the rest of the family enjoying this glorious day. There seemed to be nothing to fear living here in the Ardennes Forest hidden from the war. She made a mental note to not let down her guard. The Gestapo was everywhere, and she was sure they might be looking for her at any time. Her mother was sending letters addressed to Uncle George only and she hid little messages to her daughters in the contents. If the Gestapo were to call on Eva, she would tell them that her daughters left for France to try and find work and she hadn't gotten a letter in many months.

George was approaching her blanket. He held a basket in one hand and the rod and reel in the other.

"Well Uncle George, do you have supper in the basket?" asked Suzanne.

"Indeed I do! I wasn't the only successful fisherman today," George smiled and looked over his shoulder. Serge and Stephan came running up behind him.

"*Maman*, I caught a big trout!" Serge declared triumphantly.

174

"Yes, you did, Serge, one of the biggest!" George validated his great nephew's claim.

"Will we eat them tonight?" Serge asked.

"If you like, Serge. When we get back to the house, I'll show you how to clean them. Stephan, you'll help Serge learn," George urged.

"Yes, Papa, of course," Stephan was happy to help. He loved the Sunday outings to the river during the spring.

"Good. Then I suggest we pack up our belongings and get home so that *Maman*, and your Aunt Gaby, will know what we are having for supper tonight," George said.

Suzanne stood up and gathered the blanket and some picnic items to place in the basket. She waved to Francine and called out for them all to come along. As the family walked along the path back into the village, they were laughing and talking. The exuberance of the afternoon spilled over into every word and each step they took.

Again Suzanne thought about the good luck they had to experience this holiday after four long years of German occupation and deprivation. She felt a twinge of guilt knowing that Maurice was gone forever and that he had suffered so much in the hands of the *Boche*.

Her thoughts were broken when Nadine released her hand and stooped to pick some wild strawberries on the edge of the path. "Look, *Maman*," the little girl showed her mother.

"Those are the first strawberries of the season!" Suzanne exclaimed. "Go ahead, taste it."

Nadine put the small ripe berry into her mouth and chewed. She looked up at Suzanne and smiled, *"C'est bonne, Maman."*

"Yes, *cheri*, strawberries are very good. We'll come tomorrow with a basket and pick as many as we can find, all right?" Suzanne said.

"Oh, yes, *Maman*. Me, too?" asked Nadine.

"Of course. We'll pick them and make a dessert with cream," Suzanne said, not remembering the last time she had had berries and thick rich cream. God, how the war had changed them, Suzanne thought.

"Gaby, we're home," Uncle George called out. His wife was in the garden tending her early vegetables.

"Wonderful. What do you have in that basket?" Aunt Gaby feigned ignorance.

"We have 7 wonderful trout. Two are large and can be shared at supper tonight."

"I was hoping you had a successful fishing trip, George," Gaby said. "Clean them well and rinse them before they come into my kitchen," Gaby smiled at her husband.

Everyone in the Dejardin – Duchesne family went about their tasks to put away the fishing gear and the picnic ware and the process of cleaning the fish. Later that evening they sat down to pan-fried fresh trout, spring peas and country bread. There was a large tub of sweet butter to slather on the bread. The children drank cold glasses of milk while everyone else enjoyed chardonnay from a regional vintner in the northern part of France that was smuggled in by a farmer to make some extra money on the black market.

It's the perfect ending to a perfect day, Suzanne thought. She touched her cheek and still had the sensation that Maurice's warm breath was on her face. She felt reassured by the feeling and she let any latent worries and fears melt away while she finished the last bit of bread and butter.

******

The weather had been warm and sunny during the early part of May, but it turned cloudy with intermittent rain and even fog. The gloomy weather was a heavy weight on all of the people living in Felenne. Neighbors talked about the eventual invasion by the Allies and wondered how much longer they would have to wait. Even though there had been no physical presence by the

Nazis in this remote little corner, the village had to follow the rules of the Occupation. If they ignored them, they would jeopardize the safety of the mayor who had to maintain records. The owners of the bakery, butcher shop and the grocery had to collect ration stamps and keep records that would prove compliance.

Many families had men and women involved in the Resistance and through them they often had bits of information that supplemented what they heard on the BBC. Suzanne never made mention of her role in the Resistance. She had given her service for three years until her own identity was on the verge of exposure. Now her main purpose was to keep their family safe while waiting for the Americans and the rest of the Allies.

The residents of Felenne had been certain that the invasion would take place in May. The crossing of the Channel would have been safe with calm seas and clear skies. Yet here they were on Sunday, June 4, sitting inside while the rain pelted the windows.

Suzanne bundled the children and gathered three umbrellas so they could try to stay dry while walking to her uncle's house for dinner. Francine and Serge walked ahead of her as quickly as they could. Suzanne carried Nadine and held the umbrella over both their heads. Once inside they shed their coats quickly and were hurried into the dining room and the warmth of the fire.

Uncle George was excited and told them all to get comfortable. There was going to be a special announcement on the BBC in just a few more minutes.

"I'm sure it must be Churchill," George said to the family. His sons were seated nearby. "Francine, please go and tell your aunt that they are going to start any minute now."

As Gaby and Francine came into the room, the broadcaster interrupted the concert for the special message by the prime minister of Britain. Churchill's French had a distinctive English accent and he spoke rather slowly, but he did not make any mistakes.

Churchill gave the usual greetings to all of his French, Belgian and Luxembourg listeners and told them that their endurance of the four years of Occupation in their countries would not be unrewarded. He couldn't give any clear indication of when they should expect the invasion because the Nazis were listening as well. Just the fact that the prime minister was giving a message of hope at noon on Sunday was a divergence from the regular day and time of Mr. Churchill's speeches.

When the broadcast returned to music, Uncle George turned the radio down and asked, "What do you think, Andre?" to his oldest son.

"I think we should soon be prepared," Andre replied. "I think we should fill our glasses and toast to the invasion!"

"I hope you are right," Suzanne said as she got to her feet. "But I also think we better be prepared to see Germans in the village."

"Why, Suzanne?" Gaby asked.

"We all assume the invasion will be through Calais," Suzanne said. "The Allies will push the Germans east and perhaps north. I just think we better be ready to see them retreating, and it may be right through our village."

"Suzanne, you always think the worst. We should be happy knowing the invasion will soon start," her sister remarked.

"I am happy. It's the only way we will ever have our freedom again. But we need to be prepared. There may be fighting right here. If there is, we will have to hide or even be prepared to evacuate," Suzanne concluded.

Uncle George thought for a few moments before commenting. "You are right, Suzanne. We should be prepared. News reports will be sketchy at first. It will be hard to know what is actually happening and exactly when it happened.

"Now, let's still have a glass to the invasion," George continued. "I will talk to the mayor after dinner and ask what he thinks about preparedness."

Andre had poured wine for all but the children and they lifted their glasses as George gave the toast. "We welcome with open arms and hearts the arrival of the Americans. The Allies. *Sante!*"

The family echoed, *"Sante!"*

Invasion

It had been raining on and off for the past few days and the soldiers and paratroopers grew more ill at ease with each cloud covered dawn in southern England. The scuttlebutt was so fast and furious about the invasion of Europe known as "Operation Overlord" that the men assumed they were going to get their orders to ship out really soon. Jack and the 347th Engineers had received their orders from Colonel Hulen to hold tight in Radstock and await orders to move on to Southampton.

Jack and his buddies were relieved that they were not going to be in the first wave. There were engineers that would be a part of D-Day in order to start setting up the supply lines that would be necessary to get the frontlines equipped with jeeps, trucks, tanks and ammo once the beaches of France were taken from the Germans. The men speculated about which beach would be their entry landing and the popular guess was Calais. Jack and Steve didn't believe it. They kept telling their pals that it had to be another part of the coast. The Krauts would be expecting them to land at Calais or even Dunkirk to avenge the defeat the English had suffered earlier in the war. Jack and Steve and many of their comrades were certain Eisenhower would have something more devious in mind and make the landing easier.

The men were all on edge waiting to hear the news that the invasion was to begin. It was June 5, and the mess hall was crowded with engineers eating scrambled eggs and limp toast and strong coffee. Jack lit a cigarette and was sipping on his coffee. He leaned forward and said to his group of friends, "If we don't go in the next day or two, the whole operation may be delayed."

"Why do you think that, Jack," Carl asked.

"The moon. There's a full moon right now," Jack said.

"How do you know that? It's cloudy," Carl replied.

180

"Look at the calendar. If it clears and we go soon, the moon will still be full and help out the jumpers," Jack answered with a laugh.

"Oh, I get ya. You think that the paratroopers really need the moonlight?" Carl wondered.

"Yeah, the platoons will be able to find their rendezvous points and it will be easier for our guys to start penetrating into France," Jack said.

"Whadya think they're gonna have us do at first?" Phil asked Jack.

"Don't know. We may go in to build a landing dock for all of the heavy equipment if we go in a few days later," Jack replied.

"I don't think so," Steve remarked. "If we were going in right behind the infantry and paratroopers, we'd already have been moved down to Southampton."

"Hmm," Jack mused, "you're probably right. "Well, one thing's for sure, we're going to France sooner or later."

"You ever thought you'd be going to France?" Steve asked his friends.

The guys shook their heads, but Jack answered, "Never thought much about France but you know I've lived in Mexico and been to parts of South America. It's just another country. Another part of the world."

"You may feel that way," Carl said in a fairly serious tone. "You've had the chance to travel but most of the guys in this place have never left their hometowns."

"What are you complaining about, Carl? You're seeing the world now, ain't you?" Jack chided him.

"Yeah, sure, Jack; this is the way I always wanted to see the world," Carl was miffed.

"Aw, lighten up, Carl. Jack's world experience has already helped us win the girls here in jolly old England. I bet he's brushing up on his French since they gave us the language booklets. Right, Jack?" Steve was asking.

"Sure. I read the book. Easy. French ain't much different than Spanish and I speak that as well as

English. Just wait till we get to Paris, fellas. Just wait,"
Jack grinned as he leaned back in his chair.

They shared the laugh and pushed their chairs
back to get rid of their breakfast trays and move out of
the mess hall. All companies had been ordered to stay
on base. When the orders came to move out, no
company commanders wanted to have to go out and find
their men. The gang of friends decided to go over to the
enlisted men's club to play some cards. It was a way to
pass the time and forget about landing on some beach
with an army of krauts shooting at you.

Later that night when the men were all getting
ready to turn in for the night, their lieutenant came in and
told them to all be "at ease."

"Men, we are on full alert awaiting orders for
advancement to southern England," Lt. Marshall said.

"I'm sure you understand that it means that
Operation Overlord will be starting. I can tell you now
that hundreds of companies have just received their
orders to begin the invasion. We're finally going to go on
with our mission."

The men let out with a round of cheers and
shouted out, "YES, SIR!" in unison. Each man was
experiencing his own personal feelings. But to a man, it
was actually a relief to know that they were all finally on
their way. They were going to do what they were trained
to do and to liberate Europe. The adrenaline rush made
them a part of something that was far larger than any of
them were aware.

****

George Dejardin was pedaling his bicycle at
breakneck speed through the village of Felenne. It was
not quite eight o'clock in the morning and he had heard
the news and wanted to make sure the rest of his family
knew that the invasion had begun. George had a ham
radio set, and the first message he received was from a

182

radio operator in Caen. Caen was the largest town near the coast in Normandy and the operator reported that paratroopers had been dropping from the sky since the dark hours before dawn. Reports were coming in from villages all over the northern party of Normandy describing the thousands of men jumping from airplanes. There had been a tremendous amount of anti-aircraft gunfire by the Nazis, and they struck many of the airplanes that descended to earth as fireballs.

Since dawn, thousands of ships were seen off the Atlantic Beaches at Arromanches and along the entire coast. Landing craft were coming ashore and hundreds, probably thousands of Allied soldiers were running onto the beaches. The reports also told of an enormous amount of gunfire from the German bunkers located at the top of the cliffs that guarded the Norman beaches. Although the reports were filled with hope, they did not belie the mounting death toll along several miles of coastline.

George took off his headset and told his family the fantastic news. They had been expecting this for so long that it was difficult to believe the actual invasion was occurring right this minute only a few hundred kilometers from Felenne.

"I'm going to tell Suzanne and Francine right now," George declared.

"What about school?" his wife looked at him in surprise. "Have you forgotten that you have to teach school?"

"Why, yes, I had forgotten. Andre, Stephan," he called to his sons, "Take your bicycles and ride to the homes of the teachers and tell them there will be no school today! The invasion has begun! Tell everyone that you see that the invasion is on the beaches near Caen. Run!"

Both young men ran to do their father's bidding and George ran out of the house right behind them. He called over his shoulder, "Gaby, tell all of the neighbors on our street and the word will spread."

When George reached Suzanne's house, he put the bike down rapidly and knocked loudly on the door.

The morning was sunny and warm and Francine leaned out of a window on the second floor. "What is it, Uncle George?"

"The invasion! It's begun in France! Now let me in," he had shouted out the message.

People in the street or near open doors or windows came outside and cried out, *"C'est vrai?"* Is it true?

"Yes! I listened on the short wave radio. There are thousands of Allies on the Normandy beaches and paratroopers in the fields and villages," George responded.

Suzanne opened the door and flung her arms around her uncle's neck! "My, God, it's finally happened!"

Tears streamed down his niece's beautiful cheeks and at the same time she laughed and said, "We will have liberty once again!"

"Yes, Suzanne, liberty," George was more solemn as he spoke. The enormity of the day was finally penetrating through all of his senses and sensibility. "The Americans are saving us again. Like in the last war," George's voice trailed off with emotion.

"Come in, Uncle George," Suzanne said.

He regained his composure and his exuberance and said, "No. Get the children and Francine and everyone else in the house. I will go to the mayor's house. We need a Belgian flag to hang from city hall once more!" George shouted.

"Be careful, Uncle George. The Americans have not liberated France yet and they are not here in Belgium," Suzanne was expressing her reservation.

"To hell with Germany! We are going to celebrate the invasion and hang our flag," George said.

George picked up his bicycle and rode off to the mayor's house. Residents were pouring out of their homes and walking toward city hall. Some people had

184

small Belgian flags and a few had French flags. Their French neighbors were only a few kilometers away across the border. Suzanne went back inside, and Francine was already tugging the hand of Nadine to bring her outside and Serge was running out of the door. The other tenants in their large house were coming out and when Suzanne turned to go back into the street, there was a wave of villagers walking towards their town hall.

A few minutes later George and the mayor, Monsieur LeClair, were walking in unison holding the flag. With most of the town's people gathered, the mayor pulled on the cord of the German flag that hung from the second floor balcony of the building. He took the flag from George and went into the building. A few moments passed, and then Monsieur LeClair appeared in the window he just opened. It took him a few minutes to lace the rope into the grommets on the flag and then he secured it to the wall brackets. The flag unfurled as its weight pulled it straight and it fluttered in the light June breeze.

A tremendous cheer came from the crowd. The next cheer was instantaneous. *"Vive la Belgique! Vive la Liberte!"* The people kept cheering.

After a few moments another cheer was led by a deep baritone voice in the crowd, *"Vive la France! Vive les Americains! Vive les Alliers!"*

The cheers and chants kept on for several minutes, and then the mayor spoke from the balcony. "My dear fellow citizens of Felenne. This is indeed the most marvelous news we have had in more than four years." The crowd cheered him onward.

"While we enjoy this day of hope and recognize that it will only be a matter of weeks before all of Europe is liberated, we must be cautious," the mayor said. "When we go back to our houses for dinner, I will take down our precious flag, and hang the flag of German occupation again."

The crowd was stunned and then began to grumble and shout remarks. "No. Not possible! We can't allow that filthy flag on our village."

Monsieur LeClair motioned for quiet, and he received it. "I say this with regret. I want liberty and know we will have it soon. But we must think about everyone's safety. Suppose Germans come through here and see this. We all know terrible stories of the Nazis killing villagers for disobeying orders. We have come so far without a scratch, please; we must not risk our future freedom."

"The mayor is right," George Dejardin was speaking in front of the crowd. "It turns my stomach to have to raise this flag again," he kicked it as he spoke, "but we must."

There was some grumbling but it was less. Other voices rose above the din of the crowd. "Monsieur the mayor is correct. We must use common sense. We will have true and real victory here soon."

After a short while the crowd began to disperse. Clusters of neighbors walked together toward their streets and homes, and nothing could dampen the spirit of liberty that had fallen upon them.

George joined his family. They all were talking at once with excitement and anticipation. Finally George got them to quiet down. "Since this is a holiday, I say we put together a family picnic and go to the stream for an afternoon of eating, drinking wine and fishing. What do you all say?"

"We say, yes!" Francine shouted.

The whole family laughed and then fell in step to walk back to their homes and put together two picnic baskets. Nadine was tugging on her mother's skirt. Suzanne looked down and picked up her little girl who was not yet two-years-old.

"Oh my baby, you are probably afraid, wondering what just happened," Suzanne spoke soothingly. "One day I will tell you everything that just took place so that you'll remember."

Serge was holding a little flag and waving it as they made their way through the village. Francine told him to wave it now and to put it away until the Americans come to liberate Felenne. Serge nodded in agreement.

****

No one slept late on the morning of June 6, 1944. The men had talked well into the night about the possibilities for real success on the beaches of the Atlantic Ocean. There was a great deal of tension and excitement running through all of the barracks in Radstock where they awaited orders to move south. Jack, like the rest of them, got up early and headed to the mess hall at the first light of day. He wanted to hear the news. Had the Airborne been successful with their predawn drops? Were the ships blasting the hell out of the German bunkers? We're our guys making it to land?

They sat around in groups drinking coffee and smoking. Every so often they would look at the door waiting for one of their commanders to come in with news. By seven in the morning they still were sitting; waiting. Phil got up first and announced, "I can't stand it. I gotta do something." He turned and headed for the door.

Jack got up and followed after Phil. "Hey, Phil, wait up. Let's do something together."

Phil was at the door and waited for Jack. The two men walked out and over to the enlisted men's club, but Phil didn't want to go inside. He looked up at Jack. "I'm scared, Jack. I'm scared and this waiting is gonna kill me," Phil said.

"Hey, buddy, I'm afraid, too," replied Jack. "Every man here is afraid. We're all in this together. Don't let this get you, man; we got a long row ahead." Jack tried to calm the fears of his friend.

"How can you be so calm, Jack?" asked Phil.

"It's just the way I am. But let me tell you, Phil, I'm just as scared as you. Listen, we're going to help each other. We're going to look out for each other. You and me and Steve and Carl and the rest of our platoon."

Phil looked up into Jack's eyes and he saw the honesty and concern in them. He felt a measure of reassurance.

"Come on, Phil. You have to just take this one day at a time. We're going to make it. We're going to be supplying the front lines and they aren't going to be shooting at us. Okay, Phil?" Jack asked.

Phil nodded. "I'm a real dope, huh? I know I'm making too much out of this. Thanks, Jack. You're the best friend a guy could ever hope for."

Jack clapped him on the back. "Go on into the club. I'll go scout up the rest of the guys. Hey, eventually they're going to tell us what's going on in France, and I bet we're whipping Hitler's ass right now."

Phil smiled at Jack. "I bet you're right. Yeah, let's wait it out in the club."

On the beaches of Normandy, France the Americans, Brits, Canadians and French Armies made slow advancements towards the cliffs that protected the centuries old coastline. Inland in little villages and towns the men of the airborne companies were scattered on farms, in swamps and forests looking for men from their companies and for officers to lead them. Hitler's Army, though caught unaware, was fighting a fierce battle to keep the Allies from taking control of the coast. They knew damn well that the successful invasion of France meant the end of German occupation and probably the end of the war.

News started filtering in to the thousands of infantry, engineers, fighter and bombers crews waiting it out in southern England by afternoon. The assault on the beaches was slow and steady. Paratroopers were scattered all over the farms of Normandy. The enemy had been taken by surprise, but was fighting fiercely to maintain their positions on the cliffs looming as much as a hundred meters above the sandy shore. Casualty reports were not available.

The weather had been in their favor. Skies were clear, and the full moon helped some of the paratroopers read their maps and move along the wetlands and hedgerows to locate each other. The dry warm air allowed the landing craft to come near the water's edge so the men could disembark in shallow water and hit the beach and begin firing at their German enemies. There was a great deal of quiet conversation in the clubs, barracks and exercise yards. The talk was all speculation and very little fact.

When Jack, Steve, Phil and Carl were sitting around smoking after supper, they received orders to form up in their platoons for an update on the status of D-Day. Anxious to know if the beaches had been won, they ran to formation and were met by the platoons making up their entire company. Captain George Anderson approached them from a nearby jeep that had just pulled up outside of the barracks.

"Men, I'm going to give it to you straight," Captain Anderson began. "Today has been the biggest battle since Midway."

The men roared a cheer in unison.

"General Eisenhower has achieved his goal for today."

Again there was a huge cheer.

"But. But I'm not going to bullshit you. We took a lot of casualties today," Anderson paused, and the men were silent.

"We don't know the numbers but they were heroes, every one of them," Anderson said. "We took the beaches and drove the Krauts out of the bunkers!"

This time the men cheered even louder.

"We have victory on Omaha and Utah beaches" related Anderson. "The English came in on Sword and Gold beaches. We lost a lot of Rangers at a place called 'Point du Hoc,' but again, we were victorious!"

Again the company of engineers shouted out their approval even louder.

"I know you are anxious to get going and we will soon enough," Anderson said. "ADSEC that went in before you will be setting up the first supply lines and making an artificial harbor. You will be moving in to bring in the supplies and begin the construction of bridges and supply stations all over France. That's all for now. Lt. Marshall will keep you informed of your orders."

Lt. Marshall saluted the Captain and then turned to the company and told them they were dismissed.

The men began walking to their barracks. They were all talking at once, and they talked up the victory and, decidedly or not, didn't mention the casualties. None of the troops waiting in England knew that some of the landing craft had to wait nearly an hour before the men hit the beaches and that seasickness had ravaged the strength of many of the troops. Hundreds of soldiers died while still in the shallow Atlantic surf from the rounds of fire coming from dozens of bunkers on top of the cliffs. Bodies and body parts lay scattered for hundreds of yards as the Army was devastated by land mines, shrapnel and machine gun fire. The call for medics created a chorus amid the screams and groans of wounded and dying men. Buddies were often separated from each other, and sometimes soldiers saw their best friends lying dead in the sand.

The troops of D-Day invaders inched their way to the base of the cliffs. They remembered their training, and it was now a necessary instinct that drove them onward toward the enemy.

The big guns of the flotilla of ships blasted at the cliffs. When they ceased fire the Army took advantage of hollowed out areas on the cliffs and began the process of moving upward to be able to throw grenades into the bunkers and to begin claiming this coastline of France as theirs.

As the hours wore on, wave after wave of landing craft kept bringing more soldiers onto the beaches. The enormity of the number of soldiers invading Normandy was incredulous to the German soldiers in the bunkers and in their commanding headquarters. The Allies were accomplishing the mission of Operation Overlord with the sacrifice of many lives and the tenacity of the well-trained armies. The longest day of the war in Europe was just about to end.

Normandy

On June 12, the 347th Engineers arrived in South Hampton. They, along with hundreds of other companies, were cooped up in tight quarters. German buzz bombs and V-2 rockets were a regular hazard to their survival as the enemy tried to stem the continuous tide of Allied troops arriving at the man-made harbors at Omaha and Gold beaches.

Three days after the invasion, Mulberry A and B were ready to facilitate the unloading of equipment and supplies to fuel the troops beginning the penetration of France. The "Mulberry" artificial harbors were developed by British engineers and consisted of breakwaters, piers and roadways. These harbors were essential to the success of the Allies to defeat Germany.

As Jack and the rest of the Group B of the 347th sat around waiting, they knew they would be part of the continued invasion along with all of the equipment they would need to carry out their mission. They had been drilled repeatedly in the skills they would need until they boarded trucks taking them to South Hampton. Day long drills made them experts at sweeping for land mines, demolition of railroads and rebuilding of the same. Jack recognized that they might not be disembarking into the line of fire as did the troops of June 6, but their job was no less dangerous dealing with explosives, mines and heavy equipment.

The oppressive, humid summer air wore on the nerves of all of the troops. They were ready to board the ships and cross the Channel. Just as they approached their own D-Day, a fierce storm hit the Channel and North Atlantic Ocean. The storm blew so ferociously that Mulberry A at Omaha Beach was destroyed. In Arromanches, at Gold Beach, Mulberry B was beaten up but still intact. The reduction to one port further delayed the 347th.

At last, as the official first day of summer approached, Jack and his fellow soldiers were given the word that they would board their ships in the pre-dawn hours on June 21. As they gathered in the mess hall for supper, the chatter was in low tones. Jack knew that the anticipation was probably worse than the actual crossing and disembarkation. He worried about Phil and kept reassuring his best friend that it would be a piece of cake. Jack told Phil to stick with him or with Steve and Carl if they did become separated.

When their lieutenant talked to them that evening he explained that the following day would be very long. There was a huge amount of equipment to off-load and get into the town of Arromanches. From there the equipment would be deployed with soldiers in a variety of companies that were headed in many directions into France to keep pushing forward to liberate Paris and beyond.

Lt. Marshall told them that the 347th would be given their orders after off-loading thousands of tons of equipment. He didn't need to explain the work to be done. It had been drummed into their minds and bodies month after month. Lt. Marshall did remind them that their mission was essential to the winning of the war.

Jack and Phil went to bed right after sundown in their pup tent. There weren't enough barracks for all of the men, and if you looked around, you could see thousands of pup tents. The two friends talked for a while. The conversation revolved around home and some of their favorite things. Neither of them wanted to talk about "what if." Finally they drifted off to sleep. Only a few hours later they were awakened to get prepared for boarding.

****

ADSEC Headquarters set up inland of Utah Beach in the village of Catz in a cluster of stone farmhouses. Catz was only a few kilometers from the site of the Battle of Carentan. The 101st Airborne had fought for four days before it successfully drove out the Germans on June 14 the same day General Plank, commander of ADSEC, had landed in Normandy. As the 347th and many other engineer companies landed at Mulberry B and on Utah Beach, they met with sniper fire, strafing and artillery fire and were still able to unload as much as 39,000 tons of supplies in one day. The work was exhausting, but it was better than sitting around waiting. Their minds were occupied with the tasks at hand and there was no time to dwell on the position of the Germans. Phil seemed to be handling everything pretty well, Jack thought. He hadn't mentioned his fears and just kept working like they all did. Jack figured that most of Phil's anxiety was in his own mind and keeping busy was good for him.

The 347th was ordered to make their way to Cherbourg about 80 kilometers from Arromanches. In trucks that bounced along the rough roads, the men knew they were facing an area that had been badly torn up by several battles. Supply lines needed to be established, and Jack figured they'd have railroad tracks or roads to rebuild.

Just outside of Cherbourg, the truck stopped and Sgt. Grady, who was riding along with Jack and several other men, ordered them out. They had reached their destination. It felt good to jump down and stretch their legs and backs after a long day of unloading ships and moving equipment. Sgt. Grady told them to light up while he went to find Lt. Marshall for orders. The trucks started pulling out and Lt. Marshall gave the order to find spots for pup tents. The lieutenant knew his men were exhausted and needed a night's sleep to face the tasks ahead of them. He told them to find clearings in the woods. A Group was ordered to dig slit trenches. No mess kitchen would be set up because they would be on the march right after first light to begin repairing a railroad between Cherbourg and Carentan. It would be back-breaking work and the men were happy to eat their K rations and get some sleep.

The 347th had been repairing rails and laying new tracks for three days when they came upon the site of a recent skirmish between U.S. infantry and the enemy. There were about a half dozen German soldiers lying dead near the demolished railroad. The engineers were really glad they hadn't been taken by surprise by this renegade squad of Krauts. At the same time it reminded them that they were always vulnerable, and they remained quiet.

When they had a chance to take a ten minute break for a smoke and drink of water, Jack saw a guy named Joey from his platoon go over to the Germans. He was poking around the bodies looking for souvenirs. Sgt. Grady was sitting nearby and Jack called over to him. "Sarge, is it okay to take some souvenirs from the Krauts?"

Sgt. Grady looked over at the bodies. After a moment he said, "Yeah, it's okay. It's legal as long as you declare what you have when you ship it home."

Jack stood up and went over to the bodies. He didn't like looking at gore, but these guys weren't too torn up. He asked Joey, "Hey, are you looking for something particular?"

"Sure, I want a Luger. Every GI wants a Luger, Jack," said Joey.

"You mind if I look for something else?" asked Jack.

"Nah, help yourself. I don't think there is much here. Probably picked clean by the guys who killed them," Joey replied.

Jack wondered about that. He didn't think anyone would rummage around bodies they just killed. He also didn't want to get too close. Jack spotted a helmet about five yards from the men and went over to it. Looking at it, it must have come off the Kraut's head before he was killed. He turned the helmet over and looked at the inside and saw the soldier's name. *Reickemier.*

Jack decided to keep it and gave a quick look around. That's enough for now, he thought. Jack strapped the helmet to his back pack and went back to join his buddies just as their break was over.

195

"Whadya want that for," Carl asked.

"Just a souvenir. I'll probably take a few more as we keep going," Jack said.

"You must have angle, Jack," Steve wanted to know.

"You never know what something might be worth some day. Anyway, I like souvenirs from where ever I've been," Jack said.

"Man, Jack, I don't want to remember any of this," Phil piped up.

"Aw, come on, Phil, ain't we having a good time?" Jack kidded him.

"Back to work men," came the call from Sgt. Grady.

****

The 347th stood in formation 'at ease.' They had been told to form up because Colonel Hulen was on his way from Headquarters to see the completed railroad. Group B had totally repaired 50 kilometers of track, and the Transportation Corps railroaders were ready to operate the first train by the U.S. Army in France.

It was July 11 and it was hot. They had not changed their uniforms since arriving in Normandy, and each man stunk as badly as the soldier standing next to him. After a few minutes they could see a jeep approach, and Lt. Marshall ordered the platoon at attention. Col. Hulen got out of the jeep quickly, and with a brief salute, he turned to Group B.

"At ease, men. It's too damn hot to be at attention," the colonel said. "I'm here to congratulate you on a job well done. This railway will carry supplies and will be helpful to get wounded soldiers to the hospital in Cherbourg.

"Now I want to deliver some good news. We're pushing hard towards Paris and Belgium. Your work of repairing roads, tracks and bridges are essential to winning this war. But I gotta tell you, you look and smell pretty bad," the colonel paused, waiting for a response.

196

The men laughed and someone called out from the rear, "Well, what are you gonna do about it, colonel?"

Col. Hulen smiled and replied, "Bringin' in the showers for you!"

A cheer went up from the 347th as the colonel looked at his watch.

"Yep, I think I'll let Lt. Marshall here tell you to go over to the grove of trees and have a smoke in the shade. By that time the showers and clean uniforms will be here."

The men roared their approval. Col. Hulen turned and ordered the lieutenant to dismiss the platoon. Jack and his buddies and all of the men headed for the trees and collapsed with joy. Showers! What heaven!

They luxuriated in their clean fatigues, fresh underwear and socks. It took a few hours for everyone to get their turns and go back to the shade and take a nap. Shortly after they were treated to a hot meal and real coffee. It truly was heaven on earth. Col. Hulen and Headquarters knew how hard all of the companies had been working, and Carentan was now a safe zone in this part of Normandy.

The 347th stayed in the area around Carentan throughout the month of July. Group B repaired a bridge, set up a water pumping station and created a dump yard for supplies to get to the front lines. There was heavy fighting and resistance only 25 kilometers southeast in St. Lo. General Patton's Third Army was engaged in battle in hedgerows. Progress was difficult, and the casualties were heavy. During the last week of July, heavy bombing raids took place for three days. The bombers and their P-47 escorts flew low overhead. Jack and everyone else watched the sky in awe at the force of the Air Corps.

Word got back to the engineers that the bombers had missed their mark two times, destroying much of the town and killing many GI's. The 30th Infantry Division took the worse hits with hundreds of casualties during the battle. When the bomber pilots and navigators found out about it later, it was something extremely difficult they would live with forever.

At last they learned that Patton had broken through, and they had the Germans on the run. By August 1st the 347th and other ADSEC companies were on the move to St. Lo. Their orders would include rebuilding rail lines and bridges to keep supplies moving to the front lines.

When the trucks stopped and the engineers jumped down and got their first look at St. Lo, Steve let out a low whistle.

"Look at this place," he was incredulous.

"Yeah," was all Carl could manage as he turned his body a full 360 to take in the devastation.

"Christ," Jack uttered, "the whole town is demolished."

Everywhere they looked they saw buildings in shambles. The dead soldiers on both sides had been removed, but the destruction made it clear that a great many lives were indeed lost here in the Battle for Normandy.

Phil remained silent, and Jack was afraid he might be spooked and said, "Looks like we've got our work cut out for us for a long time, fellas."

"You ain't kidding," Steve replied. "I wonder if the Frenchies will be glad we invaded after they get a load of this town."

"Come on, Phil, let's move over there and hear what the lieutenant has for us," Jack urged his friend.

Phil nodded and the four friends joined the rest of the platoon that gathered around to get their orders.

Anticipation

Francine ran into the apartment her sister had rented in the big house at the center of the village. She had been sent to buy bread at the baker's shop, and she came into the kitchen where Suzanne was preparing dinner.

"Suzanne, I heard the news when I went to the baker."

"Oh, and what did you hear?" the older sister always wanted to know if the Allies had made progress.

"That General Patton was on the move and chasing the *Boche*!" Francine shouted in glee.

"Who said that?" asked Suzanne.

"The radio," Francine replied. "There were several people at the baker's, and they were able to tune into the Armed Forces Radio. The reporter was saying that since the battle in St. Lo, they finally had the Germans running from the Americans!" Francine was very excited.

"How do you know that? They must have been speaking in English," Suzanne wanted to know.

"I've been teaching myself English. Uncle George gave me a book and I've been studying it every day. It's not so difficult," she answered.

"You could learn it from a book without hearing the lessons?" Suzanne was surprised.

"Oh, I've heard English on the radio for all of these years on the BBC. You know, when the reporter is on before Mr. Churchill speaks to us in French. I've learned a great deal of English," Francine said with confidence.

"I'm just surprised that you could learn so easily. Is there much difference between English and American?" asked Suzanne.

"Not much," Francine said. "Remember when we would go to the movies? I always could tell if they were English or American movies. The accent is different and some of the expressions, too."

"Well, what do you plan to do with your English?" asked Suzanne.

"When we are liberated, I want to work for the Americans," Francine said.

"What are you talking about? What work?" Suzanne was perplexed.

"We're bound to be liberated before the Allies move into Germany. There will be jobs available! The Americans will need secretaries," Francine said enthusiastically.

"Hmmm, I suppose so. But you are so young. Can you type?" asked Suzanne.

"Yes, I've been practicing for several months on an old typewriter that Uncle George has in his office at the school," Francine said.

"Well, aren't you the grown up little sister!" Suzanne smiled at her.

"I just want to be ready, and, it will all be very exciting. I can't wait to meet American men!" Francine said.

"Hold on, you're only 16," her sister pointed out.

"So, look what I've had to live through. I can certainly take care of myself!" Francine exclaimed.

****

Suzanne didn't want to argue with her. She knew her mother would have much more to say about it. Actually, she was proud that her sister could understand English on the radio!

"We all want to meet the Americans, Francine. It means our liberty, and God knows we have waited a long time for it," Suzanne's voice trailed off as she thought about all the wasted years and the loss of her husband.

"When the Americans come here, I will be able to talk to them," Francine said. "Oh, I just can't wait. Come on, General Patton, come and liberate us soon!"

The two sisters burst out laughing and both of them felt an overwhelming sense of relief as well as anticipation for their future.

****

During August, the 347th replaced ties and track for the railroad to continue west and north to speed supplies to the front that was slowly advancing. Infantry moving north towards Paris were making more headway than the eastward advancement towards Germany. It was slow going and the engineers had no problem keeping up with rebuilding the infrastructure and trucking ammunition and supplies to the frontlines.

The soldier engineers worked long and hard to rebuild the rails, and when they were done in the area of St. Lo they set in place concrete forms on existing pilings for a bridge over *La Vire* River. It was vital that trucks and tanks be able to get through from the landing areas along the Normandy beaches. Col. Hulen was gratified that his ADSEC Company was able to get the work done in St. Lo in just over two weeks. He moved his men west and slightly north some 275 kilometers to Dreux where they replaced a vital railroad bridge with steel UCRB spans.

Groups A and B worked on the bridge and were able to complete it in six days. The Germans had blown bridges wherever they were able in an effort to stop the advancement of supplies, artillery and tanks of the Allies. The engineers did amazing work and they did it fast.

Col. Hulen had sent word to his men as they were nearing the end of August that they were on their way to Paris! The city had been liberated on August 19, and the Americans, along with General DeGaulle and the French Army, were part of a fantastic party along the Champs Elysee. The engineers were hoping to get their turn in Paris even if for only one or two days.

Jack and the rest of his platoon would talk about the day when they would finally reach Paris. When they finally finished a day's work and had a chance to sit around in an empty farmhouse or barn, somebody would start talking about the women and the wine.

"There are plenty of girls in Paris, fellas, and I bet those infantry guys were too tired out to take care of them all," a guy named Harry proclaimed.

"You're damn right," Joey answered. "Us engineers have stamina. Look how many fuckin' bridges we've already built!"

Everybody laughed, and the chatter kept up while the men smoked their cigarettes. It didn't take long before they started falling asleep and the chatter was taken over by the sound of quiet breathing and snoring. The engineers were exhausted. Col. Hulen understood that and promised they'd be in Paris soon.

The next morning Jack was awakened at dawn by the sound of heavy equipment moving down the road in front of their farmhouse. He went to the window and saw several UCRB pieces loaded on trucks heading west. Shit, Jack thought. He knew that they were probably going to fall in right behind the loaded trucks. Within the next minute their sergeant opened the door.

"Rise and shine men. You got another bridge to put up!"

"Where we going?" Jack asked.

"West. Now let's get a move on. We're moving out in half an hour," the sergeant said.

The men had to hustle. There were a couple of outhouses to use and a slit trench. There was no time for mess to be set up, and they had to eat rations for breakfast. All of the guys in their platoon went about their own ritual with haste. At least they had water to wash their face and hands before moving out.

Jack fell in beside Steve. "Hey, you know where we're headed."

"Yeah, I do. I heard the lieutenant talking to Sarge. A placed called "Juvisy" and they said it's right outside of *gay Paree*!" Steve replied.

"You sure?" Jack asked.

"Yep. That's what I heard," Steve said.

"Hey, Jack," Phil called from behind, "After we put up this bridge, you think they'll give us leave?"

"Beats me, pal, but I think Col. Hulen wants us to get a couple of days for R & R. I'm counting on it, Phil."

They loaded onto the trucks and pulled out about thirty minutes behind their steel bridge going down the road towards Paris.

Liberation

Suzanne and the children were sitting in the garden behind their apartment in the Eloy house. The weather was exceptionally warm as summer came to a close on September 1. Suzanne was mending socks and watching Serge and Nadine playing with a few toys under a large cherry tree that had yielded fantastic fruit earlier in the summer.

Suddenly all she heard was the clanging of the church bell that was not far away in the village. Suzanne leaped up and ran over to pick up Nadine and grabbed Serge's hand.

"What is it, *Maman*?" Serge demanded.

"Let's go and find out," his mother answered with a bit of hesitation. Her heart told her it was good news, and her head told her to be cautious.

As they ran to the front of the house and stood on the sidewalk, they watched as all of the families began to emerge. The residents of the side streets ran to see what was happening. After only a few moments, two familiar boys riding their bicycles came in view and earshot.

"Les Americains, Les Americains! Ils viennent! They are coming!"

The Americans! Suzanne was incredulous.

"Maman," Serge pulled free of his mother's hand. "It's the Americans! The soldiers, *Maman*!!"

Before Suzanne could say anything, Francine came running from the direction of the church. "Suzanne, did you hear? The Americans are here!" Francine shouted.

People scurried into their homes and within minutes Belgian flags appeared and an occasional small American flag could be seen by those lucky enough to have them. Everyone seemed to be on the sidewalks and in the street. Suzanne saw her aunt, uncle and cousins coming from their neighborhood.

Francine called out loudly, "Uncle George, over here. Come over here with us."

The Dejardin family made their way across the street. Everyone was clapping each other on the back, and cheers were beginning to go up. Finally one of the boys who had been on the bicycle shouted, "I see them. Here they come!"

Suzanne stretched her neck above the crowd, and she saw them. The Americans. Tears instantly sprang to her eyes and began flowing down her cheeks. She did nothing to wipe them away. Serge looked at her and asked, "*Maman*, aren't you happy?"

"Oh, yes, Serge, you can't imagine how happy I am. I'm so happy that I'm crying," Suzanne said.

Serge looked at her for only a moment longer and then wiggled to the front of the crowd to see the Americans as they came closer.

Just before the soldiers reached the Eloy house, a sergeant told his men to halt. There were a few platoons, perhaps 60 men, Francine thought. The mayor had made his way to the center of town and saluted the sergeant. The sergeant returned the salute and spoke to the mayor.

"I think we are in Belgium, aren't we, sir?"

Francine ran over to the mayor and told him what the sergeant had asked.

"*Oui, Sergeant, oui. Vous etes en Belgique! C'est la village de Felenne.*

In an awkward accent the sergeant replied, "*Vous etes libre!* You are free!"

The mayor repeated the incredible news. "*Nous sommes libre! Vive La Belgique! Vive l'Amerique! Vive les Americains!*"

The crowd cheered. Somehow people began communicating with the soldiers. The village asked them to stay and have a meal together and champagne to celebrate, but that was impossible. The sergeant had orders to keep marching towards Brussels. Many people asked if Brussels was liberated. The sergeant replied that they were due to get there in two days, and they hoped it would be.

Several soldiers began offering cigarettes to the men who gratefully accepted them. Chocolate bars were handed over to the children and their mothers, who kissed and hugged them. It was a scene that was repeated in town after town in France and finally now in this little border village just a few kilometers from France.

After the quick celebration the sergeant said that his men had to continue to march north. He was asked if the men were hungry, and he answered that they only had rations to eat. Women ran into their house and grabbed big loaves of bread and tubs of creamy butter and knives. Francine went in and got her camera and started taking photos of the Americans and the villagers.

Everyone began to walk alongside the soldiers. They cut slabs of bread and loaded on the butter and handed the slices to the GI's who had just set them free. Suzanne walked with them, holding Nadine. She was smiling, and tears were still running down her cheeks. Several of the men smiled at her and pinched the cheeks of her little girl. Serge kept pace with a couple of big men, and they tousled his hair and told him he had better go back to his mother.

After about another half an hour, the citizens of Felenne began to fall back and wave goodbye to the American soldiers. Never in their lives would these Belgians forget this moment of liberty and the Americans who made it happen. Never.

****

The 347th got to Paris on Sept 5, 1944. They were driven into the city of lights along the Champs Elysees in troop trucks. The weather was warm and clear and they pulled the canvas down to get a better view of the famous city. As they passed by sidewalk cafes, patrons waved at them. The soldiers whistled and hollered greetings from America in reply.

Lt. Marshall told them which hotels were open to them and asked them to try not to wreck the rooms. They had two days to see the sights, meet the girls, get drunk, and if they got lucky they could screw the nights away.

The day before they left Juvisy, they had had hot showers and clean uniforms. Several men had also been surprised to receive promotions and get their new stripes for their clean clothes. Jack was promoted to corporal and had been surprised by it. His buddies all chided him, but were good sports and told him that he deserved it.

In spite of his early reluctance to be drafted into the Army, Jack accepted his fate and figured he might learn something in the bargain. He had been right. The construction projects they had worked on sharpened his mathematic skills, and he willing volunteered to lead some of the jobs they had undertaken. His leadership and 'know how' were noted in a report to the company commander by Lt. Marshall, and Jack and a few other men received the promotions. Jack was happy to get a little more pay and figured the girls might go for the stripe on his sleeve.

The four buddies walked into the Hotel Elysee Etoile a few doors off the sweeping and breathtaking Champs Elysees. The small lobby was crowded with GI's checking in and several checking out. Jack and Steve went over to the desk to see about getting two rooms for the four of them.

"*Oui.* Yes, I have two rooms with two beds. The bath is in the hall. Special price for Americans is ten francs each night," the clerk smiled at the newest of his soldier guests.

"That's swell," Steve said. "We'll take them." Steve reached into his pocket for some French money and so did Jack. They both signed the register and asked if there were two keys for each room. There were. For now, they took only one for each so that they could stow the small bag of gear each of them had.

"Hey, Phil, Carl, come on," Steve called over to them. They climbed two flights of stairs and found their rooms.

"How much for the rooms?" Carl asked. "Ten francs a night pal. Do you believe it? Right here in Paris, two bucks a night!"

"Special American soldier price," Jack quipped.

"I wouldn't care if it cost a month's pay after the last two months! We're in Paris and we are free to do whatever we want for 48 hours!" Steve shouted out.

"Well, let's get a move on. Get your stuff stowed and let's hit the Champs Elysees," Jack said with a great French accent.

"I hope your French is up to par, Jack," Phil kidded his best friend.

"Don't worry, Phil. Have I ever let you or any of you down before?"

"No, Jack," Phil replied and was going to continue when Steve butted in.

"Stop the chatter. Throw some water on your mugs, put your crap away, and let's get to a bar!" Steve said.

They all laughed and went about squaring away their gear and washing their faces and hands. They straightened their ties, combed their hair, placed their hats on and left the rooms racing down the stairs. Steve tossed the keys to the desk clerk and remarked, "Don't wait up for us, Frenchy; we're going to paint the town red!"

With that they walked out of the small hotel and strode quickly to the grand avenue that had recently been the scene of the French and American Armies marching from the *Arc de Triomphe* past the grand hotels, restaurants, shops and parks all the way to Notre Dame Cathedral. It was a magnificent sight today to these four GI's and to all the rest of them who had been here for the liberation and during the recent weeks. None of them was ever going to forget the impression it had upon them.

Everywhere they looked they saw soldiers on two-day passes. Beautiful girls were walking arm in arm with them or sitting at the little café tables on the wide sidewalks sipping wine. Everyone was smiling. Old men clapped soldiers on the back and their wives kissed many on the cheeks. Young women blew kisses or planted a quick kiss on the lips of soldiers as they passed them on the sidewalk. There were French flags flying or draped from the balconies of almost every building along the Champs Elysees. American and British flags were prominently displayed in shop windows, flower boxes and balconies. Jack and his friends took all of this in with silence, and they felt proud at what they had helped accomplish. These people and those all over Europe were being freed by soldiers like them.

Phil broke the somber moment. "Hey fellas, let's go grab the table right over there at that café," he pointed as some GI's were exiting from the crowded sidewalk spot.

"Sure," Steve said as he bounded over to it and grabbed it before any other soldiers could get there."

When they were all seated the waiter, an older man with a crisp white apron tied around his waist, came over to clear the wine glasses and wipe the table. *"Avez vous faim*?" he wanted to know.

"Oui," Jack replied. "We're hungry."

The waiter hand them small menus handwritten on stiff paper. *"Que c'est vous recommendez?"* Jack inquired.

"Le poulet, corporale. Ils ne pas le boeuf. Avec les frites, corporale.

"Chicken with French Fries. There's no steak," Jack told his friends. "Lousy war. The Krauts probably ate all of the beef!"

"Sure, Jack, sounds good," Carl said and they all nodded.

"Oui, monsieur, quatres plats et le vin rouge."

The waiter nodded and walked away.

They were drinking a delicious red wine in glasses with short stems. The wine was in a ceramic pitcher. Just ordinary table wine. Jack reflected upon the last time he drank wine that was in a pitcher.

"When I lived in California and visited wine country just above San Francisco, they served wine just like this. Pretty little ceramic pitchers and good, cheap wine. Man, I haven't thought about that in years," Jack surprised himself with the memory of his visit to Napa County.

"Well, Jack, you didn't get to spend it with buddies in the 347th Engineers!" Steve mused.

"No, you're right. I was with a couple of old pals from New York. We had a good time, but it wasn't like this," Jack's voice was low as he continued.

"Did you guys get the same feeling as I did when we walked out on this street and saw all the flags and people making a fuss over soldiers everywhere?"

They all nodded in agreement, no one wanting to show their true emotion.

"Makes you know that there was a real reason to be here," Jack said.

Their meals arrived. Small pieces of roasted chicken, lots of French Fries and a few pieces of lettuce with tomato slices. They asked for another pitcher of wine and dug into their meal with gusto. Each soldier tasted every morsel of food as if he had never eaten chicken and potatoes before. They were in heaven and each realized he should savor this moment and each moment during the rest of their 48 hour leave.

Celebrations

The gray skies and slight chill of the early autumn couldn't damper Suzanne's spirits on this particular afternoon. She and her family had returned to Brussels two days earlier after a full day of catching rides and some walking from Felenne to her house on the outskirts of the city. They had gotten a ride with a farmer bringing the last of his crops from Waterloo into the free capital city. After the family thanked the man, they walked from the chausee the few blocks to her mother's door.

The children ran ahead of her to the back door. Francine had returned a few days ahead of them getting a ride. As they burst through the kitchen door, they found Eva in the next room waiting anxiously for their safe return.

"*Maman*, we're home!" Suzanne exclaimed.

Serge ran to his grandmother's arms and she held him and kissed him. Nadine was more reserved not quite sure what she thought of *grandmere*. Eva scooped her up and gave her several kisses while the little girl wiggled out of her grasp. Eva looked over her shoulder and saw Suzanne standing in the doorway.

"You all look wonderful!" Eva exclaimed.

Suzanne went over to her, kissed her and they held each other for several moments. "We are fine, *Maman*. We are free. We are all free."

"Yes, thank God," Eva said and wiped away tears of happiness that her daughter and grandchildren were all safe and healthy.

"Everyone in Felenne is fine, too, *Maman*," Suzanne told her.

"We'll have plenty of time to catch up on all of the news over the next few days, Suzanne. Look at you. You all need to wash up and change your clothes. Your house has been closed up the whole time you were gone," her mother said. "Tomorrow we can go and air it out and clean. Why don't you get some clean clothes and wash up while I make and early supper?"

"That sounds wonderful, *Maman*. We're very tired. I'll go and get some clothes from my house and come back in a few minutes," Suzanne said.

"Serge, Nadine, go upstairs and take off your dirty clothes and I'll come back to bathe you."

The siblings went reluctantly. A little dirt didn't bother them at all.

Suzanne sat at her dining table with a cup of weak coffee and luxuriated in the comfort of her familiar surroundings and the things she loved. She looked over at the wedding photograph of Maurice and her from 1937, and she smiled. He was so handsome in his formal tuxedo with tails and she in her fashionable fitted, satin gown with swirling hemline. With her tiara type headpiece, Suzanne appeared a bit taller than her husband. They were young, in love with each other and with life.

Suzanne had asked her mother if there had been any news from the Germans or any of their friends about Maurice. There had been nothing, Eva had answered. Although this wasn't a surprise, she had hoped there might be a message of hope from someone in the underground or from the diamond dealers who would get bits and pieces of information about the whereabouts of their business associates and friends. She hadn't wanted to believe that he was among the dead of some concentration camp in Poland.

After cleaning her house, she sat down and phoned her good friends whom she hadn't seen in so many months. The Picavets invited her to come for dinner on Saturday and to please bring the children and her mother and sister. Josette said she would invite Fred Caron and his fiancée, Marie. It was time to celebrate the liberation of Brussels together as best friends. Suzanne looked forward to the little party that was planned for tomorrow.

As she looked away from the wedding photograph, she thought about her future life. 'I've survived the war and so has the rest of my family. My husband and his family are most likely gone forever, but I must begin to plan for the future without him and for my children. Maurice told me that the welfare of the children was more important than anything, and I have to uphold his last request of me.'

Suzanne knew that her friends would help her to find work. Perhaps she could go back to designing textiles and her mother could care for the children. Maybe there would be other work with so many men still away in the English Army or in the work camps in Germany. Tomorrow she would find out more about the future of the citizens of Brussels from Felix and Fred.

****

"Oh, my dear, dear Suzanne!" Josette exclaimed as Suzanne appeared at the apartment door. They both began to cry and then to laugh at the same time. Fred Caron presented his fiancée to everyone. Suzanne had not met Marie and looked forward to getting to know her. Fred had been such a good friend to her and Maurice. Suzanne smiled broadly and was overwhelmed by the emotion in those moments.

Everyone kissed and hugged each other. The children tolerated all of the sentimentality but were glad when it was done. They had endured far too many pinches on their cheeks and Nadine was scowling. Josette brought them over to a corner of the salon where she had set up a small table with paper and watercolor paints for them to be amused. They looked at Suzanne for permission, and she nodded.

"Serge, show Nadine how you dip the brush in water, then the paint to begin your painting.

"Yes, *Maman*. I know what to do," he said. Everyone smiled as they went to the next room to begin their art projects.

After removing their coats, which Felix whisked away to the bedroom, the gathering took seats around the beautiful table Josette had set. There were tiny canapés on an antique tray that Marie passed to everyone. When Felix returned, he walked to the buffet where he had an assortment of aperitifs waiting to be served.

"All right then, may I prepare drinks for each of you?" Felix said.

"Yes!" they said in unison.

"Not for Francine," Eva reminded him.

"*Maman*, I'm certainly old enough to have an aperitif! I deserve to celebrate, too." Francine was indignant.

"Yes, it's all right, Felix," Eva quickly relented.

Francine smiled, and Suzanne thought about the differences between them. She would never have spoken back to her mother, but Francine had done so always and usually got her way.

After the drinks were placed in front of each of them, Fred spoke. "I want to make a toast. To our dearest friends; Eva, Francine and our most darling Suzanne and her lovely children. Words cannot describe how happy we are that you are all well and that we are together in our beautiful city of Brussels, finally free from the Germans. We trust that Ivan is well and will be home soon. We pray for Maurice who has been taken from us." Fred lifted his glass a bit higher and everyone took a drink.

Maurice's name had evoked a silence among all of them as each person had his own prayer or thought. Josette squeezed Suzanne's hand as she had made sure she was seated next to her girlhood friend. The quiet was broken quickly as the chatter began and grew and the laughter and sounds of the voices mingled to create an atmosphere that was so pleasurable it would be remembered as one the best times of their lives.

****

It was another blustery and cloudy day in November that greeted the men of the 347th as they worked their way from town to town and village to village across northern France. It had taken the Americans the entire summer and early autumn to advance to northeastern part of France. The Advanced Engineers had swept mine fields, laid more railroad track than they ever cared to see again, and built bridges after the Germans blew them up during their retreat to the east.

Jack thought the countryside looked a lot like New York state or Pennsylvania. There were rolling hills, a lot of farms, and plenty of woods. Many of the villages had been untouched by the Germans, and the GI's were greeted warmly by the French farmers and their wives. Jack was happy to be invited with his friends into some homes for a simple hot meal. He always asked if there was milk to drink and most of the time there was. The French found it strange that an American man in the Army would want milk with his supper, but they were pleased to be obliging. Steve and Carl would always opt for the wine while Phil would often join Jack in a glass of milk.

There was plenty of talk among the men in the platoon about the end of the war. Scuttlebutt had the war ending by Christmas and that they would all be home after New Year's Day. Whenever a platoon or company of infantry passed through their projects, the engineers would ask about their orders and what they heard from their commanders. They were moving north and east into Belgium, Jack and his pals learned. There was a part of Belgium that had not been liberated in the Ardennes Forest near Luxembourg and Germany. The engineers wished them well and would go back to work.

Jack knew that the supply depot located nearby was getting shipments of ammunition, weapons and food on a daily basis. He assumed that the generals were getting ready for another offensive and that the gossip about the end of the war was just that. Gossip. Unfounded stories spread by men who wanted the end of this war to be very near. They were fatigued and were dreaming about home and who would meet them when they disembarked in New York Harbor.

When the guys talked about the future, they were careful not to make predictions in fear of jinxing the timing of the end of the war. If Hitler was as nuts as the *Stars and Stripes* reported, then Jack knew there was no way that he would give up. Hitler would go down fighting until his last breath.

"Hey, Jack," Steve called over to him as they were stacking ammo boxes, "did you hear that we're getting a USO show?"

"No. Really? Anybody famous?" asked Jack.

"Don't know. Maybe just a regular show with music and dancers, but I didn't hear," Steve replied.

"That's great. We haven't had even a movie in a few weeks. I hope we get one of the Hollywood stars," Jack said. He was still interested in Hollywood even though it was about five years since he'd been to California.

"I'm just glad we're getting some entertainment at this depot!" Steve responded.

"They'll probably tell us tonight or tomorrow morning. You know if the show got held up along the way, they don't want us to be let down, that's why there's never much notice," Jack concluded.

"Right, Jack. I'm glad about it, too," Steve said.

They continued stacking ammo for the rest of the day, and when they were done eating their supper in the mess tent, the sergeant announced that the USO was coming the next evening to put on a show. They were told that the line-up wasn't going to be announced in advance and to show up at 19 hundred in the center of the depot yard.

The next day there seemed to be an endless number of supply trucks pulling into the depot and the entire B Group was assigned the laborious job of unloading the weapons and ammunition. The stockpile had really grown over the last several days, and Jack thought more about the offensive being planned. Jack had read the most recent Stars and Stripes, and there wasn't anything in it about a German surge. He believed, however, that something was on the horizon.

As they were finishing the unloading of the fifteenth truck, Jack noticed the stage area going up in the central part of the yard. He was glad to see that the show was still scheduled and hoped nothing would stop it.

All of the 347th were dismissed from duty a half-an-hour early to give them more time to clean up before chow. Rumors were rampant about the guest stars for the evening. Jack and his pals ate hurriedly and grabbed their heavy coats to protect them from the chilly autumn night air. It was dark when they found a good place to sit atop some crates of weapons as close to the stage as they could. Jack knew the cast was nearby in an area that had been cordoned off and blankets hung to make dressing areas for the show people.

Finally it was 19 hundred hours, and the emcee came on stage. He was an old vaudeville guy who use to do the circuit in cities and towns throughout the East Coast. His jokes were from a bygone era and were familiar to most of the men. The comedy routine was nostalgic, and the men laughed after each punch line, yet at the same time, they felt a yearning for home. He was a New Yorker and Jack felt this longing more profoundly than did his friends from the Midwest, western Pennsylvania and Massachusetts.

While the laughter was fading away and the applause was loud as the emcee-comedian finished his opening for the show, he took his bow and then began his introduction of the main act. There was a curtain behind the emcee that hid most of the stage and a couple of GI's were on duty at each end of the curtain.

"All right fellas, it's time for the big show. I have a very special treat for you tonight. Straight from one of the biggest ballrooms in London on tour with the USO is one of America's favorite bands," the emcee said. The anticipation mounted, and some of the men started to clap their hands.

The GI's jumped up on the stage ready to pull back the curtain. "Men, here is the Les Brown Band!"

The entire audience got on their feet and began to hoot and holler and applaud loudly. Simultaneously, the band began playing one of the most popular songs of the day. While they played, the soldiers sat back down and enjoyed every musical note. When the tune was finished, Mr. Brown turned to the audience and microphone.

He motioned for the men to stop their applause but to no avail. Finally, they quieted down to listen to one of the best band leaders in the United States.

"Gentlemen, I bring you greetings from the people all over the USA; especially the girls!" Brown said.

The audience burst into loud approval by whistling and clapping.

"We are thrilled to be over here in France with you boys, and I've brought a really special person to be on stage with us tonight. The best singer I've ever worked with and you all know her, Miss Dinah Shore!"

Dinah Shore walked on stage in a beautiful gown with long sleeves. The deep blue color sparkled with thousands of sequins under the two spotlights that had been rigged for the show. She also had a fur stole around her shoulders to help her endure the cold night.

The men went wild cheering her and welcoming her to their part of the war. The whistling and shouting over the applause was deafening. Finally Miss Shore got their attention.

"Okay, fellas, I know you really want to hear me sing with the great Les Brown Band, so you've gotta keep it down a little. You don't wanna wake up Mr. Hitler across the border, do you?"

Again the men went nuts and Miss Shore remarked, "You've gotta save some of that energy to drop some bombs on mean Mr. Hitler!"

The soldiers laughed and clapped their hands and settled down to listen to Dinah Shore sing some of the best known songs of the day. Some were recorded before the war and the men sang along quietly. There were newer tunes that the folks back home would have recognized, but to the 347th they were hearing them for the first time.

After a while Dinah Shore reached down and asked one of the young soldiers if he'd like to come on stage and dance with her while the orchestra played. A big grin broke out on the GI's face as he jumped on stage and she took him in her arms after shedding her fur wrap. "I surely don't need that hunk of fur when I'm in the arms of an American soldier," Miss Shore said. The men went crazy and the band struck up the popular "You'd Be So Nice to Come Home To" ballad while the couple danced.

A minute later, the singer moved back from the GI and thanked him while she motioned for some other men to come on stage. Four soldiers hopped up and Miss Shore danced for about a minute with each of them as she transitioned smoothly from one tune to the next.

After the third instrumental, Miss Shore kissed each GI on the cheek and whispered something to each of them. They jumped down and got back into their places, and their eyes sparkled with the moisture of tears forming. Miss Shore had conveyed the love of their families and the country to them as she wished them good luck.

The sentimental moment had quieted the audience. Miss Shore turned back to the band, and it swung into harmony with the ever popular "I've Got You Under My Skin." Some of the guys stood on top of the ammo crates and danced or kept time with the beat. The men clapped in rhythm with the band and there were more grins on faces than anyone could remember since they had arrived in Paris and enjoyed their brief furlough.

Jack could feel the evening coming to an end. He loved swing bands and the jazz musicians of his youth. Carl, Steve and Phil had clapped loudly alongside of Jack and they had all chimed in with hollering and whistling. It really felt good to let loose and it made them forget that they were in the middle of a war so far from home. For most of his boyhood and young adult life until 1942, Jack had been totally carefree and did exactly what he wanted. He knew those days were over, and he needed to concentrate on doing his job and keeping as safe as possible to survive. As Dinah Shore and the rest of the entertainers took their last bows; Jack wondered what was in store for him. What was his future to be? He didn't yearn for his old stomping grounds of Coney Island and he knew there was no future for him in California. He was 26-years-old and the war was almost over. Fairly soon Jack would have to figure out what he would do with the rest of his life.

Christmas

They had been in the northern region of France for several months. It was almost Christmas and the 347th was busier than ever moving supplies to the frontlines in eastern Belgium. The Battle of the Ardennes had been going on for weeks and the news was grim. Thousands of Americans were getting killed by the Germans, and the GI's were not well supplied. The extremely cold and snowy weather kept the airborne from dropping in weapons, ammo and food to the troops at the front. At Jack's depot they kept receiving supplies and loading trucks bound for the area around the town of Bastogne. The trucks were being off-loaded outside of the battle area waiting for the weather conditions to change and for the enemy to be pushed back into Germany.

The German Army still had strong infantry and panzer divisions to continue to push the frontline forward toward the west. *Stars and Stripes* displayed a map that had the Germans penetrating west creating a Bulge through the dense Ardennes forest. Bastogne was a strategic location because five major routes met in the small town. If the Germans gained control of Bastogne, they might regain territory going north to Antwerp, south into France, and west into Brussels. Giving back liberated Belgian land to the Third Reich was absolutely out of the question as far as the Allied Army was concerned. Hitler had to be stopped and his army soundly defeated on these battlefields. Once this was accomplished, the invasion of Germany could begin and the end of the war would be in sight.

It was evident to the Allied generals that Hitler would never surrender, and total defeat was the only answer. Hitler did not care if he could save thousands of civilian lives by ending the war. His maniacal and egocentric persona made surrender impossible. Many more lives would be lost in the Battle of the Ardennes and future battles and bombing raids in Germany.

****

Suzanne had been to the markets three times in the last two days trying to buy enough food to prepare supper for Christmas Eve. As she looked over the tins and packages she had managed to purchase, she was disgusted. What was she going to serve for hors d'oeuvres? Nothing was appealing, Suzanne thought as her mother entered the kitchen from the back door.

There were traces of snow on Eva's shoes, and she wiped them thoroughly on the door mat. Suzanne and her mother had cleaned the walkway numerous times but the snows kept falling during December of 1944 and you had to be careful not to fall on the slippery surface.

"Suzanne, did you have any luck at the market?" asked Eva.

"Not much," Suzanne replied. "I have enough flour and cocoa to make a nice cake, and we have canned vegetables. With the chicken we're going to have killed, we will have the basic meal. But I have nothing for hors d'oeuvres, *Maman*."

"I do," Eva said. "I saw Madame Allemon, and she had mushrooms dozens of chanterelles, and I bought some from her."

"Oh, *Maman*, that sounds wonderful. We can make them in a cream sauce and serve them as a *vol au vent,*" Suzanne said.

"Exactly what I was thinking," Eva was proud of her expedition to find something tasty.

"Oh, *Maman*, it's been so difficult since I returned from Felenne," Suzanne said. "I thought that when we were liberated, food would be plentiful, but it is worse now. Look at me. I've lost the weight I gained over the summer, and the children are thin."

"It is bad, but we'll manage with everything I canned from last summer" Eva said. "Without you and the children here, I didn't need so much for myself, and I managed to preserve a lot more than usual."

222

"I shouldn't complain, *Maman*. We made it safely to the end of this stinking war. Why isn't it over?" asked Suzanne.

"It will be soon, Suzanne."

"That's what everybody says, but the Germans are gaining in the east. If they win that battle, they may come back and take Brussels again. I just can't bear it. I can't," Suzanne said.

"Calm down, Suzanne," answered Eva. "The Allies will win. It will take a while longer, but we will not fall to the Germans again.

"Listen, Suzanne, you will have to rebuild your life once the war is over. Maybe you'll meet a man and remarry or perhaps you'll go back to designing. There are good things on the horizon for you. I promise," her mother said.

Suzanne nodded and relaxed her shoulders in order to lessen the tension she felt in her body. "I know you are right. I just would like things to be easy for once. When Maurice and I were first married, he took care of everything and I only needed to make us a lovely and comfortable home. How could that dream have just evaporated in so short a period of time? Hmmm, *Maman*?" asked Suzanne.

"Because of the Germans," Eva said. "There is nothing any of us could have done, and we need to live our lives knowing the end of the war is almost here."

Again Suzanne nodded and then spoke in a quiet voice. "I know you're right, but I miss him. I really have been lonely."

"Wars do that. Your father was wounded in the first war and later when he died, I got a nice pension," Eva sounded cheerful.

"Yes, *Maman,* I know how it worked out for you, but I don't want to raise my children without a father, and I want an income that's reliable," Suzanne responded firmly. She knew that her mother was happier without her own husband. They had probably never been in love as she had been with Maurice. Suzanne's life had been filled with romance and excitement. She wondered if she would ever have those feelings again.

Suzanne had invited Fred Caron, Marie and the Picavets to join her family on Christmas Eve. Eva had been preparing the dishes with the ingredients they had been able to assemble while Suzanne and the children decorated the small tree on display on the buffet cabinet. Serge was allowed to hang the glass ornaments while Nadine placed the tinsel on the branches. When they were finished, Suzanne rearranged a few of the decorations to make the tree more balanced.

Francine came into the house and tossed off her coat. "Hey, can I help with the tree?"

"There's not much left to do," her sister replied. "Oh, you can put the candles on and we'll light them when the guests arrive this evening," Suzanne added.

Francine took her place beside the tree and began to place the candle holders on a variety of limbs and then put the candles in their holders. "The tree is really pretty this year, don't you think, Suzanne?"

"Yes. Yes, it is," Suzanne smiled at her sister.

"*Maman*, is Père Noel going to bring us candies tomorrow?" Serge asked.

Suzanne was quick to answer. "Yes, he will as long as you are both good children this evening."

"I have my shoes ready to put outside the door, *Maman*," Serge said. "I told Nadine that she'll be able to put her shoes outside this year, too. Do you think Père Noel will put candy in her shoes?"

"Of course he will," Suzanne said. "Why do you ask?"

"Because she cries a lot at night and you have to be good all year for Père Noel to come to your house," the five-year-old boy answered.

"She cries because she is frightened, Serge, not because she is bad," his mother replied.

"Oh. Père Noel understands that?" asked Serge.

"Yes. He knows that during a war, children get afraid and can have bad dreams and cry," Suzanne said.

"All right." Serge turned to his little sister and said, "If you are good tonight, Père Noel won't forget your shoes."

Nadine looked at her brother and said, "I'll be good."

Suzanne smiled at her children and said to Francine, "Will you take them upstairs to change into the clothes I've put on their beds?"

"Sure. Come on," Francine said.

"Why do we have to change?" Serge was annoyed.

"Because it's a holiday and we all want to look nice," Francine replied. "Come on, Serge, don't always argue."

Suzanne was overwhelmed by the generosity of her friends. Fred Caron had brought a bag of charcoal and a bundle of wood as his Christmas present. It was a wonderful gift, and they were all enjoying the warmth from the stove in the dining room as they ate their dessert. Felix had brought two bottles of champagne, and the family and friends felt giddy as they sipped the exquisite wine. Marie and Josette had brought little toys for Serge and Nadine. Serge had received a cowboy hat and fake pistol with a holster while Nadine had gotten a new doll with a pretty dress. She seemed more interested in Serge's toys, and that made the gathering of adults laugh out loud.

Since they had been liberated, American films were back in the cinemas and Serge had seen several Westerns. Suzanne had remarked recently that her son was just like her brother, loving the cowboys and Indians.

They had all been talking throughout the evening about their plans for the future when the war would be over. Mostly the group tried to avoid the bad news that had come to them via the radio about the severe loss of life in the Ardennes.

"Have you heard from Ivan, Madame Duchesne?" Fred asked.

"Not for about a month, Fred, but I'm sure he is all right or we would have heard by now," Eva answered.

"I'm sure you are right. Is he with the Resistance?" Fred asked again.

"Yes, as far as I know," Eva answered. She was worried about her son, and had hoped he would be home by now.

"Of course he's all right," Felix interjected. "Ivan knows everyone and knows how to stay out of harm's way. He'll probably be home when this mess in the Ardennes is over."

"Do you realize it is past ten o'clock and the children have not put their shoes outside the front door for Père Noel?" Marie asked.

Everyone feigned a look of surprise and then set their gazes upon the children. Serge jumped up and said, "I'll get my shoes!"

"Please get your sister's shoes, too," his mother requested.

"I will," he answered as he raced up the stairs to fetch them from their frigid bedrooms. Within a minute he was downstairs. Fred helped Serge and Nadine place their shoes on the door mat upon opening the front door.

"Let's hurry, children. It's so cold we must shut the door quickly," Fred said.

"Will Père Noel be too cold to come?" Nadine asked.

"No, of course not. He dresses very warmly in fur robes and visits the houses of all of the children in Belgium," Fred responded and smiled at these two precious children who luckily outlasted the Gestapo. He kissed them both and told them to kiss everyone goodnight.

Francine put the children to bed, and they promised to fall asleep right away so that Père Noel could make his scheduled visit and then see all of the rest of the children's shoes in Belgium.

She rejoined the party as they were beginning to sing a few favorite Christmas carols. Suzanne's voice was lovely and lead the group in *Silent Night* as they enjoyed the last of their champagne and hoped beyond everything that the war would be over when the New Year began.

****

In foxholes spread throughout the Ardennes forest, American soldiers shivered under their blankets wearing every article of clothing they had on their bodies. There had been no weapons fired since sundown. Each man in both armies thought about Christmases past. Somewhere in the dense woods, two GI's began singing *Silent Night* and were soon joined by their platoon in singing the moving Christmas song.

In the distance from foxholes behind the lines, the GI's heard the tune of *Silent Night* being sung in German by their enemies. It was an unlikely harmony of two languages at this particular date and time and it made many of the soldiers on both sides wonder what the hell they were doing in the middle of a forest, barely staying alive in the freezing temperatures so they could begin killing each other again in the morning.

Supply Depot

The advanced engineers had worked and endured the winter months in small towns across northern France and then continued east to Metz and Nancy. Their assigned duty had been difficult in the freezing temperatures, but Jack and Group B knew they were far better off than the men who fought and supplied the Battle of the Bulge in the Ardennes. The war dragged on as the myth of ending it by the first of the year was blown to pieces.

By early March 1945 the 347th was in Bad Munster, Germany. After heavy bombing by the American Air Corps, Group B had been ordered in to clear debris in this border town to prepare for supplies to be moved into Germany. The engineers worked long hours with no passes. There was no fraternization with locals to prevent any kind of information falling into enemy hands. Now that they were in the enemy's country, everyone talked about the end being near. By summer, they'd be on their way home, according to the daily gossip.

After a few weeks Lt. Marshall talked to the men while they were in formation. "We have orders to go into Belgium. The 346th has been building a huge depot at Liege and we're to go in and help them finish the job. The Army will have a great need for that depot even after the war ends," the lieutenant said.

They were dismissed by their sergeant after being told that the troop trucks were arriving in about half-an-hour. Jack and his friends broke down their tents, grabbed their duffle bags, and then found a spot out of the wind to wait. Sitting around seemed like a luxury and they all lit up cigarettes.

"Well, we're going into Belgium," Steve mused. "What do you think it's like, Jack?"

"Guess it's about the same as France," Jack replied. "Why are you asking me?"

"Cause you know this stuff," Steve gave a laugh.

"Wonder what the girls are like?" Carl chimed in.

"They're just like the French girls, dope," Steve answered, "and we're probably not going to see much of them. When was the last time we had a pass?"

"Too long," Phil was quick with this answer.

"Why do you care, Phil? You never go out with any girls except that time back in London," Steve prodded him.

"I still like time off just like the rest of you. I wanna see the country, too," Phil said.

"Phil, you don't have to answer these goons," Jack interjected.

"Aw, I don't care, Jack," said Phil. "I know Steve doesn't mean nothing. Carl, too."

"Yeah, maybe not," Jack sounded resigned. "I want to see Belgium, too. Maybe we'll get a 24-hour pass in Liege. I know one thing. They've got great beer in Belgium. The French have their wine and so the Belgians specialize in beer. That's all I know," Jack said.

"I thought that all the good beer is in Germany," Carl added.

"Sure there's good beer in Germany, but you don't think Hitler's gonna let us drink any of it while he's alive, do you?" Jack joked.

They shared the laugh and heard the rumble of trucks pulling in. Troop trucks and the bad roads always made them look forward to their destination. The friends picked up their gear and lined up to climb onboard.

After bouncing across the roads past farms and through small villages, they crossed the border into Belgium and through the Ardennes Forest. They were south and west of the Ardennes that had been the battleground for the last major defense of this war. The forest was dense on both sides of the road. Jack observed that the pine trees were the straightest he had ever seen. The trees looked as if they had been planted in rows and there was no underbrush. The fresh scent of pine from the dark green woods that surrounded them during their journey to Liege was a pleasure they all seemed to be enjoying as the long day was coming to an end.

It didn't take much longer to reach their destination. The trucks pulled into the depot after dark and came to stop near some buildings that looked like barracks. Jack wondered if they'd actually be lucky enough to be housed in barracks. It was funny how priorities changed, Jack smiled to himself. He used to think that bunks inside barracks were poor accommodations, but now the sight was very welcome.

When Group B was assembled in formation, its sergeant told them they'd be housed in the "C" building. They were told to stow their gear and get a hot meal at the mess hall, which the sarge pointed out was to the north of their position. Jack felt the rumble in his stomach as he thought about hot chow. They hadn't eaten since breakfast except to snack on the chocolate in their rations.

"Man, this seems too good to be true, huh guys?" Carl said with a big grin on his face.

They headed for their barracks. "Yeah. Let's hope our duty tomorrow isn't as back-breaking as it has been lately," Steve replied.

"You bet," Jack said as they moved inside.

After looking around for a few seconds, Steve headed for two double stacked bunks in the middle near the stove. He tossed his duffle on the lower bunk and claimed the four beds for them. Some other guys who were right behind them shook their heads. It seemed that this foursome of buddies always got what they wanted when it came down to accommodations.

Phil smiled and knew he'd never have the best location or be the first in chow if it weren't for his pals. They all knew how to handle themselves and to get what they wanted. He was along for the ride and thanked his lucky stars that his best friend in the world was Jack.

Minutes later they were outside walking toward the mess. Carl was looking all around and said, "This place is damn big."

"You're right," Jack answered. "I think we'll be supplying the army but I also think this depot may supply the country when the war is over."

"I think you're right, Jack," Steve agreed. "We may be here for a while."

"Maybe," said Jack, "but I wouldn't bet on anything."

The four friends entered the mess hall and grabbed their trays. Jack looked at the selection and saw there was spaghetti and meatballs. "Oh, great. After steak, the food I like best is spaghetti and meatballs."

"You're no Italian," Steve kidded him.

"No, but I learned that if you eat Italian food no matter if you're in New York or L.A., you only need to spend a quarter and have a full stomach. And it's usually pretty damn good."

"Well, the Army can ruin everything," Carl added.

"Hey, lay off the guys in KP," Phil said, "They work hard and can't control the supplies they get."

"Yeah, yeah. Haven't seen you in kitchen since we landed in Normandy," Steve chided Phil.

"Sarge never gave me a chance. Maybe if we stay here for a while, I can get KP."

"Come on guys, just get your food and let's be happy it's hot," Jack said.

They all took a heaping tray of the Italian dish and plenty of bread. There was milk reconstituted from powder and Jack took two glasses. They sat down and were joined by familiar men from their platoon. As they began to eat, they were all pleasantly surprised that the pasta and the sauce were good. Even the meatballs were edible. They spent the next twenty minutes enjoying the first hot meal since they had been in Nancy, France.

The meal reminded Jack of one of his favorite places in L.A. that he'd frequent once a week to enjoy a good meal and stay within his budget. There was also a little Italian place in Coney Island where he'd often eat the familiar meal, but the place in L.A. was a lot better.

Jack's reverie was interrupted when one of the men from Group A of the 347th came over to their table. His name was Charlie Beck, and they had worked together from time to time since their days back in England.

"Hey guys, how you doin'?" Charlie was glad to see some old pals.

"We're doin'," Steve answered. "You guys been here a while?"

"Yep, and it's pretty good duty. The best part was a 48-hour pass we got last weekend," Charlie grinned.

"Where did you go?" Jack wanted to know.

"Brussels. We took the train from here, and it only took two hours," Charlie smiled again.

"Nice city?" Jack inquired.

"Yeah, man, real nice," Charlie replied.

"How long were you on duty here when you got the pass?" Steve asked.

"Only about ten days. The captain wanted us to get some real R and R. Nobody had any since Paris," Charlie explained.

"Your damn right," Jack interjected. "Paris was a long time ago. It's been six months."

"Well, I hope you guys get a pass, too." Charlie was sincere.

"Hey, Charlie, do you think we'll be on duty here for a long time?" Phil asked.

"Hard to tell, Phil. I heard this is a long term depot but they're going to need a lot of us for bridge details over the Rhine. Hitler can't last forever. He's hardly got an army left."

"Bet you're right, Charlie," Jack replied. "Hey, man, thanks for telling us the scoop and at least we can hope for that pass. Lt. Marshall's gotta want us to get some time off."

232

"You bet, Jack," Charlie stood up. "Hey, you interested in some cards?"

Charlie remembered that all of these guys except Phil like to gamble.

"Not tonight, Charlie. I'm beat and that bunk looked awfully good," Jack answered.

"Me too," it was Steve. The others nodded in unison.

"Maybe tomorrow, Charlie," Jack told him.

"Sure. I'll catch up with you tomorrow after supper. Have a good night, fellas." Charlie walked out of the building.

"Let's get some sleep, guys," Jack said.

"I think we're ready," Carl agreed. They dumped their trays and walked back to the barracks in the damp early spring night air. All four men were content with their newly assigned post, mess hall and barracks. Being dry and relatively warm made them feel that the worst was behind them.

One week later during formation, Lt. Marshall gave Group B the best news they had had since September of 1944. "You all will receive a 48-hour pass beginning at ten hundred hours tomorrow. I think most of you will want to go to Brussels. There will be a train waiting to take you at eleven hundred hours. Trucks will take you to the station. Just be ready to go. Sergeant Brady will give you a list of hotels that will give you a special rate. Brussels is a lot smaller than Paris, and the people are nuts about Americans. So go ahead and have a good time. You've done a great job for all these months. Make sure you don't miss your train getting back here on the 30th."

Sarge briefed the men on the hotels and handed out the army issue books on Brussels that doubled as a guide book and commonly-used phrases in French. He reminded them to behave like gentlemen and to stay out of fights and trouble. Duty for today would be over by seventeen hundred hours so they could get their uniforms in order and be ready to enjoy their first leave since Paris.

Every man in Group B of the 347th spent his day at work with smiles on their faces. Visions of cafés with beers and girls danced in their heads. When their day came to end, they all polished their boots, shined their brass, and showered and shaved to look their best. Tomorrow they'd be enjoying the privilege of being American GI's in the city of Brussels.

The Nightclub

Francine was arguing with her mother when Suzanne walked into the dining room at Eva's. "It's ridiculous that you don't think I should go out by myself. I'm 18-years-old and I don't think I need your permission."

Eva turned and saw Suzanne and she immediately dragged her into the argument. "Suzanne wouldn't have even thought to go out to night clubs without an escort or chaperone. She never went to a night club until she was engaged!" Eva stressed to her younger daughter.

"That was so long ago, *Maman*," Francine said. "Things have changed since the War. Girls go out by themselves all of the time now."

"Well, you make me sound like an old dinosaur, Francine," Suzanne said. "It wasn't so long ago that I was going out and meeting men."

"Yes, I know, but things are different now and changed, too," Francine would not relent.

"Suzanne, will you please go with your sister tonight?" her mother asked in desperation.

"I don't really feel like going out tonight, *Maman*," Suzanne sounded annoyed.

"Please, Suzanne. You'll have fun, too. You hardly ever go out," Francine was practically begging her so that she could do what she wanted.

Suzanne looked at both her mother and sister. Each had expressions of hope. "All right, I'll go. Where are we going?"

Francine gave her a look that said, 'why are you trying to ruin everything by letting *Maman* know what I want to do?

Suzanne quickly took back her question by answering herself. "It doesn't matter. Francine, show me what you plan to wear tonight so that I can dress in the right fashion for this evening."

"Sure. Come upstairs and I'll show you," Francine said.

She ran ahead of Suzanne glad to escape the glare from her mother's eyes. When they reached her bedroom, Francine turned around and grabbed Suzanne's hand. "Thank you for saving me. I found out that a whole bunch of Americans are coming in for the weekend, and they will be ready for a night of jazz and dancing."

"They'll be ready for a lot more than that," Suzanne scowled at her sister.

"Most of these men haven't even been in a civilized town for months. They just want to meet and talk to girls, buy them drinks and dance."

"Oh, you're such an expert, Francine. How do you know so much about these Americans?"

"Because I'm with Americans all of the time at the office. Really, they are the nicest people I've ever met. Now just come over here, and I'll show you what I'm going to wear. Look, you're going to have a good time, too. It's about time."

Suzanne couldn't help smiling. "Yes, you're right. I do need a night out. What time are we going and where? I won't tell *Maman*," she assured her sister.

After everyone had supper together at Eva's, Suzanne kissed her children goodnight and went to her house to change her clothes. She picked out a lovely white satin blouse that was styled in the popular Russian couture of the times. Her black fine wool skirt was cut to the knee and she had black leather pumps and small hand bag to complete the chic ensemble. Suzanne had decided to wear her hair down and it fell in luxurious brown waves to her shoulders. As she checked her appearance in the mirror, she was pleased. Suzanne liked being a blonde more than her natural brunette, but hadn't been able to afford the salon or the time over the last few years. Maybe after the war, she thought as she went downstairs to wait for Francine.

When her younger sister came in she smelled her perfume first and got up to take her coat. "I'm ready, Francine. Just let me get my coat," Suzanne said.

They walked to the chausee and waited for the tram to take them to the Grand Place. Francine knew every nightclub in the center of the city.

"So, what's the first stop, Francine?" asked Suzanne.

"Let's go to Corso," Francine said. "They always have good music and plenty of room to dance. All right?"

"Of course. You're in charge tonight," Suzanne laughed.

The nightclubs were in the cellars of the beautiful old guild buildings of the Grand Place. Many had been wine cellars but the owners had found more profitability in running nightclubs catering to all of the young people wanting to forget the German occupation. The sisters entered Corso and checked their coats. Suzanne turned to look for a table and noticed a tall American soldier jitterbugging by himself as the band played *"Is You Is or Is You Ain't My Baby."*

More people started coming onto the dance floor, and Suzanne felt she couldn't move out of the way. His eyes met hers after a moment, and he continued his lone dance as his friends, seated nearby, cheered him on.

The sisters moved to the right of the dance floor and were about to take seats at a small table when Francine saw friends from work a few meters further. She told Suzanne to follow her to their table, but her sister stayed where she was and stared at the American. Suzanne felt her face blushing as she kept eye contact with the G.I. When the tune was over, he walked towards her, his dark, wavy hair falling over one eye.

"Bon soir, je m'appel Jack," the American said to her.

"Bon soir, Suzanne," she replied hesitantly.

Jack smiled at her. "Will you dance with me?" He held out his hand so she would understand his English.

A Benny Goodman piece started to play and they walked the few steps to the dance floor.

Jack put his arm around her waist and took her hand and they began to jitterbug. Neither of them spoke as they danced. Suzanne felt that his steps were a bit clumsy; however, it didn't matter to her one bit. She looked at his dark complexion and strong features. His nose was perfectly straight and in proportion with his wide set eyes that were hazel. The GI's lips were full, and he sported a dark thin mustache that gave him a strong resemblance to the movie star, Clark Cable. She loved his dark hair that was almost black and not cut short like most of the soldiers. Suzanne couldn't believe that she felt as though she were melting in his arms.

The song was coming to an end, but the band leader didn't really stop and moved into *"GI Jive"* made popular by the Louis Jordan Five. Jack held her tighter and spun this Belgian beauty around. They separated and Jack decided he could show off his *boogie woogie* dance steps as Suzanne kept time with the rhythm with her feet and hips. He looked at her and grinned seeing that she was enjoying it. Jack's eyes were riveted to her face. Her beautiful pale skin, high cheek bones were perfect and her blue eyes sparkled. He looked at her strong nose and full mouth and thought they were a perfect combination. Jack wanted to reach out and touch the luxurious brown hair that fell around her shoulders, but didn't want to make the move too soon.

As the tune was ending, Jack took Suzanne back in his arms and they finished with an enthusiastic jitterbug finale. Smiling at him, Suzanne said, "thank you. I enjoyed the dance."

Jack spoke in French with a very strong American accent and several grammatical mistakes, "my pleasure, mademoiselle. Can we sit for a while?"

"Of course," Suzanne led the way to a small table and sat down.

Jack seated himself and a moment later the waiter came over. "What can I get you, Suzanne?"

"I'll have a red wine, please."

Jack ordered a beer for himself and turned back to look at this fantastic looking lady. "You live here in Brussels?"

"Yes. Just outside of the center of the city," Suzanne said.

"This is our first day here. It's a beautiful town," Jack commented.

"Are you stationed here?" Suzanne probed.

"No, I've got a two day pass. We haven't had any time off since we were in Paris in September," Jack told her.

"Oh, only two days," her voice trailed off.

Jack thought he heard a trace of disappointment in her voice. "Do you come out to the nightclubs, often?"

"No. I love the music but have a lot to do at home," Suzanne said. "My sister asked me to come with her tonight," Suzanne finished.

"Your sister? Is she here?" asked Jack.

"Yes, right over there at the bar. The girl with the light brown hair and blue dress," Suzanne saw that Francine was looking at them.

"Oh, she looks like a kid," Jack said without thinking.

Suzanne reported, "She's my younger sister," and didn't reveal by how many years were between them.

Jack noticed they both had the same strong, but fine features and that Suzanne was a lot taller. He liked that this woman was tall; perhaps only a few inches shorter than he. "Well, I'm glad you decided to come out tonight, or I wouldn't have been able to meet you."

Suzanne smiled and lowered her eyes. She hadn't corrected the soldier's use of the word *mademoiselle* and let him know that she was *madame*. She thought about it and decided they would probably never see each other again, so why bother with details.

The band began playing a soft melody and Jack stood up and took her hand. Suzanne followed him to the dance floor and they began to sway in unison with the ballad. Steve had moved onto the floor with a girl he asked at the bar and he danced over next to Jack. "Hey, pal, seems like you made a friend right away," Steve was speaking in English.

"Yeah, I have, so make sure you and the rest of the guys keep your distance tonight, got it?"

"Sure, sure. Hey, Jack, meet Paulette," Steve said.

Paulette was a slight, young woman with a pretty face. Jack replied, *"Enchanté."*

Paulette just smiled and they moved away as Jack turned his attention back to Suzanne. "He's a friend of mine. Been through the war with him and the other two guys I came in with."

"It's good to be with friends, I think; especially in this war," Suzanne replied.

"Yes, it is. They are really good guys and we've been together since 1942," Jack said.

Suzanne nodded. "Did you come in at Normandy?"

"Yes, but not in the first few days. We're engineers and we destroy and build things, like bridges and railroads. We just got stationed in Liege after being mostly in France and also in Germany for a couple of weeks," Jack concluded.

Suzanne liked what she heard. He was an engineer which was a fine profession. "I'm glad to know you have been safe since Normandy."

When the song ended, Jack guided her through the crowd on the dance floor to their table. Suzanne's wine was done, and he ordered drinks for them. She thanked him and wasn't sure where to go next in the conversation.

Jack began, "You're a beautiful woman, Suzanne, and I'm looking at your blouse, and I think it looks Russian. Is it possible that you're really a Russian girl?"

Suzanne laughed, and he loved the sound of it. "No. Russian style has been very popular in Belgium for years. Before the war, we had a lot of Russian aristocrats settling in Brussels. They came after the Russian Revolution and the first World War. They entered the universities and brought a great deal of their culture here, and our country really embraced them," Suzanne paused. "I'm sorry I'm probably talking too much and you may be having a hard time understanding me."

"No," Jack replied. "I understand most of what you said. You see I speak Spanish and learning a little French was easy for me. I know I'm not speaking very well, but I'll get the hang of it."

Suzanne almost blurted out that her husband had a difficult time learning French and it took him several years to be really fluent. But, she caught herself and said, "I know you will. Obviously your time in France has given you a good start. I really don't know any English."

Jack smiled at her, "You don't need to, doll."

Francine had practically never taken her eyes off of her sister and the GI. She decided to see what was going on and came over to their table.

Suzanne looked at her and wasn't sure what to say and didn't have to because Francine spoke first. "Hi," she said in English and put her hand out for Jack to shake.

He stood up. "Hi," he shook her hand.

"My name is Francine, and I'm Suzanne's sister," she smiled at Jack thinking he was really handsome, but wondered what they could have been trying to say to each other.

This time Jack answered her in his broken French in order not to leave Suzanne out of the conversation. "My name is Jack, and I've been enjoying meeting Suzanne and dancing with her. She's a much better dancer than I am."

Francine was taken aback of his skill at speaking French even if his grammar and accent were pretty bad. "Yes, Suzanne has always loved to dance. I see you have some pretty good moves yourself," Francine commented.

"Too bad there aren't any open chairs, or we could ask you to join us with your friends," Jack said to Francine.

Francine understood the hint. "Thanks, but I'm fine over there. Go ahead you two, have a good time." She turned and went back to the bar.

Suzanne looked annoyed at her sister and Jack broke the ice right away. "Tell me about yourself."

"Oh, there's not much to tell," Suzanne lied.

"What do you do? Do you have a job?" asked Jack.

"Oh, well, I did before the war," Suzanne said. "I was a designer. Textiles. I graduated from art school and got a job with a design firm. Belgium makes and exports a lot of carpets and other textiles," she informed him. "Let's say, we did. Everything changed with the war."

"Can you manage without a job?" he was curious.

"We do. My mother, sister and I," she didn't mention the children. "Francine is working with the Americans at an office in the city. She's a secretary. She was smart to learn English. Not very many girls know English, and it was easy for her to get the job. My mother has always been a seamstress and gets work and she has a widow's pension. We manage," Suzanne concluded.

"A lot of women work in the United States since the war started," Jack told her. "My mother always worked because my father isn't healthy."

"Where did you live in America?" asked Suzanne.

"I grew up in New York," Jack replied.

"New York. It must be wonderful there," Suzanne sounded wistful.

"Yeah, I like it. I grew up in Coney Island. At the beach. But we go downtown for a good time. I spent a lot of time in Los Angeles. You know, Hollywood," Jack was trying to impress her.

"Really, Hollywood?" asked Suzanne.

242

"Yes. It's really nice there. The weather is beautiful. But I think I like New York better. My folks moved to Jersey right before I was drafted. I don't really know if I'll like it there when we get to go home," Jack said.

Suzanne nodded at his details. "Do you have sisters or brothers?"

"I've got one brother who's two years older than me. He's in the Merchant Marines."

"Oh, that's dangerous," Suzanne sounded concerned.

"Yeah, but he's always loved the sea. I get a letter from him once in a while. He's Okay," Jack said.

They went back to the dance floor and were moving back and forth slowly as Suzanne tried to figure out why her emotions were so strong towards this American soldier. It made no sense, she was thinking. She was lonely, but she had so many responsibilities. She felt a very strong attraction and almost overwhelming desire for him. In the next moment Suzanne was ashamed of her desire.

At that moment Jack whispered in her ear, "Do you have to stay here with your sister?"

She leaned back and looked at him quizzically.

Jack quickly added, "I just thought we might go to another club and hear a different band. I understand there are several nightclubs right here in the Grand Place."

"Oh, yes, there are," Suzanne forgot her feeling of shame. "Why, no, I don't have to stay here. I'll get my handbag at the table and tell Francine we're leaving. Will you get my coat?"

"Sure. Do you have a ticket?"

Suzanne went ahead of Jack to the table, pulled the ticket from her purse and gave it to him. "I'll meet you at the door."

She crossed the room to the bar and tapped on Francine's shoulder. "We're going to another club," was all she told her.

"Oh. Then what?" asked Francine.

"What do you mean?" asked Suzanne. "Then nothing. We're going dancing at another club. Just make sure you get home by midnight or *Maman* will be angry if she hears you later than that," Suzanne admonished her sister.

"I will, but you need to make sure of the same, Suzanne."

"Goodnight, Francine."

Jack was waiting at the door with her coat. His pals were at the bar having a good time drinking beers and talking to pretty young girls. They all gave Jack a couple of winks thinking he had scored with this beautiful dame. Jack gave a wink back but was thinking differently.

He wondered what was wrong with him. Sure she was beautiful and had a great laugh, but there was something else he was feeling in his gut. Or was it his heart? Jack felt compelled to seek out a long visit with this foreign woman. She wasn't just a silly girl; there was much more to her. Not knowing why this attraction felt stronger than any other he had ever had, he decided it must be because of the six months of duty without any time for living life.

He gave his head a rest. "Do you know a nice place to go, Suzanne?"

"Yes. The Majeste. It's very close by and has a bigger dance floor and good orchestra," Suzanne said.

Jack took her arm and placed it in his and Suzanne told him the direction to walk. A few minutes later they were at The Majeste and were seated at a nice table near the dance floor. It was fancier than Corso, and the orchestra was bigger. After ordering their drinks, they danced. While dancing they both began to learn more and more about each other. They spoke of Jack's travels which were mystifying to Suzanne. She told Jack about her forgery work with the Resistance and he was impressed and felt proud to be with a woman of such character.

They were walking arm in arm on the Chausee Ninove. A very light rain had been falling for about thirty minutes. Jack had kissed Suzanne lightly on the lips at The Majeste, and she had responded by kissing him back. He held her tightly and she spoke softly as she asked Jack to go home with her. Jack leaned down and asked her if she were sure. Suzanne nodded and they left the dance floor and the night club.

Suzanne led Jack to the tram stop and they climbed onboard. He took her hand in his and squeezed it lightly. "How far do you live?"

"Not too far. We'll go by tram to the chausee and then we'll walk the rest of the way," Suzanne answered.

"Sure, I don't mind. I was wondering what your mother might think if she hears us?" Jack asked.

"She won't. I have my own house. It's next door to my mother, and we often eat meals together, but we sleep in our own houses." Suzanne decided she needed to tell Jack why she had her own house.

"You see, Jack. I was married."

"Oh," Jack was definitely surprised. "What happened?"

"He was killed."

Jack looked deeply into her eyes and asked, "Was he a soldier?"

"Not like you think. He was a soldier like me; in the Resistance."

"I see," Jack relaxed a bit.

"But that's not all. Our stop is next and I'll tell you the rest while we walk." Suzanne decided that if he wanted to run away after she told him, then he would just have to do it.

They got off the tram and Suzanne told him they had to walk several blocks. The soft rain began then and he tried to protect her.

"Don't worry about the rain. In Belgium you get used to it," Suzanne said.

Suzanne was quiet for a minute and then began. "I will tell you about my life. I married a very fine man who was originally from Poland. He was a Jewish man."

Jack interrupted her. "Really?"

"Yes, does that bother you?" her body stiffened as she asked.

"No." Jack gave a little laugh. "I'm Jewish, too!"

Suzanne looked at him, and the both shared a laugh. "Let me continue," Suzanne relaxed more than she had before. "Maurice; that was his name in French, was a jeweler and very much a gentleman. We got married in 1937 and our life was very nice. I had a son before the war began. His name is Serge."

Jack kept quiet and wanted to understand her life and encouraged her to continue.

"When the Germans occupied our country, Maurice was in great danger. We all were. My brother had a false identity so that he would not have to go to a German work camp. He hid all over Brussels for years and the Gestapo looked for him many times. They were searching for Maurice, too. Then in the spring of 1942 Maurice was arrested with several other men as a political prisoner. He was taken to the prison here in the city. When they realized he was a Jew, they moved him to a concentration camp just north of Brussels called Breendonk. Meanwhile I was pregnant. I tried to get him out of prison by bribing the guards. They took my bribes, but they never released him." Suzanne took a deep breath and decided to move the story along quickly.

"I was able to send him packages of food and clothing, but I don't think he ever got much of the food. He was able to write to me a couple of times and told me that he had given some of his business friends' jewelry and money for me to use to survive the war. Believe me, I have needed it," Suzanne said.

"My daughter was born in November of forty-two, and I was able to send a message to him in Breendonk. It wasn't much longer before Maurice was deported. I received a very short letter that was smuggled out for him that told me he was being sent to another camp in Germany or Poland. I've never heard from him since."

Jack stopped walking and looked at her. "How do you know that he isn't still alive?"

"Because I have many friends who are involved with the Resistance and in politics. One of them was at the deportation site in the town where the trains took all of the Belgian Jews they could catch and send them away. My friend told me that Maurice was so skinny that it would have been impossible for him to survive. And we know now that the trains leaving from Malines took them to Auschwitz in Poland and that by 1943 they were killing the arriving Jews by the thousands. If someone couldn't be useful working, they would be killed. I am certain he is dead."

They began walking again in silence. Jack pulled Suzanne closer to him and said, "When I saw you on the dance floor, I felt an overwhelming desire to hold you in my arms. Not just because you are a pretty woman. Something told me that I wanted to know you. Now after you've told me about your life, I want to know you even more," Jack said.

"I haven't frightened you with my story? With my children?" Suzanne asked as she looked into his eyes.

Jack responded by leaning over and kissing her.

"We're almost home," she said. They entered the street leading past the shops and walked to rue Virgile. "Please be quiet or the geese will start honking and wake everyone."

Suzanne slipped the key into the back door, and they were in the dining room a moment later. The room was dark since all of the shutters were closed and she quickly turned on the switch for the chandelier. Jack helped her out of her coat and she hung it on the hook by the front door. Suzanne turned to walk back to him and suddenly she felt nervous as she realized she had made her decision to invite this American soldier into her home and into her bed.

Jack smiled at her and she felt a little more at ease. "May I get you anything to drink?" Suzanne asked because she didn't know what else to say.

"No. No, there's nothing I want except you," Jack answered and reached out for her at the same time. They embraced and kissed a long and deeply passionate kiss. As they moved apart, Suzanne took his hand and led Jack upstairs.

When they reached the second floor Suzanne switched on a small lamp on a dresser in the hallway. The soft light set a romantic atmosphere and Suzanne glanced in her bedroom and instantly thought of Maurice. She didn't want to think about him. He was gone forever but she couldn't bear the thought of bringing Jack into her marital bed.

Suzanne quickly reached for Jack's hand again and guided him to the little bedroom at the back of the house over the kitchen. The bed was smaller and was seldom used. Jack looked around as Suzanne put on a very small lamp. He didn't say a word about her choice of rooms.

"I'll be right back," she said to Jack. "I want to freshen up in the bathroom."

He watched her go and decided to undress quickly to ease the tension. Jack realized this beautiful widow had probably not been with a man for a long time and was probably nervous.

The room was barely illuminated as Suzanne came back. She had put on a beige peignoir and looked beautiful in the low light. Suzanne saw that he was naked. Jack's body was lean and his arms and chest were muscular and well defined. Her nervousness melted as he took her in his arms and they kissed again and again. She broke away for a moment and untied the bow on the peignoir and let it drop to the floor.

How beautiful she is Jack thought as they lay down and he began to make love to this very special woman. Suzanne felt such a deep desire it overwhelmed her, and their passion carried them as if on a cloud in the

248

dark universe as they explored each other's bodies and ended in glorious satisfaction.

The Promise

Jack's arms were wrapped around her as they stood by the window in the little room looking out at the moonlight. Suzanne had gotten out of bed after they had made love two times. She turned out the lamp and opened the window in order to fling open the shutters. Closing the glass to keep out the chilly night air she turned towards her soldier-lover.

He saw her silhouette illuminated by the light of the moon. "Come, look, Jack, the moon is full."

As he moved next to her she turned and looked out and he put his arms around her and Suzanne put her hand over his strong hands. "Isn't the moon beautiful tonight?" she asked.

"It is and it allows me to see you in the dark. I never want to take my eyes off of you, Sweetheart." He held her more tightly.

"I... I wish you could stay here with me, Jack," she said tentatively.

"Oh, baby, you don't know how much I want to do that," Jack said.

"Do you have to leave tomorrow, I mean today, Jack?"

"No. I've got another day off. Have to be back in Liege on the 30th."

"It will be morning soon, *cheri*, and I have to ask you to leave here before then," Suzanne said.

"I know, I understand," he said. "I'll go soon. Can I take a tram back?" asked Jack.

"Yes, they run at night again now that the Germans are gone. I'll tell you which to take," Suzanne said.

"Can I see you tomorrow? You know, later?"

"Oh, yes," she was so glad to hear him say that. "Will you come for dinner?"

Jack was surprised. "Sure, I'd love to. Are you sure it's Okay?"

"Yes, *cheri*," Suzanne said.   "I will invite my mother to meet you. Francine has brought some soldiers home from the office. Everyone tries to invite soldiers to show them how much we appreciate being liberated."

"Great! What time should I come?" asked Jack.

"At noon. I will try to find something decent at the butcher first thing in the morning," Suzanne was excited that would see him again.

They fell silent and looked at the moon together. He turned her to face him and kissed her tenderly. "I want to tell you this was very special for me, Suzanne. I feel something very different than I've ever felt before."

Suzanne embraced him and whispered, "I feel something in my heart for you, my American soldier."

Jack reached his hotel about 30 minutes after walking to the tram stop. He entered the room he was sharing with Phil and heard his light snoring. On the way back, Jack wondered why he told Suzanne how he felt. He never shared his emotions with a woman the first time he was with her. Yet, he knew this was truly a different experience for him. He must have let down his guard because female companionship had been rare over the last couple of years.

While he was lying in bed, he realized that he was trying to convince himself that Suzanne was just another dame, just like all the others. She was not. Jack fell asleep and dreamed he was in the arms of the loveliest woman he'd ever known.

Phil was trying to be quiet as he got dressed in their small hotel room. He didn't hear Jack come in during the night but he guessed it was pretty late. As he reached for his jacket on the hook on the back of the room's door, Jack turned over and asked with his eyes still shut, "What time is it and what are you doing?"

"It's nine o'clock, Jack, and I'm going downstairs for some breakfast. Comes with the room, you know."

"Right," Jack said.

"Jack, you gotta hangover?" asked Phil.

"Nope." Jack opened his eyes and swung his legs out of bed and sat on the edge rubbing his face to wake up. "I never felt better."

"Good. Did you have a nice time?" Phil asked.

"Yep. Best night of my life, buddy," replied Jack.

Phil was surprised by the answer his friend gave him. "Okay. Good for you, Jack. Hey we're all going to take a look around the city after breakfast; wanna come?"

"Sure, for a little while. Go on to breakfast. I'll get washed up and meet you in ten minutes," Jack said.

"Yeah, sure, Jack." Phil left the room and Jack got up after putting on his pants. He grabbed a towel and his shaving kit and went down the hall. The bathroom was open, and he got cleaned up quickly. He wanted to pal around with his friends before going to Suzanne's house.

When Jack entered the dining room, his best friends were waiting for him. Jack sat down and a young girl came over and poured him a cup of coffee. Jack thanked her and didn't look up. He always looked at the girls. He helped himself to a roll and butter and looked at the faces of this buddies.

"Why are you all staring at me?"

"Give it up, pal," Steve told him.

"What?" Jack asked.

"You left the nightclub with that brunette bombshell and you ask 'what?'"

"Yeah, Phil told us you had the best night of your life," Carl chimed in.

"Yep."

"Well, what happened?" Steve pressed him.

Jack recounted their next nightclub visit and then the short tram ride and long walk to Suzanne's house.

"She brought you to her house?" Phil was again surprised. "She has her own house?"

"Yep. Nice house and nice neighborhood. Right on the outskirts of the city. I'm going there for dinner at noon today to meet her family," Jack concluded.

They stared at him and Steve asked, "Why?"

"Because she invited me and because I feel something is very special about this woman."

"Hey, man, you must have lost your mind," Steve remarked. "This isn't like you."

"I know, I know, and I'm not sure why," Jack admitted. "She is different. Hell, the world is different. This fuckin' war has made life different. If I feel like she is someone special, I don't want to miss the chance I might have with her," Jack said not really knowing why he felt this way.

"Geez, buddy, there are millions of girls back home waiting for us to come back," Carl reminded his friend.

"Yeah, well maybe that's the reason," Jack said. "The girls at home are all the same. Everybody grew up with nothing, and nobody knows what they want to do with their lives. People here are ready to start living again. They know what they want," Jack stopped talking when their sergeant entered the room.

"Listen up, men. I just got word from the lieutenant that when we move out tomorrow morning, we're going to Germany. Make sure you are at the rendezvous point at eight hundred hours."

A soldier at another table asked, "What are we doing in Germany, Sarge."

"You'll get your full orders tomorrow. All I can tell you for now is that we're joining up with General Patton's Third Army and we have in important mission to carry out."

"We're not picking up our gear in Liege?" Steve asked the sergeant.

"Yeah, we are stopping there for one hour. Get in your fatigues and pack your essentials and get your rifles. That's all, men. Eight hundred hours tomorrow."

The sergeant left the room to go on to the next hotel. The room started buzzing with chatter about the possibilities of their next mission. Jack stood up and said, "That's for tomorrow. Come on, fellas, let's go take in some sights, I'm in a hurry."

253

Jack got off the tram on the chausee and found his way to the little suburban city of Mortabeek without a hitch. He had bought flowers at an open air market he passed finding the tram. His buddies and he had spent the morning touring the little streets off the Grand Place. They saw the statue of the little boy pissing in the fountain called *Mannequin Pis* and had a good laugh and took photographs of each other in front of it. All them stopped and bought a few postcards to send home. Jack looked at some beautiful lace in one of the shop windows and decided he would buy a piece for his mother when he came back to Brussels.

Jack realized he was making plans to come back to Brussels without really thinking it through. What the hell was wrong with him? He thought about Suzanne. Is she really that special, he wondered? Jack also thought about what he had been saying to his friends over breakfast. Did the war really change everything in their lives forever?

As he approached her house, Jack decided he better knock on the front door. He didn't want her mother to know he was familiar with the back entrance. He knocked and Suzanne opened the door only a few moments later. She held the door open for him to enter, and she offered her hand which Jack took and shook it tenderly and then handed her the flowers. Suzanne took them and turned around quickly and led the GI through the small salon into the dining room. She immediately introduced him to her mother, and Jack instantly shook her hand, nodding and smiling.

Suzanne turned to Jack and said, "I think you remember my sister, Francine, from last evening."

"Yes, of course." Jack took Francine's hand which was extended.

"Hello, Corporal," Francine said with a knowing smile on her face.

"These are my children, Jack. Serge and Nadine."

Jack stooped down and took the hand extended by Serge. *"Bonjour, Monsieur."*

254

"Bonjour," Jack replied.

The little girl wasn't shy and walked over and kissed him on the cheek.

"Well, what a sweet little girl you are," Jack was elated.

Everyone smiled, and Jack was offered a chair at the table. "Well, let me put these lovely flowers in a vase," Suzanne said. "Thank you very much. Francine, offer him a drink, please."

Francine spoke in English, "What would you like to drink, Corporal?"

"Please call me Jack. What are you offering," he replied in French not wanting to be rude to the rest of the family.

"How about vermouth?" Francine asked in French

"Please."

Suzanne re-entered with the vase of flowers and placed them on the buffet. Jack looked around and realized how stylish it was and what beautiful furnishings filled the room. He hadn't been the least interested in the room the night before noticing only Suzanne. She took the chair next to him and when everyone had a drink, Eva spoke.

"Let's toast our American friend and all of the Americans who have come here to help us," Eva said.

Everyone's glass was lifted, even the glasses of water the children had. *"Santé!"* they said in a chorus.

After a short while Suzanne busied herself with serving dinner. Francine helped serve the children, and Serge was asking a hundred questions of the American soldier. They ate and talked and were quite surprised by Jack's ability to speak French without too much difficulty. When he couldn't find the word in French he would say it in English and Francine would repeat the word back in French. She could see that he was a quick study at language as she was.

When they were through with the meal and had had dessert and coffee, Suzanne suggested that she and Jack take a walk. He agreed instantly. The children began to complain that they wanted to go, too, but Suzanne answered that Nadine needed a nap and Serge should play quietly and rest for a while.

Suzanne took her coat and led Jack out through the front door. He took her arm and placed it in his and she looked at him and smiled. "Well, what did you think of them?"

"Your family is very nice, Suzanne," Jack said. "Your children are well behaved and Serge seems like a very smart little boy."

"Hmmm," Suzanne kept looking at him as they walked. "Yes, they are fairly good children. I have trouble at night with Nadine. She cries during the night. I think the war did that to her. I think she becomes afraid when she awakens in the dark or when she heard the planes overhead so often."

"You didn't say what you think of my mother and sister," Suzanne pressed him.

"Oh, well, your mother seems very nice. She certainly was nice to me. Your sister has a lot of questions in her head, I think," Jack said.

"My mother was fine today, but she can be difficult. I know she wants what's best for me. And my sister; she loves Americans. She has brought home many since the liberation. I believe she is determined to find a husband!" Suzanne laughed.

"Isn't she too young?" Jack inquired.

"Perhaps, but she knows that life is so uncertain. Her entire adolescence was spent during this damn war. I doubt she wants to miss out on something in life and wants to make sure of what she is getting," Suzanne said.

Jack thought for a minute as they continued walking along the chausee. "I guess it's been really difficult for civilians all over Europe since 1939. I really didn't think about how many years it's been. From 1939 until 1942 I was living in California and Mexico having the time of my life. I read about the war over here, but it was so far away. You know?"

Suzanne steered Jack to turn right into the park in Dilbeek. "You have had an interesting life so far, Jack. I want to hear all about it. And about your family, too."

"Sure, I'll tell you some day. Hey, what is this place?" Jack was looking at the beautiful park with the chateau in the distance.

"It's a park, and the chateau is closed. No one lives there any longer. We come here with a picnic sometimes and for long walks. There's a little lake just ahead and it has a Medieval tower on it. Let's walk over there, she steered Jack to the left. I love the woods, and there is a long foot path."

They arrived at the wooded path and began to walk through the woods. There were buds on many of the early blooming trees, but the oaks were totally bare. Suzanne could see that they were alone and she stopped and turned to Jack.

"*Cheri*, I really felt that last night was special. I have only made love with one man before, my husband, Maurice."

"It was special for me, too, Suzanne. You have ignited something inside of me that I didn't know was there." He pulled her into his arms and they kissed for a long time.

"Oh, Jackie," she said it as Americanized as she could. "I don't want you to have to go back to the war. Something may happen to you."

"Don't worry, Sweetheart," he called her that in English. "I've been okay all this time and the war has to be over soon. We've got them on the run. I don't know what our mission is in Germany, but I'm sure we're going to build something to push further inland and to keep the Krauts on the retreat."

"But I do worry. I want to see you again, Jack. I don't want this to be the end," she said anxiously.

"Don't worry, *cherie*, I'll be back," Jack said. "Don't know when, but I will." They kissed even harder this time and stayed in each other's arms for several minutes.

"Suzanne, I'll write to you, but I don't know when. I don't know if we'll be in a place where I'll have time to write, but I promise you I will."

"I'll write to you, too, Jackie. When we get back to the house, write down your address and I'll give you my card so you won't forget the address."

"I don't think I could ever forget the address of your house. It's the place of the best night of my life, Sweetheart," Jack said.

They embraced and began to walk back toward the park and the chausee. Suzanne didn't want her family to become suspicious if they were gone too long. She didn't want her mother asking too many questions.

Jack left 33 rue Virgile at half past eight that evening. He had spent time with Suzanne's children telling them about America. Serge was very interested and asked Jack to tell him more stories about when he was a cowboy in Montana. Suzanne thought about her brother and wished he were here to listen to Jack's stories of his time in the American West. She suspected that Serge was going to be just as crazy about cowboys and Indians as Ivan.

Eva had gone back to her house and returned with a pot of soup for supper. Jack spoke about his mother and father to her, and Suzanne could tell that her mother was pleased that this American had a great respect for his parents, especially for his mother. Jack told her that his mother was a seamstress for her entire life and worked for two large department stores in New York. Eva recanted that it was a very dignified profession for women.

Suzanne smiled and couldn't help but think that Jack was very astute in his method to gain the acceptance of the matriarch of this family and thus the permission to spend time with her eldest daughter. She was also certain that her mother would interrogate her later and most likely throw several blockades in her path, but Suzanne was determined not to let her mother interfere.

Francine had gone back to work after dinner and had just returned from the office when supper was served. She told them all that the office had been very busy and she had met a very nice American named Tommie and that he asked her to go out on Saturday evening. Suzanne knew that her sister made the announcement with Jack at the table so that her mother would hold her tongue and wouldn't forbid her from dating a soldier. Jack asked a few questions about Tommie's duties and learned that he worked in records.

"There will be plenty of work for the next several months to make sure the records and whereabouts of GI's that are MIA and KIA," Jack remarked.

"Yes, and that means I'll have a job for a while and can continue to learn English so that I can do something with my life when this war is over," Francine was very confident.

Eva glared at her youngest daughter. "What do you mean? You can't think you can go and live in America."

"Why not? Although that's not what I mean. I want to be able to get a very good job later and I may want to live anywhere in the world if I want," Francine said.

Suzanne knew it was time to interject into the conversation. "If everyone is done their soup, I'll get some cheese. Francine, please clear the soup plates."

The change in subject worked and Serge began a new onslaught of questions about America which Jack was happy to answer. His French vocabulary was limited and it was fun to talk with the little boy. Jack wondered if he could be a father to these children. He surprised himself with the thought and quickly moved on to other conversation with Eva.

When Suzanne came back with a platter of cheeses and basket of bread she said kindly to her mother, "*Maman*, please don't bore Jack with stories of the ancient relatives in the country."

"Yes, of course, I'm going on and on. I hope I didn't bore you, Jack," she only sounded slightly annoyed at her daughter's interruption.

"Of course not, Madame Duchesne. I hope to learn more about your family when I get my next leave of duty."

"But you're going to Germany now," Eva was perplexed by his remark.

"Yes, I am. I don't think the war will go on much longer. I've heard talk that many of us will get a good amount of leave time when it is over. Those of us that have been over here the longest will get some leave," Jack told her.

"And you intend to come to Brussels when that happens?" Eva pressed him.

"Ah, sure. I have often thought that I wanted to go to Switzerland, but Belgium is really a nice place," Jack smiled.

"*Maman*, let's have our cheese. I don't think Jack needs to make his plans right now. Isn't that true, Jack?" Suzanne said turning to him with the plate of cheese.

"That's right. I really don't know how long I'll be in Germany," he said.

Suzanne walked Jack to the tram stop and again reminded him to write and to be very careful. She was extremely worried that he may have been overwhelmed by her family and may never want to return even though he said he would.

As if reading her thoughts, Jack pulled her into his arms. "Look, Sweetheart, I do plan on coming back here. I want to get to know you better and I like your family. Your mother didn't bother me; she's just trying to protect you. She doesn't know me, and she should be suspicious."

260

"Oh, Jack, I'm so happy to hear you say that." She put her head against his strong shoulder and he squeezed her tightly.

She heard the sound of the tram but didn't move. "Here's your tram, *cheri*. I have to let you go," Suzanne said.

Jack loosened his embrace and looked into her face. "You are the loveliest woman I have ever known. I'll be back, Suzanne. You can count on it."

The tram was almost there, and he kissed her quickly and squeezed her hand in his. "See you later, Sweetheart," he said as he jumped onboard.

"Bye, *cheri*," Suzanne said and waved to him as the tram pulled away. She stood there watching the moving vehicle until it disappeared from her sight. Suzanne was overcome by a mixture of emotions. She was happier than she had been since before the war, and she was sad because she worried if he would ever return. How could her life totally change in two days, she wondered, and what was in store for her and her American soldier?

Patton and F.D.R.

On March 30 the troop trucks rolled and bumped their way across Belgium, through Luxembourg and into the eastern border of Germany. The men of the 347th had been briefed about the orders. They were going to the Rhine River to build a bridge into the city of Mainz near Frankfurt. A bridge had stood at this location for centuries and was destroyed by the German military engineers only two weeks earlier to try to stop the Allies from crossing the Rhine. This mission had high priority since General Patton intended to bring battalions from the Third Army into German and wiping out the final remnants of the enemy's resistance.

The weather was mild and sunny and the landscape was beautiful. There were rolling hills filled with vines that produced some of the finest Rieslings. The men had tasted some of the wine when they had entered Germany once before. This time, they were under strict orders to build this railroad bridge at record speed. It was critical to the success of Patton's strategy. The general kept pushing troops across the Rhine by rail and floating heavy artillery and equipment on barges to the other side of the river. Company C of the 333rd Engineers had finished a bridge over the Saar River in just the last four days, and Patton was anxious to keep moving forward.

Jack was amazed by the amount of troops on the road, each company with orders to reconstruct railways and bridges. Since the Battle of the Bulge had finally been won, the Army had been occupied with rebuilding infrastructure and supplying the troops to win the War. Patton had been a major part of the eventual victory in the Ardennes Forest, and now he was bound to be the driving force for the final triumph inside the enemy lines.

During their transport, Jack's friends had questioned him about his time in Brussels. Jack was coy. He told them 'he had the time of his life,' but wouldn't give them any details. When they were away from Jack, they speculated about the depth of Jack's attachment to the gorgeous woman they had seen at Corso Nightclub just a couple of days before.

Arriving at their destination, Group B was informed that the 333rd would be attached to them to complete the bridge to Mainz. The next day the engineers began assembling the materials to construct the new single track railroad bridge. Almost all of the materials being used were captured from German stockpiles. It was definitely the most ambitious project the engineers had undertaken from the time of their arrival in Normandy.

While they were cutting piles for the pier and assembling the beam sections they would put in place, Jack thought about Suzanne a great deal. He was thinking about his future and concluded that he needed to plan his life rather than letting circumstances plan it for him. After a few days on the job, Jack got a letter during mail call. With only a thirty-minute break to eat and have a smoke before getting back to the construction, Jack carefully opened the letter. It was dated March 30, the day after he had said good bye to Suzanne at the tram stop.

Cher Jackie,

I have thought about you all day. Did you have a good trip? There is a very cold wind. I will write often if you enjoy receiving letters. I don't have any photos developed yet because of Easter.

Today I've worked in the garden all day and am very tired. Mother is in bed and Francine is in town for the evening.

Smile, Jack, I don't want to think that you are sad. I'm thinking of you often and wishing you good luck.

My thoughts are with you. Affectionately, Suzanne.

Jack folded the letter and slipped it back into the envelope. He was very happy to have received it and knew he should write to her, but there was no time. Every man was getting back on their feet and back to work. He promised himself that he would write, even if it was a brief note.

As the 347th and 333rd finished the bridge to Mainz, the men received news from their commander that the next day they would be visited and inspected by General George Patton. While they were eating a hot supper from the field mess, Jack and his pals talked about the visit.

"I think it's a big honor," Phil announced.

"Sure it is," Steve said sarcastically. "I bet the general doesn't give two shits about the engineers. He's all about killing, and we didn't do that for him"

"Aw, come on Steve," Jack piped up. "General Patton knows he couldn't have some of his victories without us. No supplies, no victories."

"Yeah, Steve, Jack's right," it was Carl.

"Well I don't give a rat's ass if Patton or even if Ike comes here for a visit," Steve was belligerent.

"So, stay out of the limelight tomorrow, buddy," Jack told him.

"You bet I will," Steve said.

"Carl, you got film in your camera?" Phil asked.

"I sure do, Phil. I was just thinkin' the same thing. I'll take plenty of pictures of the general at our bridge tomorrow."

"I heard they are going to dedicate it tomorrow and call it the "FDR Bridge," Jack told them.

"That's fine with me," Carl answered.

"Me, too," Phil said.

"I guess you don't care about the president, either, huh, Steve?" Jack was egging him on.

"I'm just glad the damn bridge is done. Now I'm turning in for the night," Steve walked away.

The three friends laughed as they finished their smokes and decided to call it a night, also.

On April 8, 1945 General George S. Patton arrived at the eastern side of the Franklin Delano Roosevelt

Bridge that would be taking supplies by rail across the Rhine in order for the Third Army to push further into Germany and have final defeat of the German enemy.

The engineers of Group B of the 347th and the 333rd that was attached to them temporarily assembled for inspection by the general. When the general arrived by jeep, he immediately stepped out of the vehicle and gave a long evaluating look at the bridge that had been built in only 7 days. After several minutes he turned to the Captain and returned his salute.

"General, the companies are assembled for your inspection. Will you do us that honor, sir?" the captain asked.

Patton moved towards the engineers standing at attention. He walked slowly in front of the first row. Jack was in the third row along with his buddies. He felt an air of electricity as the general passed by in review.

"The bridge looks like an engineering marvel," Patton spoke to the assembled troops. Engineers, you've done a fantastic job moving me closer to kicking the ass of Hitler himself!

"Captain, order your men 'at ease,'" Patton said.

The captain turned to Lieutenant Marshall, "Give the order lieutenant."

Lieutenant Marshall turned to face the troops. "At ease, men."

The engineers stood at ease, most of them thinking they had not had such formality in their ranks for a very long time.

General Patton continued and turned to the troops. "You can be proud of what you have accomplished here and in many of the other demolition and construction projects you've done. I want you to know that I pissed in the Rhine a couple of weeks ago, and I think all of you should do the same!"

A cheer went up from the men and Patton gave them a nod. "We all belong to the same club, men. We came here to beat the crap out of the Krauts, so let's make sure you piss on them, too!" Patton said.

There was laughter from all of the troops. Patton turned to the captain. "I'd like to inspect the bridge now, captain, after I salute your troops."

Lieutenant Marshall took the command to order the soldiers back to attention. They did so gladly and seemed to stand taller than before.

General Patton turned to the men and saluted. Dropping his arm he turned to walk with Captain Stuart to inspect the bridge. "Captain, dismiss your men, so they might take me up on the challenge to piss in the Rhine." The order went to Lt. Marshall who dismissed the men.

Carl poked Steve in the arm, "You see, Steve, the general was swell. Really swell."

"Yeah, well, I gotta admit, he surprised me," Steve relented.

They had a good laugh and Carl ran over to his pack and got his camera and began to shoot a whole roll of film. As Patton looked over the work they had busted their asses doing, Carl clicked away on his Kodak Brownie.

Several minutes later, the friends ran down to the edge of the river making sure they all pissed in the Rhine River, Germany. The rest of the day was spent mostly at leisure after the equipment was loaded onto trucks. They all needed a few hours to relax, eat a hot meal at a slow pace and play some cards or write letters home.

The next day, Jack received another letter from the woman he left behind. It contained photos they had taken together at her house during his daytime visit to meet her family. Jack smiled as he looked at her beautiful face. There was a good one of the two of them in her back yard and Jack was happy to share that with his friends who remarked that she truly was a great beauty. That evening he sat in his small tent and wrote a brief letter.

April 9, 1945
Dear Suzanne,

Thank you for your hospitality and good times. I'm working hard for the war to be over. There will be no leave time for the near future. I'm enclosing two photos with me and two of my best friends. The other friend is taking the picture.
Your Jack.

****

Suzanne and the children were sitting in their dining room with the radio playing the music of Louis Armstrong. Tapping her foot to the beat of the band, Suzanne busied herself with mending a few of Serge's play clothes. Suddenly the broadcaster interrupted the program to bring important news from the United States of America. Her heart leapt with anticipation of an announcement that the war was over.

"We have received official news from the White House just minutes ago," the broadcaster said in a serious voice. "President Franklin Roosevelt has died."

Suzanne dropped her mending and let out an audible gasp. Both of the children looked at her and Serge ask, "*Maman*, what's wrong?"

"Sssh, listen," Suzanne said.

The broadcaster continued, "At one o'clock in the afternoon, the president died in Warm Springs in the state of Georgia. There is no cause of the death at this moment, but the president had not been in good health for a while and was in Georgia to regain his strength. The Vice President, Mr. Harry Truman, will be sworn in as president today."

Suzanne looked at her clock indicating it was half past seven on this Wednesday evening. She calculated the time difference and knew the president had only been dead for a little over an hour. Serge was tapping her arm.

"What does it mean, *Maman*? The American president is dead, really?"

"Yes, Serge. He was an old man and sick," Suzanne said.

Serge thought for a moment. "Will that mean that the Germans will come back here?"

The little boy startled his mother with his question. "No. No, Serge. There is already a new president. President Truman," she continued, "will make sure that the American soldiers continue to win the war. No, my *cheri*, the Germans are gone."

Suzanne knew she was right. The war was nearly won and nothing could stop the Americans and all of the Allies now. She wondered if Jack had gotten the news. Her mind was racing and she hoped that her soldier was safe and not coming under any enemy fire. Oh, how she wished for a letter from Jack telling her he was fine and that he would come back to her.

With thoughts of her own circumstances on her mind, she was again surprised; this time by her mother who came in the back door. "Suzanne, Suzanne," her mother entered breathlessly.

"Yes, *Maman*," she got up from her chair. "I know."

"It's not possible that President Roosevelt is dead," Eva announced.

"It's hard to believe but in the recent news reels he does look ill," Suzanne answered.

"Yes, I think you're right," Eva said. "I came over because I didn't know if you were listening to the radio."

Suzanne nodded and sat again. "Where's Francine?"

"She's in town again. Seeing that new boy, Tommie," Eva frowned.

"She'll know more than we do when she goes to work tomorrow," Suzanne said.

"Probably. I hope the new president will be as strong as Roosevelt. He has to finish this war and then finish with Japan."

"Yes, *Maman*, I know."

Suzanne didn't feel like resuming her mending. "Stay for a while, *Maman*. We'll have a little bread and cheese and a glass of wine."

268

"All right. Have the children had their supper?" asked Eva.

"Yes. I didn't feel like anything earlier. Let's enjoy something together," Suzanne said.

As they ate their light supper the two women reminisced about the great accomplishments of Franklin Delano Roosevelt. The children listened and Serge wondered if his mother's reassuring remarks about the new president were true. He certainly hoped that the Germans were gone for good. He hoped the American soldier that had become friends with his mother would come to visit again soon.

Eva and Suzanne decided to travel to Hannut and Villers later that week. The warm spring air tempted Eva to visit her cousins and she made arrangements to stay for several days with her eldest daughter and grandchildren. Suzanne was still hoping to receive a letter from Jack, and although she wanted to spend some time relaxing in the country, she was afraid she might miss a return visit from the American.

Guarding her anxiety from her mother, Suzanne also didn't show her joy at receiving a short note from Jack only hours before their departure to Hannut. As she read the letter dated April 9th, she was overcome with happiness. He had signed it "Your, Jack." At that moment she was certain that he did care for her and now she would continue to correspond with him. She also realized from the letter, that he would not be back in Brussels for a while. Germany was a very large country and there was much to do to win the war.

Suzanne and her family boarded the afternoon train with the destination of Liege at the *Gare du Midi.* Both children were excited about the ride that would take less than two hours to reach Hannut. Serge remembered past train rides where German soldiers and police would patrol the passenger cars, and he would feel his mother tense her body each time one passed near them. This time was different. His mother and grandmother were filled with smiles and laughter as they stowed their small suitcases and got comfortable in the second class carriage. Serge smiled broadly at the conductor as he passed through their cabin taking the tickets and punching holes in them. Serge placed his own ticket in his pocket. He would keep it as a souvenir of this trip along with the stamps he collected and put in a book.

The entire family was totally at ease as they rolled through the green countryside. Suzanne had a small smile on her lips thinking about Jack and what might be in her future when he returned to Brussels after the war ended.

Germany

As the 347th moved deeper into Germany, they continued to stay within the Rhine valley. There had been several layovers to repair railroad tracks or to move supplies in for the 1st Army. Everyone kept wondering how much longer it would take before Hitler would surrender. Betting pools were becoming massive as unofficial bookies set the odds and took bets for the date Hitler would finally throw in the towel.

At times the Allied troops felt comfortable and worry free from the threat of being killed or wounded in action. They were brought back to realty when word would come that fellow soldiers had fallen under the fire from German soldiers still along the Rhine and further inland toward the center of the country. The Russian Army was pushing into Germany from the east while the Americans pushed from the west. Their goal was to have obliterated the German Army by the time they met in the middle. German civilians feared the onslaught of the Red Army more than anything else. Many were aware of the atrocities inflicted on the Soviets in Stalingrad and all along the eastern front. They knew there wouldn't be any mercy from the Reds, and many prayed that the Americans would get to their particular towns first.

Jack and the rest of Group B were moving southward not far from the Rhine when the convoy stopped in a heavily wooded area. The countryside was beautiful here in the legendary Black Forest. They were ordered out of the trucks and told to wait for orders.

Carl was next to Jack and asked, "Why do you think we're stopping?"

"Don't know," Jack replied. "Seems pretty quiet. Just the woods."

"I don't like it," Steve chimed in.

"Why?" Phil asked with a very worried look on his face.

271

"It's too quiet, and it could be the site of an ambush," Steve replied as he removed his rifle from his shoulder.

"Don't get too charged up," Jack told them "Let's wait and see what the orders are."

They were all having a smoke when their sergeant came over. "All right men, leave all your gear except for full canteens and your rifles. We're going into the forest."

"Why, Sarge," came a question from a bit of distance.

"We received intel that there's a POW Camp several hundred yards into the forest, and we may be the troops liberating it."

"Are they Americans?" another voice asked.

"Don't think so. They think they may be Russian soldiers."

There was a low rumble of voices as many of the men remarked they were glad they wouldn't have to see their own men being freed. The GI's were afraid of what they might find. They had been reading stories in "Stars and Stripes" about camps of all sorts being freed. The concentration camp stories were going around, and no one was looking forward to having to see the horrors being uncovered.

Within a few minutes, the 347th moved into the forest. There was no real underbrush, and they made fast time going through the dense pine trees. After about fifteen minutes they saw the buildings of the camp from a distance. Everything looked all right, many of the soldiers thought, as they continued toward their objective.

Less than 100 yards away, they were ordered to remain in the forest and to wait for further orders. A few scouts went ahead with Lieutenant Marshall. They had moved to the right and then forward into the darkness of the woods. The men assumed they were going to check out the front gate and see if there were any guards left. At least twenty minutes passed and Lt. Marshall came back to rest of Group B.

"Listen, men. It appears as though the German guards have abandoned their posts. We're going to proceed with caution and enter the camp through the front gate. Be sharp and look for snipers. Let's go!"

Jack moved out with the rest of the platoon and wondered what they would find. He guessed finding a POW camp would be a lot better than one of those concentration camps. As they proceeded cautiously, they were assaulted by an odor of decay. The farther they went inside the gates of the camp, the stronger the smell became. Some of them pulled out their handkerchiefs to cover their noses and mouths to lessen the stench. Finally they saw a rotting pile of corpses. Jack saw a few of his comrades turn away and fall out of ranks because they had to vomit.

Phil poked Jack and said, "What the hell's going on over here?"

Jack could see the fear in his friend's eyes. "I'm not sure, Phil. Maybe this is one of those concentration camps. You know, they call them 'death camps.'"

"No, Jack. Look they have uniforms on. Military," Phil said.

"You're right, Phil," responded Jack.

Just then, Lt. Marshall came alongside of them. "Look men, I'm not sure what we're going to find when we open the doors on the barracks, but we have to do it. They may all be dead, but maybe not. I can tell you those dead men are in Russian uniforms. Let's break up into groups of five and start opening the doors."

Several of the men nodded at the lieutenant. Everyone knew that Jack and his friends would stay together making up a group of four and a fellow they often played poker with, Harry Gold, fell out with them. As they made their way to a cluster of buildings, no one was hurrying as they moved forward holding the rifles out, ready to fire if they were walking into a trap.

Approaching the second building on the left of the yard, Steve and Carl moved to push open the door with their guns. Jack and Phil stayed back on the right of the door and Harry was on the left side. As the door opened, it creaked and the sunlight fell inside the barracks. Jack could barely see inside as Steve and Carl moved inside. Jack saw them let the rifle barrels aim downward and then saw the men inside standing with their arms raised up as if surrendering.

They all moved inside and as their eyes adjusted to the dim light the story unfolded in front of them. There were only three windows in the building letting very little light inside. Rows of bunks were three high and had straw instead of mattresses. Some men were on the bunks, too weak to stand. The soldiers that they could see were all emaciated, and their uniforms were in tatters. Harry told the guys that he knew a little bit of Russian. He was the son of immigrants and had remembered the language of his parents.

Harry said cautiously, "We are American soldiers. You don't have to surrender to us. We are here to free you."

One of the Russians moved forward. They could see that he had some rank on the other men and he lifted his right hand into a salute to Harry and the rest of them. He spoke in a weak voice, "We are grateful that you have come to save us. We have been prisoners of war for a long time and were afraid we would not live. Is the war over?"

"No, it's not," Harry answered. "It should be over very soon. The Allies are moving into Germany from the west and the east. Your comrades are coming from the east. We are going to finally crush Hitler and it will be over."

Harry turned to the rest of the men, "What do we do now?"

Steve said, "I'll go and find Lt. Marshall and ask him."

"Okay," Harry agreed with the plan.

Phil had moved closer to Jack and seemed to be very afraid.

"Phil, are you all right," Jack was worried.

Phil nodded. "I'm okay. I don't know what's going on here, but just don't leave me alone, okay, Jack?"

"I won't. Stay next to me," Jack tried to reassure him. "Harry, why don't you tell them they can come outside?"

"Shouldn't we wait for the lieutenant?" asked Harry.

Carl stepped backwards and looked around. "Harry, I see other Russians coming out of the buildings. Go ahead and tell them that's it's all right."

Harry did and the Russian officer turned toward the men and told them they were free and could go outside.

Once they were outside, the GI's began offering cigarettes to the Russians. Many of them were happy to take the cigarettes and puffed on them. Some of them let little smiles creep onto the corners of their thin lips. When Lt. Marshall stood in the center of a cluster of buildings, he told the men to not give them any food. They could offer water, but no food. The lieutenant had been instructed by orders to do so. Experience of liberating other camps had made the Allies aware that the prisoners could not handle food they might have.

Lt. Marshall had already telephoned headquarters company and reported what they had found here in the forest. He told the men that the Red Cross, along with some administrative army staff, was now on their way to handle the liberation of this camp. They would stay here until ordered to leave. There were still several buildings that were not opened and the soldiers were ordered to continue opening barracks. Harry stayed with his group and was able to communicate with the freed prisoners in each of the next several barracks.

It was almost evening by the time the Red Cross arrived. They came in with trucks filled with supplies and immediately began to set up a mess tent and the cooks were preparing large kettles of cream of rice. They had clean water supplies and soon were feeding the starving Russians small cups of the hot cereal and cool water.

Some of the GI's asked the lieutenant what was going to happen to all of the dead bodies and the really sick men that were still in the barracks. Lt. Marshall told them that the bodies were to be cremated. The Russian officers told them that their identification tags had been removed before the bodies were placed outside in hopes of reporting the deaths one day. The sick would be dealt with one by one by the Red Cross.

They were all happy to learn that they would not be a part of the cremation. A team was coming in to take care of that by morning. The men of Group B were relieved of this duty by nightfall, and Lt. Marshall was glad to lead them back through the forest where they had bivouacked much earlier in the day.

They camped along the roadside that night. Some of the GI's slept in the trucks while others were asleep underneath. Guards changed duty every four hours so that they could all get some sleep. Jack thought it would be difficult to fall asleep after everything they had seen that day, but he and every other man was so physically and mentally exhausted, they slept. What they may have been dreaming wasn't known and how long the memory of what they had experienced would haunt them would be discovered for years to come.

In the early hours of the morning, Group B of the 347th Engineers was preparing to move out of the Black Forest. Lt. Marshall had ordered the men to assemble in the roadway. They were a little surprised that they just weren't loading up and figured Marshall was going to tell them that they had performed a good duty the day before. All any of them wanted to do was forget about April 12th as fast as they could.

"Men," the lieutenant began, "yesterday while we were busy liberating that POW camp, important news from the United States came in. President Roosevelt died yesterday afternoon."

An audible buzz of remarks of disbelief was immediately heard. The lieutenant continued. "I know it is shocking," the officer said. "We have all grown up with

President Roosevelt as our leader. The man we can depend on in the White House. The President died of natural causes, and President Harry Truman has been sworn in and is our Commander in Chief. That's all men. Let's load up and move out."

The men loaded up in the troop trucks in silence. As they began their ride, they all started talking and discovered that hardly anyone knew who was president before FDR had come into office in 1933. He had been president since they were kids and now he was gone. April 12 was certainly a day none of them would ever forget, although it was one that they needed to put behind them.

Victory in Europe

The late April weather was extremely warm and daffodils and tulips were in bloom throughout the villages. Suzanne hadn't enjoyed visiting her cousins very much over the last few years. Villers held strange memories. She remembered pleasant times with her grandparents, but they were always overshadowed by her mother's stories about family members. Eva was jealous of anyone that lived a happier or more prosperous life than she. Her repeated memories of the husband she truly despised made it no secret that she was thankful Nestor was dead at 40 years of age. As Eva recited this litany, she never failed to mention that at least Nestor had left her a decent pension because of his service during the First World War, as they called it now.

Even these continuous diatribes weren't bothering Suzanne now. She took long walks in the country with the children and with cousins or friends she had known years ago before the Nazis had changed their lives. Occasionally when she felt real happiness thinking about a future with Jack, she would feel twinges of guilt about Maurice. Everyone told her he was dead, and she knew he must be. Few spouses had a friend who witnessed their loved one being shoved into a cattle car on a train headed for Auschwitz. Suzanne realized that she would have to wait until the war was over and records opened to verify his death even though she knew in her heart that he must be gone.

After a long late afternoon walk, Suzanne found the family gathered in the garden of her grandparents' home. They ate a supper of country bread, fresh creamy butter and sliced radishes. Everyone was enjoying each bite of the traditional springtime dish. Glasses of white wine washed down the final pieces until nothing was left. Throughout the lovely evening, Suzanne's mind kept straying to memories of her night with Jack.

When she went to her room after putting the children to bed, she took out her stationery, pen and ink and wrote to Jack. Suzanne felt she must write her thoughts carefully and didn't want to seem aggressive.

My Dear Jack,
I received your letter of 9 April. I thank you and am happy to have your news. Thank you for the photo; it is very nice and very welcome although it would be better to be together.
You have a lot of work, I think, with the rapid advance of the army.
For the moment I am in the country at friends and family near Liege. I will return to Brussels tomorrow.
I hope for your return soon. Write to me soon, please. It gives me great pleasure to have your news.
Good luck, Jack. Take care of yourself and know that you have my best wishes.
Your, Suzanne

She sealed the envelope and decided to mail it from Brussels the next day. Suzanne felt a wave of happiness and felt positive about her future and hoped to find a letter awaiting her upon their return.

Turning out the light by the little desk where she had been seated, Suzanne slipped into the comfortable bed and fell asleep hoping to dream about her reunion with her American soldier.

Suzanne filled her days with spring cleaning and planting a vegetable garden for the summer upon their return to Brussels. She did not have a letter waiting for her and convinced herself that Jack was far too busy to stop and write her. Each day the news reports were brighter. The end of the war seemed very close. Hitler hadn't been heard from for a while and the Allied Armies pushed into Germany from the east and the west. Bombings of strategic cities were devastating to factories and to civilians. There was no empathy for the civilians by neither Suzanne nor any people she knew. They were all civilians and had endured five years of occupation. She and many others had been under surveillance, arrested, tried, and many people Suzanne knew had disappeared or been killed. The bombs had dropped all over Belgium, and she understood how lucky her family and friends were to have not been killed by a bomb.

When news reached them that Hitler had committed suicide on the 30th of April, it was a shock. As family and friends gathered, they discussed Hitler's final actions and realized that most people had not thought how the end would finally arrive. Thinking about it now, people understood that Hitler would never have surrendered. Surrender would have been the ultimate defeat and humiliation. Suicide showed what a coward he truly was to leave all of the horrors of the war and the accountability to his generals.

Radio broadcasts kept asking the citizens of Europe to be patient while the armies put into place the actions and maneuvers to end World War II.

****

It was nearly four o'clock in the afternoon on May 7 when Francine called her mother from the American office where she was employed. Her excitement overwhelmed the conversation after Eva picked up the telephone.

"*Maman*, the war is over!"

Eva was silent for a moment. "What? What did you say?"

"It's over, *Maman*, it's over. I heard it about thirty minutes ago when the wire picked up the message from Eisenhower. Oh, *Maman*, finally!" Francine's voice cracked with emotion. "Please go and tell Suzanne."

"I will! Of course I will. Are you coming home this evening?" Eva asked.

"I don't know," replied Francine. "We may have so much work to do. Or, we may go out and celebrate. Don't worry about me, *Maman*. I have to hang up. Bye." Francine put the phone in the cradle and ran back to the central office where chaos included drinking glasses of champagne and typing memos at the same time. This had to be the best day of her life, Francine thought.

Eva didn't hesitate to push open the kitchen door at Suzanne's and shouted, "The war is over! Suzanne, *la guerre est finis!*"

Suzanne ran down the stairs to find her mother standing breathless in the dining room. "Are you sure? Is it really true?"

"Yes. Francine telephoned from her office. They received the news on the teletype from General Eisenhower. Oh, Suzanne......." Eva's voice broke with tears.

The mother and daughter embraced each other. They were both laughing and crying at the same time.

Serge came running down the stairs leaving the toys he had been playing with behind. He wanted to find out why there was shouting. "*Maman*, what's happening?" he asked wondering why his mother and grandmother were now almost dancing together.

Suzanne released her mother and grabbed her son into her arms. "Serge, the war is over. The Allies have won. There will never be Germans here again, *cheri.*"

Serge was wide eyed, and he understood what his mother had told him. He was almost six years old and all he had known was war. As soon as the Germans were gone, they were free to do anything they wanted. His mother never had to tell him to be quiet when they were on the tram or at a café.

"*Maman*, can I go and play with Emil and the other boys? Do they know the war is over?" Serge asked.

"Yes, you can go," Suzanne said. "Tell them if they don't know to turn on their radio," she called after Serge who was nearly out of the house.

Eva and Suzanne hugged each other once more, and then Suzanne went to the radio and tuned it to the best news station. Her thoughts immediately turned to

Jack. He'll be safe now, she thought. Soon he can come back to see me.

May 8 was officially declared "Victory in Europe," and the celebrations lasted for four days. Suzanne went into town with her dearest friends, the Picavets and Carons. They ate supper and then went from one night club to the next. They danced together and with Americans. Happiness was etched on every face of people they encountered. No one acted as strangers; they were all Belgians or Americans and they were free!

Francine brought her friend Tommie and a couple of his friends to dinner the next day and they celebrated again. By the time the Americans went back to their office, they were more than a little drunk on the wine and champagne they drank throughout the noon meal and afterwards.

By evening, the neighbors on rue Virgile gathered around the large tree that stood in the middle of their little street which created a traffic circle. Everyone brought wine and cognac and glasses to the street while men went back to their homes and carried out chairs. Someone had an accordion, and they sang and cheered and laughed throughout the evening.

Jean van Leda came over to the party from his house a few streets away and joined them. He stood next to Suzanne and placed his hand on her shoulder giving it a little squeeze. Jean had been a good friend to Maurice and had helped her by making beautiful pieces of jewelry out of many of the gems her husband had left for her to survive the war. She had indeed sold several pieces to buy food on the black market, but she also enjoyed wearing them and would always be grateful to Jean.

The weather was mild and sunny on the third day of celebration, and it was decided to have a big picnic at the top of the hill in the pasture. It had been a place where Francine remembered watching planes flying over on their way to bomb Germany. It was also the direction from which the Germans had marched into Brussels just five years before. As the Duchesne – Morgen family spread out their picnic next to the Temperman family they were joined by long-time friends Madame Allemon and her son, Leon. As they settled down Suzanne watched two figures riding on bicycles toward them.

She thought one of the men looked like Amand but wasn't sure. She had not seen him since their Resistance Group had disbanded and she went to hide in Felenne. Suzanne stared at the figures and suddenly realized the other was her brother, Ivan. "Look, everyone, it's Ivan and Amand!"

Suzanne was standing and waving madly. Francine jumped up and waved, too. "It is them!" she was sure.

Finally they were there and laid down the bicycles. Everyone began to embrace and to kiss, and Eva had tears flowing down her face. She scolded her son, "It's so long since I had even a word from you!"

"It wasn't safe, *Maman*, I couldn't write or call you," Ivan stated and hugged his mother once more.

"Amand and I are famished! I hope you've made a good picnic!" Ivan teased.

Ivan looked at Serge. "Don't be shy. Don't you remember me?"

Serge nodded, "Yes, I remember you, Uncle Ivan."

"How about the little one, does she remember?" Ivan was reaching for Nadine.

"No!" she screamed and ran away.

Ivan roared with laughter. "Stop, Ivan, she's afraid of a great many things. Don't try to frighten her," Suzanne admonished her brother.

"Oh, all right," Ivan said. "Well she'll have to get use to me. I plan on being around for a while. I'm done sleeping in alleys, attics, woods, wherever! We are free and the war is done!"

The celebration continued and lasted until sundown. They were all giddy from drinking too much wine, and as they walked down the hill and to their little street, they felt the comfort of homes in a very free state of mind.

Their final day of celebration was in the Grand Place. There was a parade led by ministers and the mayor followed by horses and some Belgian military. There were bands that came from the nightclubs, and there were Americans and British soldiers and office personnel. The loudest cheering came when the American soldiers marched by followed by a tank. The noise was so loud on the cobbled streets that children covered their ears, and many of them cried in fear. Finally the tank came to a stop in the center of the square and turned off the engine. Cheers went up, and the bands joined together next to the tank and played the most popular tunes of the year. It was difficult to dance on the curved stones but people were dancing on sidewalks and café platforms.

Suzanne had come with the children and Ivan. It didn't take long to find other long-time friends in the crowd, and the festivities lasted through the evening. Suzanne was tired and knew the children were as well. She left her brother to celebrate throughout the night. Brussels had not seen such a party since the end of the First World War. No one had thought there would ever be another, even more devastating war after 1918. Suzanne pushed these serious thoughts aside. The suffering and dying were over, and they had celebrated their newly won freedom. Now it was time to get back to living.

Suzanne would have to figure out what she needed to do to earn her own living to ensure her family would have enough of everything. Again she wondered how Jack would fit into her life, if he would.

After the celebrations ended, Suzanne spent a few days cleaning and organizing everything in her home. She finished planting her garden and helped her mother with hers so they would have an abundance of vegetables. Neither of them knew what food would be available in the markets. There were many farms destroyed throughout the country and in Holland and France. Suzanne surmised that many farmers would need a year to rebuild their barns and to cultivate the earth.

When she came back into the house the postman was ringing the bell and Suzanne rushed to open it and took the mail with great anticipation. On top was a letter from Jack. Carefully opening it, she was glad to see it was written entirely in French.

In Germany   *12 May, 1945*
My Dear Suzanne,
I received your two letters at least two weeks ago but I haven't been able to respond sooner because I was extremely busy. In one of your letters there were photos and I found you and Francine very, very pretty. Truly, you are the most beautiful woman in Brussels.

I will be getting a leave and will want to have a vacation but it will be much better if you are with me.

I am still in Germany and since my time here I have seen a lot more of the country of the savages. Now my primary desire is to return to you and for the time I have in Europe, I cannot think of any better place than Brussels with you.

I think Brussels must be the most beautiful city with nice days and fun times since the war is finished.

I hope you will forgive me for not answering for such a long time to your letters. It will truly please me to receive letters from you frequently and I will try to respond to them right away.

The first chance I get to have a leave, I will be there to see you.

I hope you are all well. Give my best wishes to your family and to Serge and Nadine, give them a big kiss for me.

I have to finish my letter now and hope to have a response from you soon. Always with you,
Jack

Suzanne folded the letter and returned it to its envelope and pressed it to her breast. She leaned back in her chair and for the first time in years, she felt a strong sense of hope. Hope was something she lost after the last letter Maurice had written her before he was transported out of Breendonk. Suzanne knew she would re-read the letter again and again, but for now, she was content to hold it close to her and to revel in the hope that invaded every sense of her being.

Return to Brussels

No more letters were received by Suzanne since Jack had written her right after VE Day. She understood that the Army was still extremely busy throughout Germany, Austria and some other countries. The Army, Red Cross and civilian governments in some instances were setting up Displaced Persons Camps throughout Europe in hopes of reuniting family members. News of war atrocities, especially from concentration camps, was written in the newspapers and filmed for news reels playing in the theatres across the liberated cities in Western Europe.

Any doubts Suzanne had harbored that Maurice may not be dead were totally crushed after seeing the films shown in the news reels from the liberated concentration camps. Auschwitz was already being called the largest of all of the camps with the its sole mission the extermination of Jews. She knew it was not possible that her husband could have survived two-and-a-half years in Auschwitz after being starved and beaten in Breendonk for six months. Suzanne read the newspapers daily for news about the government's actions of verifying deaths of prisoners, and she grew impatient after realizing she would have to wait a long time for official action on behalf of her husband's declaration of death.

At 27 years of age it was rather difficult to imagine what life as widow had in store for her. Suzanne knew she had to plan her future with the welfare of her two children foremost in her mind. At times she felt ashamed when she was thinking about Jack and longing for him. She wondered if the desire was only physical or had their immediate attraction meant that her future would rest partially in what the young American decided he wanted for the rest of his life.

And so her mind was leaping to conclusions and her feeling of worry and even despair became a constant companion. Wondering why she had not heard from him in over two weeks, Suzanne wrote a long letter to Jack on May 29th asking what had happened to him and conveyed her hope that he was safe and well. She explained the details of all of their celebrations in Brussels upon the end of the war and asked him if they had had a chance to celebrate. In conclusion, she let him know very clearly that she would be in Brussels waiting for him to come back and visit her again.

****

There hadn't been time for the engineers to do much else than clear roads, railroad tracks, bridges and every other piece of infrastructure throughout the Rhine Valley and into central Germany. Jack and the men of Group B wondered how long they would have to continue their seven-days-a-week, back-breaking work since the war had ended. There were always rumors floating around and no one seemed to be able to separate fact from fiction. Jack, along with every other soldier wanted to know when they would get leave. The worst of the rumors was that they would be shipped back to the U.S. just to be transported to the Pacific to help end the war with Japan. With the exception of some senior officers, no one wanted to be deployed to another theatre of war. They had done their job and beaten the Germans. Their unit, along with countless others, was given ribbons for meritorious service along with stripes they had to sew on their sleeves indicating how many continuous months of service they had given since D-Day.

Jack worried about his friend Phil more each day. Phil had been on kitchen duty for several weeks and really liked the job, but the mess sergeant had something against him and found ways to dole out punishment almost on a daily basis. Phil's sensitive personality took all of the reprimands to heart. He didn't sleep well and that caused him to have many nights filled with bad dreams. The dreams conjured up everything from the sergeant's demeaning treatment to memories of the Russian P.O.W. Camp and the death and dying that had

288

assaulted every man's sensibilities. Phil couldn't shake it and Jack was afraid his pal was headed for a breakdown. Steve and Carl were in agreement with Jack's evaluation, and the three friends tried to bolster Phil's morale each day. They may not have known it at the time, but because of their actions they were able to stem the onslaught of a total mental collapse.

Each day moved along rapidly with the work they performed. Jack was glad he had the opportunity to see a lot of the German countryside and realized that it was a beautiful land. Throughout the small towns and villages, most Germans treated them with respect. Jack figured they were probably afraid of the Allied Occupation Army thinking that the Americans would want retribution. The men had heard about isolated incidences by soldiers murdering or raping some civilians, but they were reminded repeatedly that this was not allowed and if caught, the soldier would be court marshaled. Jack also assumed the civilians had heard about the very harsh treatment doled out by the Russian troops in many towns in eastern Germany. It was not universal, but it was well known that the Red Army had vowed revenge against the German people for the millions and millions of civilian Soviet lives lost due to starvation and mass killings.

Days passed into weeks, and the weather kept getting warmer and the engineers often worked in only their undershirts their faces and arms becoming bronzed by the sun. They helped move field hospitals and evacuate seriously ill patients to hospitals. Many of the ill were lodged in Displaced Persons' Camps, and were so sick they had to be moved to hospitals in Paris and other large cities.

By the middle of June, news regarding their future finally arrived. Soldiers with enough points to be discharged were granted 60-day leaves. If the Army still wanted them after the leave, they would probably be sent to the Pacific for duty. Men without enough points had to remain on duty in Germany and continue with the reorganization of the country. The 'replacements' didn't have enough points, and the look of disappointment on their faces was evident. To Jack, Steve, Carl and Phil there was pure elation! When they were dismissed, they patted each other on the back and began talking feverishly.

"Let's go out tonight and get drunk!" Steve commanded.

"Great idea," Carl chimed in.

"It is a great idea, fellas, and I'll join you, but...." Jack stated.

"But what?" Phil needed to know.

"But, I'm outta here on a train tomorrow!" Jack laughed out loud.

"Are you really going to Brussels," Carl asked?

"You bet," Jack said with certainty. "It's the only thing I want to do. I've been thinking about it, and her, since we left at the end of March."

"Jack, you only knew her for two days," Phil almost whined not wanting his best friend to leave him on his own. Phil didn't know how he would get by without Jack there to help him.

"Yeah, so? That's why I have to go back, to make sure I really feel something special about Suzanne," Jack said.

"You should go home and find a wife there, not a foreign girl, buddy," Carl told his friend sincerely.

"Why?" Jack asked. "I've dated dozens of girls from New York to California, and I never felt this way before."

"You're just lonely over here, Jack," Carl insisted.

"No, you're wrong, Carl. She's special and she's smart. Too many girls at home are just looking for a husband. Suzanne's been married so she knows what it's like to have family and take care of a husband and children," Jack said.

"See, Jack, I don't get it that you want this gorgeous woman with two kids attached to her," Steve really was perplexed.

"Why don't you?" Jack asked all his friends. "After everything we've seen over here we should be smarter. We're grown men now, and we helped to liberate all of these people. Maybe falling in love with a widow is a good thing. Maybe I'll be helping a family put their lives back together at the same time as I build my future."

"Maybe you're right, buddy," Phil said quietly. "I've got Marilyn waiting for me back home, and I'm glad I'm going to make it back to her alive. Suzanne's got her children, but her husband was murdered by the bastards."

"That's right, Phil. Thanks for understanding," Jack patted him on the back.

"Okay, fellas. This is getting too serious. Jack you go have your romance and figure it all out. Meanwhile the rest of us, uh, Carl and I will see how many girls we can find to romance," Steve said lightening the mood.

"Come on, guys, let's get going to celebrate!" Carl added.

They hitched a ride with a transport truck back into the little town a couple of kilometers from their camp. The local taprooms were doing plenty of business with GI's savoring the beer. The pals who had been together since Ft. Bragg decided this would be their celebration of the end of World War II. Jack wondered if any of them would remain friends when they shipped back to the states in a couple of months. That night they vowed eternal fraternity and promised to visit each other and to attend reunions of the 347th.

****

Jack quietly opened the small gate that led to garden behind the house and walked quickly past the open windows. Suzanne was hanging laundry, and he could only see her back. She was wearing a short red skirt and a white blouse. Her hair was pulled up and Jack saw the beautiful curve of her neck. He didn't take his eyes off of Suzanne while he lowered his duffle bag to the concrete walk and leaned it against the house. He stood watching her for at least another minute and then saw her turning around very slowly.

Suzanne felt the hair stand up on the back of her neck and immediately knew someone was in her garden. She didn't feel fear. She turned and saw Jack watching her, and in a split second her heart skipped a few beats. Suzanne's eyes met his and in that very instant she knew that she was in love with her soldier. Dropping the apron she had been ready to hang on the line, Suzanne ran into Jack's arms. He held her briefly and then they looked at each other before they kissed.

Suzanne ended the kiss and grabbed his hand and guided Jack into the kitchen where she turned and let her body fall against his chest and kissed him deeply. She didn't want her mother or anyone else to see them kissing. After another deep kiss, the lovers separated and looked at each other.

"Oh, Jack, I can't believe you are finally here! How long do you have?"

"Sixty days. We have the whole summer together, Sweetheart."

"This is fantastic!" Suzanne was exuberant.

"Where are the children?" Jack asked.

"They are playing at the Temperman's. They live only a few houses away," Suzanne said.

"Will I be able to stay with you, Suzanne?"

"Yes, of course. I have it all figured out, *cheri,*" Suzanne said. "I've been thinking about this since you left. You'll have the little room in the rear of the house. I'll put Serge and Nadine in another bedroom. The little room is ours, remember, Jack?"

"Of course I remember, Suzanne. I'll never forget that night. The full moon shining through the window and the early, warm spring air on our skin. I've relived that night over and over again, darling."

"Oh, Jack. Thank you for coming back to me. I missed you so," Suzanne said.

292

Jack took her into his arms and kissed her gently. "We have two months to get to know each other. I hope we can start tonight."

Suzanne smiled at him. "Get your bag and let's arrange everything upstairs. While you wash up, I'll go get the children, all right?"

"Yes, darling. I'm looking forward to seeing them again," Jack said sincerely. He felt as though he had just stepped back into the real world, and he felt good.

The Romance

A week had passed since Jack arrived in Brussels in late June of 1945. He had settled on nicely in the little bedroom of his beautiful lover's house without any sort of resistance by Suzanne's mother or by her children. Eva seemed to be sizing him up during their conversations, and he understood her concerns for her daughter's welfare. The kids were happy to have this unlikely house guest in their lives. Jack showed Serge how to catch, and the little boy taught Jack how to kick a football. Nadine, who was not quite three years old, seemed to like him, but he was surprised by her waking in the night and screaming for her mother. Suzanne would leap from bed and pick her up and try to soothe her little daughter. He wondered how Suzanne got any rest with this happening many nights.

Francine would take the children next door to their house a couple of nights a week so her sister could sleep through the night. Of course the two lovers made the most of those nights, and neither of them got very much sleep, yet the next day they both felt re-energized and very cheerful.

Suzanne told Jack about the many trying months during her pregnancy with Nadine. She was sure that the fear she felt during Maurice's imprisonment and her own arrest affected the growing baby inside of her womb. Bombing raids were frequent during 1942 and waking in the night, picking up Serge to run to the little cellar for protection most likely added to the internal fright the child experienced before birth. Suzanne would reassure Jack that with the passage of time in a peaceful world Nadine would become calmer. Jack agreed with her realizing that as civilians they had often experienced similar fear as the soldiers on or near the front lines. Jack shared how his friend, Phil, had been reacting very differently to many of the terrible things they had witnessed throughout their time in France and in Germany. Many of the men just pushed the sights and smells to the furthest recesses of their minds, while men like Phil were not able to do so and we're suffering because of it.

As time progressed, Jack rapidly grew stronger in his ability to speak French and understand a more complex vocabulary enabling Suzanne and him to share many of their experiences of the war. Soon the talk of war was pushed away and they began to share stories of their families and of their youth. Suzanne was amazed at the many places Jack had traveled and lived and how adventurous he was. She had only ever traveled outside of Belgium once when she had stayed with cousins in Paris for a summer and visited all of the grand sites and museums.

Together they had gone into town and Jack bought himself civilian clothing. He ordered a fine brown wool suit and two custom made dress shirts for his tall, lanky frame. The suit had an extra pair of pants and he chose three silk ties to complete the outfits. Jack added two casual pairs of pants and a few shirts along with a cardigan sweater for the evening. He didn't want to wear his uniforms when they were around the house or in the town at the clubs or going to the cinema. Suzanne admired his handsome and sexy appearance in his civilian clothes, and she liked the look they made as a young couple deeply in love.

It didn't take long for Jack to become good friends with Fred and Marie and Felix and Josette. He liked them very much, and they were swept away by his outgoing demeanor and candor. Jack was truly an American and they admired him. They were also astonished at his mastering their language while none of them knew more than a few words of English. The six of them often visited one of the nightclubs, listening and dancing to jazz bands each weekend. Jack was amazed by the big American musicians who were playing all of the clubs. Many of them were Negroes and he loved their music and realized that they were accepted as equals in this foreign capital city.

Fred Caron was very involved in the transition government in Belgium since their liberation the year before. He had a lot of insight about the economic future of the little country that had been the crossroads of this war and so many before. Jack talked with Fred often about the possibility of setting up a business to import goods from the United States. Fred agreed with him that there was a big need for essential goods, and that it would take years for all of Europe to get back on its feet. He promised Jack that he would help him with government red tape however he could. Jack was very pleased and began thinking of ideas for the future.

Meanwhile he asked Fred to continue to help Suzanne in obtaining the documents she needed to be declared a widow of the war. She could not move forward in planning her future until this occurred. Fred did help his long-time friend whenever there was an opportunity to receive news from the Victims of War Bureau and other agencies. He promised his American friend he would always be there to help Suzanne even when Jack had to leave for the U.S.

Sunday afternoons were usually spent at Suzanne's house. The summer weather had been unusually fine, and they would find themselves in the garden sitting in the sun or in the shade of the large cherry tree. Their friends often came to visit as their apartments were stuffy in this glorious weather. Marie would always stop at one of the marvelous patisseries in town and bring a wide assortment of excellent baked goods. They drank chilled white wine and indulged in the sweets without guilt. For years there had been little or no access to the fabulous Belgian chocolates and bakery items and they felt they needed to make up for the last five years. They laughed as they watched the expressions on each other's faces tasting a puff pastry filled with delicate crème fraiche and a touch of powdered sugar on the outside. Jack's favorite was a mocha – a delicate sponge cake cut into small rounds, layered into a tower with mocha butter cream between each layer, then covered with more of the buttery frosting and the sides covered in slivered, toasted almonds and topped by dark chocolate curls on top. He declared that he had never eaten anything as delicious in his lifetime and nothing like this existed in the United States. Suzanne and their friends watched him and would laugh in delight at the enjoyment he experienced almost every Sunday.

Many afternoons were spent walking to Dilbeek and winding their way up the long path into the beautiful woods alongside the old chateau. The children joined them from time to time, and Jack and Suzanne would spread out a blanket on the large lawn in front of the chateau and lay in the sunshine. Serge would run and kick his football and try to get his little sister to kick it back, not understanding that at her age she was not yet very athletic. The children had fun running and enjoying the warm summer air. They would run down the hill to the pond that was on the property. A pair of swans were always swimming side by side; they, too, were lovers. Suzanne told Jack that the swans mated for life and would be there together until one of them died. The survivor would never take on another mate.

Jack looked into her eyes after Suzanne told him about the swans. "Sweetheart, I'll never leave you. I might have to leave for a while, but you'll come to America and we'll be together forever," Jack said.

It was the first time that Jack had spoken with such certainty to her and Suzanne was taken aback. "Jack, I didn't know you were thinking about me coming to America."

"I feel as though you are my wife, Suzanne. I probably should ask you to be my wife, but I honestly feel that we both think this way," he said without hesitancy.

"Yes, *cheri,* I do feel as though we are married in many ways, but I never have thought about going to America. It frightens me a little," Suzanne said.

"Why, darling? There are many women here who are going to marry GI's. Even your sister is thinking about a future with Tommie," Jack said.

"But Francine speaks English and she wants to go to America. I don't know if I could ever learn to speak English," Suzanne said in anguish.

"Don't be silly. Of course you can learn English. I learned French, didn't I?" Jack asked.

"Yes, but you already knew Spanish. You're just good at it, Jack." Suzanne was really starting to worry thinking about leaving the only place she had ever known and realizing how badly her mother would react.

"Listen, Sweetheart, we don't have to make any of those decisions yet," Jack said. "I'll still be here for another month. It's only July, and I don't have to leave till the end of August probably. Maybe Fred will be able to get you the papers you need to be declared a widow and you might be able to follow to America on a ship after mine. If not, I'll come back here as soon as I get discharged from the Army. Okay, Sweetheart?"

"Okay," Suzanne said in English.

He kissed her lightly. "Don't worry so much. The war is over, and you don't have to be worried all of the time." Jack held her chin in the palm of his hand.

Suzanne nodded and then smiled at him before continuing. "Yes, Jack, you're right. Listen, *cheri,* I was talking to Josette, and she and Felix are going to the beach for a week in August. Before the war many people took the whole month at the beach. Now only a few hotels are re-opened, and they still are sweeping the beaches for mines. Do you think we might be able to join them? I have some money I could spend....."

Jack cut her off. "Of course we can and don't talk of money. I have plenty saved. Where was I going to spend it during this crazy war? Find out what we need to do and let's go!"

"Oh, thank you, Jack. We'll have so much fun. Wait till you taste all of the wonderful fish and crustaceans!" exclaimed Suzanne.

"You forget that I grew up at the beach, remember? Coney Island," Jack said.

"I remember," Suzanne replied.

"If the beaches are closed, what will we do?" asked Jack.

"Some may be open, but there's plenty to do without going to the sea," Suzanne said.

"Okay, I'm ready," Jack said laughing.

Suzanne called for Serge and Nadine to come back so they could begin their walk back to Mortebeek. She decided not to tell them about the seashore vacation wanting to make sure they could get reservations. They walked arm in arm with Nadine holding Jack's hand on their walk down to the chausee. Serge ran ahead filled with all the energy of a boy who had just turned six years of age.

They had had a wonderful time at the resort town of Knocke-sur-Mer on the coast of the North Sea. Their little suite at the hotel had two bedrooms and a small sitting room. Josette and Felix were in the room next to them, and they shared a bath at the end of the hall. Breakfast was served in a lovely, airy room with large windows looking out on the garden that was filled with roses and hydrangeas. They walked along the promenade each morning and would find a different restaurant each day for dinner. All of them enjoyed the delicious and fresh seafood and vegetables from nearby gardens and little farms. Jack was thrilled to have fresh milk every day, and Suzanne encouraged the children to drink their milk just like Jack did although she didn't understand how he could drink milk with his meals.

There was one small beach safe for people to sunbathe, but not to go into the water. Mines could move with the tide and the government warned that it would take at least another year to make sure the coast was cleared of all explosives. None of them minded the restriction to the sea, and Jack loved lying on the blanket on the warm sand. The air was much cooler here than it had ever been on Coney Island during the summer. He helped the children build sandcastles and told them to dig a big hole and he would lie in it and they could cover him with sand up to his neck. They laughed and dug furiously at the sand. Serge had no memory of ever being at the beach, and Nadine, of course, had never been.

Suzanne couldn't remember ever being this happy although she must have been when she was with Maurice before Serge was born and the Nazis had marched into the city. When she thought of Maurice, the memory brought with it a sharp pain in her heart. She figured that this was guilt, and then she told herself she did not need to feel that way. Suzanne shared her feelings with Josette and was always reassured by her dear, sweet friend that she deserved happiness and to rebuild her life. Josette would tell her that although all Belgians had suffered throughout the last five years, Suzanne had had a heavier burden than most. She had been so brave trying to save Maurice from Breendonk and working with the Resistance. Now it was time to think about her future and the life they would have with Jack. Josette hoped Suzanne would not leave to live in America unless Jack would want to go to the United States.

Although their vacation was short, they arrived back in Brussels feeling better than they had in years, and everyone agreed that the sea air and sunshine had been an excellent idea. The family resumed its regular routine while Jack wondered when he would receive orders to ship home. It was August 13 and in only one more week his sixty days of leave would be over. Jack decided he would go into town the next day and report to central headquarters to see if he could receive his orders there.

There were so many soldiers on leave in Brussels and throughout all of the major cities of Europe that central headquarters was receiving orders for Army Companies. On Friday, August 18, Jack reported again, in uniform and orders were waiting for him. Before opening the papers, he hoped he might be able to stay in Brussels longer. The war with Japan had ended only a few days before, and GI's in Europe would not have to ship to the Pacific. Jack knew that soldiers were being sent home every day from ports throughout Europe but there weren't enough troop ships to get the millions of men back to New York quickly. Redeployment would take many months.

Finally Jack opened his orders and after a moment a big grin was on his face. "Good news, corporal?" the clerk asked him.

"You bet!" Jack was really grinning.

"You goin' home?" the clerk asked.

"No! I've got thirty more days leave right here in Brussels!" Jack almost shouted.

"Gee, and you're really happy about that?" the clerk sounded puzzled.

"Yes, sir, I've got a great girl right here!" Jack folded the papers and stuffed them in his breast pocket and turned to leave.

"Hey, corporal, good luck."

Jack turned half way around, "Thanks pal."

As he reached the pavement, he took out a cigarette and lit it. He decided to stop at the flower market and take Suzanne a bouquet. They would definitely be celebrating their good luck that evening, he thought with a lascivious smile creeping up on the corners of his mouth.

Jack was riding the tram up the Chausee Ninove and making a plan for that evening. Actually, he thought, I'm making a plan for the rest of my life. He had felt sure he wanted to marry Suzanne within days of their reunion in June. Now he was positive, and he planned to ask her when he got back. All of a sudden Jack realized he didn't have a ring to offer her as his fiancée and wondered if he should get off at the next stop and go back to town to buy one. Realizing he didn't have enough money with him, he stayed on the tram. Jack decided that they would go into town together and buy an engagement ring. The ideas were flying around in his head when he also remembered she was not yet 'officially' a widow and might be offended by the ring but he was certain he would ask his sweetheart and they would discuss the details together.

Walking through the curving streets that led up to rue Virgile, Jack composed his proposal. Suzanne would be anxious to know what his orders were, but he was going to surprise her with the proposal first. He continued on his walk and was whistling a little tune he had heard earlier on the radio. Jack glanced at his watch as he turned into the yard and walked down the concrete walk to the rear door. It was 4 o'clock and Suzanne would probably be placing coffee and a few little sandwiches on the table for them.

"*Bonjour, cherie,*" Jack called out as he came in through the back door.

"I'm here, Jack," Suzanne called from the salon hanging up the phone.

Jack came into the dining room and Suzanne met him next to the radio. He pulled her towards him and kissed her hello and then presented her with the flowers.

"Oh, Jack, they're beautiful. Thank you, *cheri.* What happened at headquarters?"

"Where are the children?" Jack asked.

"At my mother's," Suzanne was a bit alarmed by his question. She began fearing that he had bad news.

Jack dropped to one knee and took her hand in his. He spoke quickly not giving her a chance to say anything. "Sweetheart," he said in English, "will you marry me?"

Suzanne looked at him quizzically for a moment. Why did he say something in English, she wondered? She thought about the words for a few moments, knowing that she had heard them in movies.

Still looking into his eyes, she replied, "You are asking me to be your wife?"

"Yes, darling," he returned to French. Will you marry me?"

"Oh, Jack, *cheri*, of course I will. Tears began forming in her clear blue eyes and Jack returned to stand before her.

"I know we've talked about being married, Sweetheart, but I've never actually proposed to you. Today when I got my orders I knew I had to come here and ask you to be my wife," Jack said.

"Jack, what are your orders?" Suzanne was afraid of the answer.

"Don't worry, Sweetheart, I'm here for another month!" Jack was smiling.

Suzanne threw her arms around his neck, and they kissed. She was laughing in joy as they pulled apart. "Oh, that's wonderful news. Another month. So much can happen in that time, Jack. Perhaps the government will give me the documents I need."

"Yes, Suzanne. We have to press Fred to find out what you need to do to get rid of all of bureaucracy so that we may be officially engaged or married!" Jack was excited.

"We will. Let's telephone Fred when he's home from work later. Now sit and have some coffee and sandwiches. I'll go and get a vase for the flowers."

She turned to find a vase in the buffet and Jack stared at her. Suzanne is going to be my wife, and we're going to be a family with two children, he thought. Later we'll have our own child. While she went to fill the vase in the kitchen he thought about writing to his parents to tell them. He was sure they would be surprised, but probably happy since he was now 27-years old.

Suzanne placed the flowers in the center of the table. "Let me pour your coffee, Jack."

He watched her movements and couldn't believe his good fortune to know this fabulous woman with whom he would spend the rest of his life once they got all of the red tape out of the way.

The End of Summer

Jack was sipping a cup of coffee at a sidewalk café in the Grand Place. Suzanne and he had gone into town after dinner, and she had asked him to wait for her at the café while she did a few errands. He was curious about the errands she wanted to do without him, but decided not to press the point with her. He strolled around the square looking into windows of the lace shops, and would ask Suzanne to help him choose something for his mother.

As he finished his coffee, Jack was managing to decipher some of the newspaper that he had bought at the tobacco shop. His speaking ability was getting better all of the time, but reading and writing in French was still quite difficult. Finally he reached the comics and began reading all of them. Jack had discovered that the cartoons were a terrific method to tutor him in his new language. He was chuckling to himself when he felt Suzanne's hand on his shoulder. She quickly slipped into the seat next to him and put down two small bags that contained her purchases.

Jack held up his hand and the waiter headed to their table. "A coffee, please," he ordered for her.

"Another for you, monsieur?" the waiter asked.

"Yes, please," responded Jack.

As the waiter turned to go, Suzanne reached for a little package in the small bag. She moved it towards Jack. "What's this?" he asked in surprise.

"Open it and see," she smiled at Jack.

The waiter returned with the coffees and Jack waited until he was gone before he tugged on the string to untie the package. There was a rectangular jewelry box and he opened it slowly.

"Sweetheart, it's very nice," Jack said as he picked up the silver bracelet.

"Do you really like it? Do you see your name is engraved on it?" Suzanne asked.

"It's wonderful, *cherie*. I love it and will wear it so I will know you are with me all of the time," Jack told her.

"Here let me put it on you," Suzanne said.

Jack held out his right wrist, and Suzanne picked up the open link silver chain with the small central plate where Jack's name was engraved. She fixed the clasp and admired how nice it looked on his wrist.

Jack took her hand and held it and then brought it to his lips and kissed it tenderly. Suzanne blushed slightly at the public show of affection and then said, "I'm glad you like it, *cheri*. Let's have our coffee before it gets cold."

As he drank the coffee Jack thought about the gift. No woman had ever bought him a gift. He realized this was mostly his fault since he never got close enough to a woman. Jack thought about a girl he dated when he was in Montana with the C.C.C. She had been special, but he supposed he wasn't special enough for her.

He came out of his thoughts as Suzanne began telling him about the plans she hoped they would make for the weekend with their friends. Jack agreed to her plans and left some francs on the table. They made their way off the sidewalk platform. Jack tucked her arm in his, and they walk across the rounded cobblestones that had been there for over 500 years. The ancient buildings had withstood the time of the most recent and vile war, been a part of the Belgian Revolution and probably had been the stage for Napoleon to parade across. Jack remained quiet as they kept walking. He liked it here, but he missed home, too. But where was home now? A small town in New Jersey which was certainly no match for Coney Island and all of the rest of New York.

"What are you thinking about, Jack?" Suzanne broke into his thoughts.

"Oh, just about how much I like it here," he said and paused. "I like it here because I love you, Sweetheart."

Suzanne squeezed his arm and they arrived at the tram stop and got on the car to take the short ride to the Chausee Ninove. "Jack."

"Yes, Sweetheart?"

"I'm going to tell my mother that we are going to be engaged as soon as I receive the documents from the government," Suzanne's voice was low and a bit shaky.

"Why don't you tell her now?" he was surprised.

"Oh, because she thinks everything has to be so proper, and it wouldn't be right. She would want to make a written announcement and really can't if I'm legally still married."

"I understand that, but why not tell her that we are engaged, just between us, and that we want her to know that we are serious and plan to marry?" Jack asked.

"You're right, I guess," Suzanne said. "I'm also a little afraid. My mother can be so overbearing and if she asks me if you will be living here always, what will I tell her?"

"Tell her we're going to live in America," Jack said.

"That could be a big problem, *cheri*," Suzanne said. "My mother will not want me to leave. She counts on me for a lot and of course the children are a joy to her."

Jack didn't say anything at first and then spoke reassuringly. "Listen, Suzanne, your sister and brother live here, and they will get married and have children here. Why do you have to put your mother first instead of us?"

"I'm sure you're right, Jack, but she has always made me accountable and has put all of the responsibility of the family on me," Suzanne said. "Because Ivan is a man, he can do what he wants, and Francine is a new type of woman and does what she wants."

"Suzanne, we have to be married," Jack said. "I like it here with you, but I know you will love living in the States. You can't put your mother first. Our love is too great a thing for that."

"Oh, Jack...." she couldn't finish.

306

"You tell her when you want to, Darling, but I wouldn't wait very long."

Suzanne appreciated Jack giving her more time and felt a bit of relief. "Thank you, Jack. I promise I will tell her soon. I have to figure out how I'm going to do that."

Jack squeezed her hand. "Okay, Sweetheart, let's just put this aside and we need to concentrate on getting your papers. We'll call Fred this evening."

Suzanne nodded her head. "Yes, we'll talk to Fred. There must be some way we can expedite the process."

****

Over the next several weeks the young lovers spent most of their time enjoying the end of summer in their garden and taking long walks. Many evenings were spent at the cinema or at the apartments of the Carons or the Picavets. Fred had found out all he could for Suzanne to file applications for the official declaration of death of her husband, and she had filed the forms. All they could do now was wait. The depth and horror of the concentration camps became more and more evident as the weeks passed. Film was shown during the news reels at the movies and although Suzanne was sickened by them, she wanted to see them and to understand. Her beloved Maurice had been tortured and then gassed and finally cremated in the largest of all the extermination camps.

Suzanne had also filed papers requesting the whereabouts of the other members of Maurice's family. He had sisters and brothers, and she wanted to know if any had survived. After all, she thought, her children were their nephew and niece. Maurice's Aunt Ginsbourg had survived by hiding right here in Brussels. Suzanne did talk with the aunt and told her she was seeing an American soldier because of the reports she had received of her husband's certain death. The aunt did not chastise her, and Suzanne felt that was probably because Jack was also a Jew.

After the first week of September passed, Jack received orders sent to Suzanne's address, which he had given as his, that he should report to Camp Top Hat in Antwerp where he would board a troop ship bound for New York. He had spent nearly another month with Suzanne and her family and knew that he would have to return to Brussels as soon as he was discharged from the Army.

He put the orders down and found Suzanne in the garden. She had just finished picking some apples and was busy peeling them at the little table they had in the yard. When she saw Jack, she put down her knife and wiped her hands on her apron.

"What do your orders say?" Suzanne asked.

"That I have to go to Antwerp and take a ship to New York," Jack reported glumly.

Suzanne didn't reply. Tears were starting to fall and her throat felt strangled.

"Oh, Sweetheart, please don't cry. Listen, there's good news, too," Jack said.

"What?" she croaked.

"I don't report until September 22 so we still have over a week," Jack said smiling at her.

"Oh," Suzanne managed and wiped the tears with her handkerchief. "That's the day after my birthday. At least we can celebrate my 28th birthday together," she tried to smile back at him.

"That's right, *cherie*, we'll be together," Jack said. "Let's make sure we're alone that night, okay?"

"Yes. And let's make sure we go out on the town on the weekend before with our friends, all right, Jack?" she asked.

"Of course! It'll be my last time, for a while, to enjoy the clubs here," Jack said.

"Oh, Jack, it all sounds fine, but then you'll be gone and how will we bear it?" Suzanne voice was anguished.

308

"We will because we will be working on getting things in order so we can marry. You'll keep working on those papers, and I'll try to find out how we can make a living in New Jersey," he reassured her.

"Listen, Suzanne, my father and mother have the farm and maybe we can make it larger and it can provide a living for all of us," Jack said.

"But you're not a farmer, Jack."

"I know, but it's chickens, darling. How hard can it be to raise chickens and sell them for slaughter? It doesn't matter. I will find ways to make money. There will have to be a lot of new job opportunities with the war being over. You let me worry about that, okay?" Jack said confidently.

"All right, Jack. I will try not to worry," Suzanne said. "We should tell the children soon that you'll be gone for a little while. It will be difficult for them. Serge will understand, but not Nadine."

"Yes, let's explain it to them this evening. What are you going to make with the apples, *cherie*?" Jack asked.

"A tart," she replied. "We'll have it later this afternoon with coffee."

"Mmmmm," Jack uttered, "should be delicious. You're the best, Sweetheart!"

As the days passed quickly, it seemed as though they celebrated with everyone Jack had ever met. Eva had hosted a dinner for all of the family. Ivan was there with his girlfriend, Rosa, and Francine had invited Tommie who would be leaving Brussels soon, also. Serge wanted Jack to stay, and although he understood that he had to go back to America to be discharged, he was afraid his future stepfather wouldn't return.

Over the weekend, Suzanne and Jack dined with their best friends. On Saturday night they went from club to club dancing, drinking champagne, toasting to each other's health and happiness, and for Jack's speedy return. Jack made the four of them promise to keep

Suzanne's spirits high while he was away and they all did so willingly. She was very much loved by each of them, and they were all fond of Jack and let him know it.

On her birthday, Jack presented his beautiful fiancée with a spectacular bouquet of pink roses. He had gotten a card for her and wrote a lovely message in it that he planned to leave under her pillow so she would find it after he left the next day.

After their noon dinner with the children and Eva, they went for a long walk in Dilbeek. Jack loved it there, and he knew it was Suzanne's favorite place when she was happy or sad. If she was feeling down, a walk through the path in the woods would help her reflect upon her troubles, and she would be able to formulate a plan to deal with the difficulties. When she was happy, the park and the forest made her feel alive, and she felt that the beauty of the place embraced her and her lover.

Jack and Suzanne lingered in the park as long as they could and then walked slowly back to her house. They passed Suzanne's long-time friend, Jean van Leda, and stopped to speak to him briefly. Jean had helped her immensely throughout the war. He had hidden much of the money Maurice had given him for his family. Jean was glad that Suzanne had found a man who was in love with her. Jean wished Jack much luck and hoped he could hurry back to Brussels.

When they arrived on their street they went to Eva's. Jack played a game of dominoes with Serge and later Nadine sat on his lap while he read a children's book to her. At least he could read French on that level, he joked to himself. Suzanne brought the coffee to the table and Eva produced a huge assortment of pastries from Wittamer in the Place du Grand Sablon in town. These were the best Brussels had to offer and Jack appreciated the gesture from Suzanne's mother. The children clapped their hands with happiness as the gazed at the fine assortment.

"Thank you very much, Eva," Jack said sincerely.

"It is your going away party and a birthday celebration for Suzanne, too," Eva pronounced.

"Where are the candles, *Maman*?" Serge asked.

"We have one candle, Serge," his grandmother replied and placed it on top of the small, elegant mocha cake with marzipan roses on top.

Jack lit the candle and they all sang Happy Birthday to Suzanne. "Make a wish, Sweetheart," Jack said tenderly.

Suzanne only had one wish; come back to me very soon, Jack. She leaned forward and blew out the candle and they all clapped in unison.

The family enjoyed the late afternoon eating several of the pastries and then just sitting and talking. Suzanne looked at her watch and saw that it was nearly six o'clock.

"Serge, Nadine, it's time for you to say goodbye to Jack. He has to leave very early in the morning on the train. You are going to stay here at your grandmother's for the night not to disturb Jack," Suzanne knew they would protest, and they did.

Jack took Nadine on his lap. "Hey, kid," he said in English and then returned to French. "Be a good girl and let your mother sleep through the night, all right?" Nadine nodded her head and Jack gave her a kiss and hugged her. She wiggled free and ran around the table.

"Serge, you have to help your mother when you can. She has so much to do around the house so keep your room neat and try to be helpful," Jack said.

"I will Jack. Will you send me some stamps for my collection from America?"

"Sure I will. I'll start saving them and sending them as soon as I get there," Jack promised.

Jack embraced the boy, who gave him a quick kiss on the cheek and then left the room. Suzanne was beginning to get tears in her eyes and she fought them and finally they subsided.

Jack stood up and went over to Eva. "Thank you for being so kind to me. I've missed my mother very

311

much over these last few years, and it was wonderful to be with you. You know I care very much for your daughter and for everyone in this family."

Eva stood in front of Jack and kissed him three times on the cheeks and thanked him for coming into their lives. "You are a fine young man, Jack. I hope your voyage is safe. Please give our best wishes to your mother and father."

"I will, thank you," Jack said.

Suzanne kissed her mother. "Thank you, *Maman*, for the wonderful birthday and for everything. I'll be over tomorrow after Jack leaves."

As her mother nodded in affirmation, the couple left the room and went out the back door and into their own house. "I'll go around and close the shutters, Jack."

"No, let me do it for you, Sweetheart."

Suzanne nodded and went into the dining room quickly as Jack went back outside. She felt herself unraveling from the poignant departure Jack had made from the children and her mother. How would she get through their goodbyes, she wondered? Pushing that thought aside, she thought about the moment. This is our last night together for a while and we'll remember it forever.

The next morning Suzanne got up from bed at five o'clock. She had hardly slept even though she was exhausted from their night of making love and talking about their future lives as husband and wife. Jack needed to be at the Gare du Midi by seven o'clock and she wanted him to have a good breakfast first.

Suzanne washed herself and dressed quickly in the chilly early autumn morning. When she got downstairs, she stoked the ashes in the stove and put some coal on the embers to warm the room. Next she put water on the gas stove to make a pot of coffee and she got the bacon and eggs from the ice box. She took a cup of coffee and added a little sugar and milk and sat and drank it before going back upstairs to wake Jack.

312

Jack was sitting on the edge of the bed. He had gotten dressed in his military uniform and was putting his shaving kit into the duffle bag he had arrived with. Suzanne went to the side of the bed and sat next to him. Jack slipped his arm around her waist and held her tightly. Suzanne's head was pressed against his shoulder and neither of them spoke.

Finally Jack released her and stood. "I need to get going, Sweetheart."

"Yes, but you must have breakfast. I have everything ready; I just have to cook your eggs," Suzanne said.

"Okay," he looked at his watch. "I have enough time."

As he ate his breakfast, Suzanne sipped another cup of coffee and watched him. "I'm going with you to the station, Jack."

"No, Sweetheart, no," Jack said. "We talked about this, and it will be too crazy at the station. I want to say goodbye to you here. I want to see you in my dreams right here in this room and remember all of the wonderful times we had here when we were alone or with the kids or with our friends. Please, Suzanne, do this for me."

She nodded. "All right, Jack. Please write to me all the time, please."

"Of course I will. You know my writing is not very good," Jack said.

"It doesn't matter, *cheri*, just tell me how you are, and your family, too," Suzanne said. "I want to know everything from America. And tell me that you love me, and that when you think of me I'll be right there next to you."

Jack wiped his mouth with the napkin and stood and took her hand. Suzanne got up and moved into his arms. "I will love you forever and ever, Sweetheart. You'll be with me with every thought of you I have and I'll be with you. When we lie in bed a night, we'll know that each other is there right beside us in the bed. I love you my darling."

313

Suzanne lifted her face to his and they kissed deeply and sweetly for several moments. After holding each other for another minute, Suzanne knew she must release Jack and let him go.

Jack put on his jacket and picked up the duffle bag. They walked out the back door and Suzanne walked behind him on the concrete walk, and they arrived in the front garden by the gate. He turned to her and kissed her briefly and touched her face with his free hand. "I'll love you forever and I'll be back, Sweetheart," Jack promised.

Suzanne couldn't stop a tear from falling down her cheek. "I love you forever, too. Be safe, my *cheri*."

Jack went out of the little gate and began walking down rue Virgile. When he reached the bottom of the street and just before turning down the next street, he turned and saw her standing there with her arms wrapped around herself. Jack lifted one hand and waved and Suzanne returned the wave. Jack walked away.

Going Home

Suzanne was in her bedroom making the bed when she found an envelope with her name in Jack's writing. The birthday card had a large rose on the front and inside he had simply written 'I love you forever. Your, Jack.' She held the card to her breast and wondered how she would be able to live without him. She sat at the small desk in her room and took out airmail stationery and wrote to him.

My dearest,
You're only gone for two hours and I can't believe it still. I regret not holding you longer when you were leaving but I couldn't believe it was true.
Please wear the bracelet I gave you to always think of me. I can only hope that soon we'll be together again. My heart is heavy.
I'll put a number on each letter that I write so that you'll know that you have received all of them.
The flowers you gave me for my birthday are beautiful. I'll try to learn English and write.
Later this evening…
You must have sailed by now from Antwerp. Please don't take long to write. You said, when you close your eyes, you will be here next to me. I will do the same and dream of you.
Your loving, Suzanne

Jack had not sailed on September 22nd. After reporting to Camp Tophat he was told that all ships were full and had sailed, but that returning ships came in every day and there was a bulletin area in the camp to check the rosters daily for your specific sailing. Of course he inquired if he could go back to Brussels and was promptly denied. He was told that the engineers were on base waiting also. Jack found his way to an empty bunk in one of the hundreds of 20-man black tents serving as barracks. He stowed his gear and started asking around if anyone knew fellows from the 347th.

The camp was similar to military camps in the United States. There were movie theatres and a PX along with mess halls serving decent and fresh food. GI's who were transient could come and go as they pleased but needed to check the bulletin board daily to see if it was their turn. Soldiers were being shipped home by the amount of points they had and when Jack inquired how many points the men had who had recently been transported, he knew he would have to wait a while. Hopefully he would find his pals since they all had about the same amount of points, sixty-five.

Jack also started to think that perhaps Suzanne could come to Antwerp for the day taking the train back and forth wouldn't take too much time. He decided that if his name wasn't on the list the next day, he'd go into Antwerp and telephone her. She sure will be surprised, he thought.

At supper Jack made his way to the mess hall. He had also learned that German POW's did all of the labor in the camp and that GI's who were not there on duty, didn't have any work to do at all. Looking at the POW's made him wonder how they liked it here knowing all the while they were probably better off here than if they were civilians trying to dig out of their own towns that were mostly piles of rubble.

There they were! Jack was walking through the large Quonset hut serving as the mess hall, and he saw his three old buddies sitting together eating their suppers. He immediately called out. "Hey, Phil!"

Phil lifted his head and looked in the direction of the person who shouted his name. A look of pure surprise filled his face as Carl and Steve turned around and saw Jack, too.

"Jack," Phil called back and got up out of his seat. Jack reached the table and the two men shook hands. They shook hands and clapped each other on the back laughing and talking all at once.

316

"Look, fellas, I'm starved. Let me get my chow and I'll be right back," Jack said hurriedly.

"Okay, buddy, but we want to hear all about her," Carl said smirking.

It didn't take Jack long to get back and the guys were still eating. "The food looks pretty good," Jack commented.

"Not bad," Steve mumbled stuffing more spaghetti into his mouth.

"How you guys been?" Jack asked looking at each one of them.

"Good," Carl answered. They all chimed in that they were pretty good. They had stuck together and gone back to Paris and then traveled down to southern France. They told Jack they didn't like it much there. It was very hot this summer and everything seemed poor. After a while, they went back to Paris and had a lot of fun. They arrived in Antwerp two days ago. Now it was Jack's turn, Steve told him. Was he married, engaged, what?

"It's a long and beautiful story, boys," Jack said. "Why don't we go over to the Enlisted Men's Club and have a couple of beers, and I'll tell you the story?"

The club was filled, but they found a table in a corner after picking up some beers. Jack told them about his time with Suzanne and her family and about the good friends she had and how they were all good friends now. He explained what happened to Suzanne's husband and his pals were really surprised. After seeing the Russian P.O.W. camp they liberated, they couldn't even imagine how bad it must have been for the man.

"So, fellas, now we have to wait for the red tape to be removed so that she can be legally determined a widow. Then we will be able to get married," Jack concluded.

"You're really going to marry her?" Steve asked.

"There's no question about it," replied Jack. "I love her and want to be married to her and her kids will be mine. I'm going to ship back here just as soon as I can

317

after I get my discharge and after we get married, we can go back to the states to live."

"Good for you, Jack," Phil said. "I'm going to marry Marilyn as soon as I get back. You two," he pointed at Steve and Carl, "You'll want to find wives when you get back. Take my word for it."

"Yeah, yeah, you're probably right," Carl said and Steve nodded. "Hey, Jack, I'm happy for you. Too bad you saw her first that night at the club in Brussels!" Carl laughed out loud.

"She wouldn't have looked at your ugly mug, Carl, she saw me and that was it!" Jack said and laughed.

Steve lifted his beer bottle in a toast and his pals followed suit. "Here's to you, Jack. May you find happiness in the arms of Suzanne."

They clicked their bottles together and took long pulls on the cold beer and Jack replied, "Thanks boys, maybe I'll invite you to our wedding!"

The next day Jack and his friends checked the bulletin board and didn't find their names. They all went into the city by hitching a ride on a transport. Jack told them he wanted to find a phone in a quiet area so he could call Suzanne and tell her what was going on with being shipped back to the states. Steve recommended that they find a nice hotel with a lobby bar, and he could place the call with the operator and then they could tell him when his call went through.

After wandering around a bit they found a good hotel and followed Steve's advice. They were at the bar enjoying some of the terrific Belgian brews when the barman told Jack he could go to the table in the rear and use the house phone; his party was on the line.

Jack leaped off his stool and dashed to the table and picked up the receiver. "Hello, Suzanne?"

"Yes, *cheri,* what's wrong? Are you all right?" Suzanne was worried.

"I'm fine, Sweetheart, but I don't know when I'm sailing," Jack said.

"Why not, your orders said yesterday?" Suzanne said.

"Not really. I was ordered to Camp Tophat yesterday," explained Jack. "It's gigantic here, and there are thousands of men waiting to sail home. I'm in downtown Antwerp now with my three old buddies. We have to check the bulletin board every day and see if it's our day to sail."

"Oh, no. We could have been together longer, *cheri*," Suzanne's voice trailed off for a moment. "I miss you so much already and you're still in Belgium!"

"I know, Darling, I miss you, too," Jack said.

"Is the camp called 'Tophat' like the cigarettes?" asked Suzanne.

"Yes. Actually the main gate has the emblem of the cigarette pack," Jack said. We have 20-man tents and sleep on cots, but there's a good mess hall and the food is good. There are movie theatres and clubs on base."

"That's wonderful, Jack. I'm glad you are with your friends," Suzanne said.

"Suzanne. You could come here for the day and we could spend time together. We could even get a hotel room, but I have to be on base at night to sleep," Jack said.

"Oh, *cheri*, I don't know. That means traveling on the train both ways in one day and leaving the children with my mother," Suzanne said.

"But, Sweetheart, we can still have time together," Jack paused for a moment. "I'm being selfish. It's a lot of bother for you just to spend a few hours with me."

"It's not that, Jack, it's...."

Jack stopped her. "Look, if I still haven't sailed after one week, then I'll come into town and call you early, right after they put the board up. If you can, then you will."

319

"Yes, Jack, that is better. Shall we make it one week from today? That way I can tell my mother in advance, and I'll be ready early in the morning and can rush to the station to get the next train. All right?"

"Perfect," Jack replied happily. He heard in her voice that she was feeling better with a plan in place.

"It will be next Sunday, then," Suzanne said.

"Sweetheart, can we make it next Saturday? I'm afraid there won't be too many trains on Sunday."

"Oh, Jack, of course, you are correct. Next Saturday. *Cheri*, this phone call must be costing so much. We should say goodbye," Suzanne said.

"All right, Sweetheart, but not goodbye; *a bientôt.* I love you, Sweetheart," Jack said.

"I love you, *cheri. A bientôt.*"

Jack hung up the phone and returned to the bar. His pals were looking at him expectantly. "We're going to wait until next Saturday morning. If we're not on the list, I'll come into town early, call her and she'll take the train here, and we'll spend the day together."

"Sounds like a good plan, Jack. Hopefully we'll be on our way sooner than that," Steve declared.

"Damn right," Carl added. "I like this beer a lot, but I wanna get home!"

"Hey, let's finish the beers and see the town," Phil chimed in.

"Sounds good to me," Jack said. "Barman, do you have my charge for the phone?"

"Yes, sir," he pushed a slip of paper towards Jack.

Not too bad, Jack thought. It was about three bucks and worth every penny. They paid the bar tab and went out to explore Europe's second largest port city that was famous for its diamond dealers and jewelers

****

It took an entire month before Jack, his friends and about five hundred GI's finally boarded the *SS Williams Victory* bound for New York City. The weather had turned cold, and there were storms almost every day.

They were supposed to sail the previous day but the vicious winds and high seas kept all of the ships in port until Monday, October 22nd.

Jack quickly finished a letter he had begun to Suzanne and put it in the A.P.O. before going on board to let her know that he had sailed. Suzanne had come to Antwerp twice during Jack's time at Camp Top Hat. After having dinner at midday they checked into the nice little hotel Jack and his friends had found on their first visit. The rest of the afternoon was spent in each other's arms, making love and talking about their future together. Although Jack wanted to live in the United States with his wife and children, he assured her that if they needed to stay in Brussels, he was willing to do so and would think about what type of work he might be able to do. Suzanne would always tell him that Fred Caron would be able to find him a job and Jack agreed that Fred probably could.

The last visit by Suzanne was on October 13 and she took the latest train home. They both found it extremely difficult to release each other from their embrace as the conductor blew his whistle and was ready to board himself. Suzanne decided she couldn't come here again because each time was more painful than the time before. She told Jack she couldn't bear it and would wait for his return in "their" little house on rue Virgile. Jack only nodded and assisted his beloved fiancée to the platform of her car and stepped down quickly. When she found her seat by a window she blew a kiss to him. The train was beginning to pull out of the station and Jack waved to her and then started running to keep up with the pace of it. He kept waving and Suzanne waved back until finally the train was out of the station.

The *Williams* had been built as a cargo and troop ship and was only finished in May of 1945. She was fairly small and could out distance her Liberty ship cousins, making the soldiers feel confident they would be back in the U.S. in record time. However, the series of storms they encountered made their progress slow with some days barely gaining any distance at all.

They were sick. Almost every man couldn't stop vomiting. For the first five days Jack had not eaten anything and had only sipped a little water which was generally followed by more vomiting. The troops were in the bottom of the ship in one common area with no beds. They felt like cattle, and Jack thought that cattle were probably treated better. Finally the ocean became calm and they picked up speed heading due west.

When the worst was over, the men started to behave as they normally did. Poker and craps games took place in every corner of the room, and Jack managed to win a hundred dollars before they reached the United States. As they got closer to port the men talked about their families and the girls they left behind. They all had high expectations for their lives even though most of them didn't know what they would do for jobs. Some guys talked about working on family farms or at the factories near their homes while a few spoke of going to college and getting the free education they had been reading about in the *Stars and Stripes*.

Phil had clear plans. After marrying Marilyn, he would work in the paper mill in his hometown in western Massachusetts. Carl would probably wind up working with his father on their farm while Steve figured he could work at the steel plant in Pittsburgh and was thinking about going to college. Jack knew his commitment to Suzanne and the children meant that upon his discharge and after a visit with his parents, he would find a way back to Belgium and would have to decide upon his career later. Meanwhile, he was sure his father would appreciate help on the little chicken farm he was building in New Jersey.

On the morning of November 5th the *SS Williams* sailed into New York Harbor. It was a clear and chilly autumn morning and every man was topside looking at the New York skyline. As they passed by Long Island, Queens and Brooklyn, Jack could make out familiar images of Coney Island. He paddled his buddies on their backs and arms and couldn't speak for a few moments as a lump formed and was stuck in his throat. His eyes were filled with tears that he managed to squeeze back. His long-time friends returned the pats on Jack's back knowing that if they had just seen the buildings of their hometowns, they would all be crying.

A collective cheer went up as the ship approached the Statue of Liberty, and then the horns on board sounded their arrival into the United States of America proudly delivering soldiers who had served their country and had been victorious in the defeat of Hitler. They couldn't stop hooting and hollering as the sights of the greatest city in America, and the world waited with welcoming arms to embrace them.

The soldiers had all of their belongings with them, anxiously waiting to disembark. When the gangplank was in place the process began, and the men saw the line of buses waiting to take them to the processing center. They soon learned they would be going to Camp Shanks across the river in Orangeburg. Many of the GI's had boarded troop ships to Europe after their last state side camp. It was generally known as "Last Stop USA" by the tens of thousands of troops that were encamped there. Now that the war was over, Camp Shanks served as a welcoming center and embarkation base for the soldiers to get transportation assignments to camps or forts where they were to be discharged or receive orders.

Jack and several men from the 347th boarded one of the buses and began their ride. They crossed the George Washington Bridge and continued north along the Palisades. Although much of the fall foliage was on the ground, shades of yellow and red were still clinging to branches on the heavily wooded banks of the river. The New York skyline had faded away and Jack enjoyed looking at the scenery while thinking about his future. His emotions were conflicted. Jack thought about his upcoming reunion with his parents, his brother and his cousins and he was happy. His next thoughts were about Suzanne and how he already missed her more than he ever thought was possible. Jack would have to explain all of this to his folks and hoped they would understand that he would be on an airplane or a ship back to Europe as quickly as possible.

The trip to Camp Shanks only took about forty-five minutes and although the busload of soldiers were not thrilled to see the sprawling Army base, they knew it was only a matter of filling out forms and waiting for their discharges. Jack and his pals decided that, given a chance, they would make the most of this night as it was probably the last time they would all be together.

Getting off the bus and grabbing their duffle bags the soldiers lined up for information. A sergeant approached them quickly, checked off their unit numbers, names and serial numbers. Jack could tell that they did this same routine day in and day out and were very happy to speed up the process. The sergeant told them to stand at ease and told them in which building they were billeted, where the mess hall was and to report at zero seven hundred the next day to this exact spot to get to their next transportation. He read off the names of the army bases they would be going to in order to be processed for discharge. Jack heard his name and Ft. Dix in New Jersey. He smiled to himself remembering that this entire journey started at Dix.

Soon they were dismissed and the group of four good friends walked off to find their barracks. Stowing their gear, they quickly went to the latrine and washed up. All of them were hungry and they hoped that American food, real American food, would be good.

Standing in the chow line they looked around at the men who were walking with their trays and saw large steaks and mashed potatoes and big glasses of milk. Jack was salivating. He had lost at least twenty pounds on the troop ship after being so sick and not eating. When they got their turns in line, the men on duty told them they could have as much as they wanted and could come back for more.

With their trays loaded, they found seats not far from other long-time friends in the 347th. Jack had taken two glasses of milk and started his meal by drinking the entire contents of one.

"It's real milk, guys!" Jack exclaimed. "I never thought I'd get to have a glass of real milk again, and I'll never drink that powered shit as long as I live."

His buddies laughed and all toasted each other and downed their glasses of milk. They attacked their steaks and couldn't believe the delicious flavor of the sirloin beef. Steve admitted that he had never eaten steak before going in the Army. Their family had been too poor during the Depression. "But I'm gonna have me a big steak at least once every week," Steve declared with gusto.

The gang laughed and ate, and joked and enjoyed every moment of this welcome home meal Uncle Sam was providing. Jack thought about Suzanne at that moment and secretly said to himself that he would provide her and their family steak once a week, too. And with French Fries, he remembered to add to his little vow.

Jack found his way to the telegraph office. He knew Suzanne would be terribly worried about him. The trip had taken two weeks and should only have been about ten days. He sent a brief telegram telling her he arrived in New York and would see his parents soon. Jack promised to write very soon and that he loved her. The clerk smiled at him when he took the message slip and made change for the five dollar bill Jack gave him.

The evening had passed quickly. In many ways, too quickly for Jack and Phil and Steve and Carl. They made many promises to write to each other and stay in touch and to try and get together once a year or so for a reunion weekend. It was very difficult to comprehend that you could live; work and fight to keep alive together for more than three years and then just separate and probably not see each other again.

Men all through the barracks were speaking quietly to each other after "lights out." They were going over their promises and making sure they exchanged addresses so they could communicate after settling down at home. Jack promised the fellows that he'd let them know when he was finally getting married and bringing Suzanne back to the states with the kids.

"Do you think you'll live in that little town in Jersey or find an apartment in New York," Steve asked.

"For now I'm going to stay with my folks at their farm. When I find out what my brother is going to do, I'll see if I can stay in New York. He's married already and got an apartment in Forest Hills. That's in Queens, New York," Jack explained.

"Well, you won't be there for long," Phil added. "I know you'll be going back to Belgium."

"You're right, Phil," Jack replied.

They continued to talk about their future lives and didn't get to sleep until past midnight. In the morning, it was all business as they got cleaned up, dressed and in formation by zero seven hundred hours. The orders were read telling them which bus number to look for and to report and board immediately. There was hardly a minute left to shake hands and wish each other luck before hurrying to their separate buses. None of them were the least bit sad, but they all felt a tinge of melancholy as they rushed away in different directions.

Jack gave his name and serial number to the sergeant at the door of bus number 508, stowed his bag underneath in the luggage compartment and got on board. It took three hours on US highways to reach Ft. Dix in the middle of New Jersey. Jack remembered the scenery and saw that nothing had changed except there were more barracks on the grounds.

Standing in formation, Jack wondered how many days it would take to get his discharge. He was tired of army life and wanted his independence back. The taste of freedom he had enjoyed with Suzanne for three months were joyous and had broken the habits that were

326

developed by being in the military and following orders every day.

Over the next three days, Jack and the hundreds of men in the barracks nearby his underwent a series of medical examinations. They also had to talk to psychiatrists and discuss any type of depression or stressful emotions they were having. Jack thought about Phil during that exam and wondered if his old friend would talk about his feelings with the shrink. Jack told the doctor he felt absolutely fine and seeing his family and getting back to his fiancée was the only medicine that he would need.

Additionally they had to watch films that the army had made with the help of Hollywood to discuss getting back into the swing of life. Jack wondered why they would bother. Most of the GI's had terrible lives and circumstances before they went into war. They were mostly poor, out of work and didn't have any plans. If they had rich folks, then why would they have a care in the world? He went through the motions, just as each soldier with him did. Lastly they heard lectures about the souvenirs of war that many had brought with them or shipped home just to make sure they weren't carrying any items that didn't qualify as souvenirs.

On November 8 Jack boarded a civilian bus at the station in Wrightstown located just outside the gates of Ft. Dix and in two hours he stepped off in front of his parents' little farm house which was on state highway 47 also known as Delsea Drive. The driver wished him good luck as he opened the luggage compartment, and Jack found his duffle bag. Walking down the dirt drive towards the house he couldn't tell if his folks were home.

Jack dropped the bag on the front porch and knocked on the door. His father opened it as Jack was already holding open the screen door.

"Son," his father was surprised to see him.

"Hello, Papa," Jack said.

The two men shook hands and Joe opened the door wider and Jack grabbed his bag and came inside.

"Vera, Jake is home," Joe called to his wife who was in the kitchen at the rear of the house.

"Ma," Jack called out as he moved through the living room. "Oh, Ma, it's good to see you!"

Jack hugged his mother and kissed her on the cheek. "Jakey, Jakey," his mother said as her pale blue eyes filled with tears.

They were standing in the dining room and Jack said to them both, "It's really good to see you."

"You're a day early, son," his father was still surprised.

"They processed us faster than they thought when I called you from Ft. Dix. I'm sure glad to be out of the army," Jack said.

"Vera get something for us to drink and celebrate our son's return," his father said.

Jack was surprised at the emotion in his father. He had never shown much even though Jack knew his father loved him. Joe had aged a great deal, Jack thought. His hair was pure white and his skin tone was sallow. His mother also had more gray hair and looked older, but not to the same degree as Joe. His father's tuberculosis was taking a real toll on him.

"Oh, Jakey," Vera was ecstatic, "dinner is almost ready, and we will have a wonderful celebration. Look how skinny you are!"

"Yeah, well I lost over 20 pounds on the damn ship coming home. The seas were so rough we couldn't eat for days. I know you'll fix that, Mama," Jack winked at her. "Hey, what's new with Marx," Jack wanted to know about his brother.

"He got back to New York about ten days ago. He and Lena, his wife, have a little apartment in Forest Hills, and they are going to have a baby," his mother told him.

"No kidding. Good for them. I'll call him in a day or two and probably go up to New York as soon as I can," Jack replied.

Marx had gotten married right after the war had ended. Being in the Merchant Marines he earned civilian wages and he got time off. Somewhere during the last year he had met this girl who grew up in Massachusetts and was as petite and pretty as they come. Jack had gotten a letter and a photo of the couple while he was staying with Suzanne.

"Well, what do you want to do first, son?" his father questioned.

"Tomorrow I'll go into Vineland and buy a car. It's not New York with subways and buses around here, is it?" Jack laughed.

"No, a car is a good idea. Do you have enough money, Jake?" Joe asked.

"Sure, Pa, where did I have to spend my money during the war?" Jack replied.

"You had a few months off. It was a vacation," Joe said.

"Yes. Let me tell you about some of my time in Brussels. In Belgium," Jack added. He proceeded to tell them about the wonderful woman he had met and that she was a widow with two great kids. When he told his mother that Suzanne was Jewish, Vera smiled broadly and patted his hand in approval. Jack knew everything was going to go well with his folks from that time.

"Let's have dinner," his mother announced and proceeded to set the table while Jack was shown to his room by his father. He changed into civilian clothes and intended to be in them for the rest of his life.

Red Tape

Suzanne sat as close to the stove in the dining room as possible trying to stay warm. It had rained nearly every day in early November, and the children were both ill. Eva went to Felenne to visit with her brother and get away from the sickness in their houses. Suzanne was writing to Jack and telling him their most recent news. Sergeant Choban, a friend of Francine's and of the family, had brought some food supplies to them earlier in the day. Choban didn't have enough points to get out of the army, and he worked in the same building as her sister. Since the war was over, it seemed more difficult to get good food than it had been and she was very grateful for the extra food.

As she closed this letter, Suzanne told Jack about government pensions being offered to displaced persons and Jews of 2,000 francs per month. The law had just been passed and she intended to find out if she and the children could qualify. Knowing her stash of money and jewels were dwindling, Suzanne knew she would need other sources of income. The pension would be a Godsend and she was also trying to find some type of work that would incorporate her skills with textiles. Suzanne didn't let Jack know how worried she was becoming about her finances because he had so many things he needed to figure out to be able to come back to Belgium and what type of work he would seek to support all of them.

By mid-November Suzanne went to the North Sea city of Ostend with Maurice's longtime friend Monsieur Sloma. Sloma, his wife and two daughters had managed to evade the Gestapo roundups with the false identity cards Suzanne had made for them and by keeping a very quiet life. He intended to buy a store and set up a fashionable shop with high quality handbags and other ladies' accessories he had made before the War. Sloma wanted Suzanne to help him select the right location, and he hoped she might supply him with her hand-woven scarves that could be sold and would give her some extra money. He assured her that if he didn't open a shop at the seashore, he would in Brussels knowing people would have to get back to normal lives eventually.

Suzanne nodded in agreement and then confided in her friend, "I wonder how long it will take? I have filled out all the forms to get a declaration of death for Maurice and each time I check, there are new forms and new laws."

"I know you are disgusted, Suzanne, but there were so many lost," Sloma spoke kindly.

"Lost? They are dead," she announced.

"Yes, there are millions dead, Suzanne, but there are also thousands and thousands that are lost. What would happen if Maurice was found alive in one of the Displaced Persons' Camps? Hmmm, my dear?" Sloma asked.

"Monsieur Sloma, you told me yourself about your friend that saw Maurice when he was getting on the train to go to Auschwitz and that he could barely recognize him. How could he have survived?"

"You are probably right, Suzanne, but there is a very small chance that he may have," Sloma said.

"Fred Caron keeps checking all of the lists for me. If anyone can find out if Maurice is in one of those survivor camps, it will be Fred."

"Yes, Monsieur Caron is very knowledgeable and works for the government. I know you want to move on with your life, but you must just keep a little hope that he did not die at the hands of those bastards," Sloma said.

"I can't live like that any longer, Monsieur Sloma. I wept for him; I risked my life and the lives of my family by trying to bribe the guard to get him out of Breendonk. Maurice wrote me that last time, right before they sent him to Auschwitz and told me how to take care of myself and the children and then he said 'good bye'," Suzanne's voice cracked as she held back a sob.

"Oh, my dear, I didn't mean to upset you so much. Forgive me, please," Sloma said.

Suzanne nodded. "I'm all right. But now I must only think about the future. I am in love with Jack and he with me. He's going to come back and marry me, and we are going to raise our family together. Maurice will always be in my heart, and I will tell the children all about him but I cannot look backward anymore."

"I understand, dear. I won't mention it again," Sloma said. "If Caron finds out anything, I'm sure you will tell me. I'll help you in any way I can." "Thank you. I know you are thinking about our future. I really do appreciate that, Monsieur Sloma," Suzanne said.

He patted her gloved hand, and they were both silent during the rest of the train trip back to Brussels. Suzanne lost herself in thoughts about Jack. She had hardly received any letters and was worried that he may be losing interest in her now that he was back in America. She had expressed those fears in a letter to Jack last week and wanted him to reassure her of his love and that he would be back in her arms very soon. The train was on the outskirts of Brussels coming in from the north. They had passed the town of Malines, and Suzanne's thoughts immediately jumped to Maurice and his last journey to his death from that very location. Soon it would be the anniversary of their marriage, she thought, eight years and four of them she spent alone. Suzanne knew that she couldn't stand being without a husband and a lover. When Jack entered her life, she felt hope and happiness more than she thought was possible after Maurice's imprisonment.

The trip ended at the Gare du Midi, and Sloma put Suzanne in a taxi and paid the driver after wishing her a good night. She was grateful for the ride after the long day they had spent and would be able to get home and have a plate of soup with her family before putting the children to bed. She planned to write to Jack later in the evening and give him all the latest news.

After she entered her house she went straight to the mailbox and found a letter from Jack. Suzanne grabbed a knife and sat at her table still wearing her coat. She scanned through the letter and smiled. Jack reassured her throughout the letter and wrote, *I, too cannot live without you. I will marry you, believe me. Please have patience, cherie.* The rest of the letter revealed to her that he had bought a used car, a 1933 Plymouth. There were also big shortages in the U.S. Meat was scarce, and the shelves were not well stocked in any of the stores. On a brighter side, he was enjoying his time with his parents and his mother was cooking and baking all of his favorite dishes. He had gained three pounds and hoped to continue to gain weight.

Suzanne folded the pages and put them back into the envelope. Picking up a little bag that held some chocolates she had bought earlier in the day, she went next door to Eva's and her children.

****

Jack had been busy ever since he arrived at his parents' little farm in southern New Jersey. He and his father bought 1,000 chicks to raise as meat birds. With the shortage of fresh meat, they figured they could make a good profit when they sold them. Jack talked to his father about building more coops to handle a larger number of chickens so that they could both make a living at it. He had never thought of himself as a farmer, but considering the number of men coming home to look for jobs; being a chicken farmer was not a bad idea.

He had visited his brother and sister-in-law in Queens. They had a small apartment and Marx was not anxious to go back to sea as a merchant marine. He told his brother that he wanted to be closer to home. Jack asked him if he would consider moving to Vineland. They could invest in a much bigger farm and raise at least 10,000 chickens at one time. Lena made it clear that she didn't want to live on a farm and liked it in New York.

Jack stayed with them for a few days, sleeping on the sofa at night. He visited all of his cousins and his aunt and uncle. They had great times exchanging stories and catching up on the events of their lives over the last few years. Judy was pregnant, and Willy wasn't sure what he wanted to do. Miriam was enjoying the single life and figured she'd settle down soon enough. Jack's older cousins were married and had kids or were off on some type of adventure.

During Jack's last evening with Marx, he brought up an idea that had been growing for the last few weeks.

"Look, Marx, there are shortages all over the world, and I think there is opportunity to start a business and really make a go of it. In Belgium and France, the stores are virtually empty. I've been thinking of starting an export company here in New York and importing into Belgium."

Marx looked at him for a moment. "Interesting idea. Did you get it from Nat?"

"Not really, but I talked to him about his business and he's making some real money," Jack said. Nat was their oldest cousin and he owned an import/export business dealing primarily with the Caribbean and South America.

"Yeah, well, seems like you got some big ideas from Nat. What do you think should be exported to Belgium?" Marx asked.

"Tires. Good Year, Firestone, all the best brands," answered Jack. "There are taxis running around in Brussels, but most cars are sitting on blocks in driveways and garages. In Europe they haven't even had a boom with cars for the middle class folks yet. I'm telling you, brother, tires are going to be big."

"Well, you make sense talking about that. Did you look into any details while you were there?" asked Marx.

"Not really," Jack said. "I have a friend there, Fred, who can help set up a business because he works for the government and can help out with the red tape.

"Look, Marx, I want Suzanne to come here and live with me, but we don't know when she'll be able to do that legally. I want to get back there as soon as I can and start my life with her, and I've gotta be able to have employment. I'd rather be my own boss, and it would be difficult for an American to work as a laborer with jobs being scarce right now."

"Suppose you can get this going," Marx mused, "how do you think I fit in?"

"You want to stay in New York. You and I can be partners with you taking care of the export side and I'll set up the contracts in Belgium. Once we get going with the tires, we can look for other goods to export from Belgium and we can diversify," Jack sounded enthusiastic.

"I sure won't rule it out, Jack, but you have to do the work of setting up the business and figuring this out. I've gotta go to work every day and make a living to take care of my wife and baby that's coming," Marx concluded.

"Swell. I was hoping you'd say so," Jack said. "First I've got to find my way back there. Meanwhile I'm going to help Pa with the farm. Winter's almost here so I won't have much to do in Vineland after this batch of chicks get sold."

"Good luck getting back to Europe. The only way you're going to do it is on a merchant ship, Jack."

"You think so?"

"Yeah. I heard on the radio that no passports or visas are being issued to travel for pleasure to Europe. There's still too many troops over there and the mess with the displaced persons and all of that. You can't just buy a ticket and go."

"Yeah, I know you're right. I've been thinking of going to Philadelphia's ship yard and seeing if I can sign up for work," Jack said.

"Oh, you'll get it, but you need a ship headed for Belgium and they'll offer you all kinds of ships," Marx said.

"I know, but it'll be worth it. Meanwhile I'm going to work on a business plan for the import/export business," Jack said.

The brothers enjoyed the evening eating a nice dinner prepared by Lena and listening to the radio. Jack left Forest Hills the next morning in his old car and made his way back to the little farm in the rural part of the New Jersey.

About a week after Thanksgiving, Jack was sitting in his bedroom at his parents' house. He had been home for nearly a month, and all he thought about was Suzanne and a way to get back to her. He had read one of her letters in the afternoon and was disturbed that she had so many worries and doubts about his love for her. He wrote her a long letter and hoped it would cheer her.

Cherie,

The first thought I think is that I love you. I will wait as long as it takes till we're together. You are the nicest woman in the world. I think that all the pretty songs in the entire world were written especially for you. Now I am thinking of a new one, 'Kiss me once, and kiss me twice and kiss me once again, it's been a long, long time.'

Have you heard it, Sweetheart? It's by Harry James Orchestra and it makes me think it was written for you and me.

Jack finished the letter by telling her about his family and that he's working on the business plan. He told her that an old friend offered him a job for $75 a week to travel to Cuba and South America. This man is no good, he told her, and the police are always looking for him. Of course he turned him down and will stay focused on the plan to get him back to Belgium. He ended by telling Suzanne that he was buying toys and candy to send to the children for St. Nicholas' Day.

Before he went to sleep, Jack kissed Suzanne's photo. He did this every night hoping to dream of only her. Jack reread the letters she had written him when he was in Germany right after they had met and knew he began falling in love with her the first time he saw her at the nightclub. He was convinced that one way or another they would be together in 1946 and would marry as soon as they were allowed.

Letters

It was only two weeks until Christmas 1945, and Suzanne opened the package Sgt. Choban delivered after receiving it from Jack. Packages were received in about two weeks rather than a month using the American Army postal service. There were new brown leather shoes, some rayon stockings and a beautiful red blouse for her. Jack explained in his letter that nylon was still not available in the United States and as soon as they were on the shelves he would send her tons of them! She dug deeper into the package and found several packages of cigarettes and tin boxes filled with candy for the children for St. Nicholas' Day and a few toys. Jack didn't forget his future mother and sister-in-law, either. He included gloves for both of them and a pair for Suzanne.

When she wrote to Jack that evening thanking him for the wonderful gifts, she mentioned that Francine had been going out with Sgt. Choban almost every night of the week since he was on military leave for ten days. Suzanne wasn't sure how much her sister really liked Choban and decided to leave it alone. Francine was still so young, and Suzanne knew she wanted to meet an American with whom she could make a life.

In the same letter she reassured Jack that her mother told her that she really did understand how much the two of them were in love and were determined to be married one day. Suzanne told him that the news had reported that 300 wives would be sent to the U.S. to join their husbands each day beginning next week. There are 50,000 wives and 30,000 babies in Europe and England right now, she explained. *"Why does it have to be so difficult for us? My mother even said that one day I'll have children with you, Jackie!"* She ended the letter telling him there was still no news about the widows of lost prisoners, but that it should be soon.

Suzanne put the letter aside thinking she might add something else in the morning before putting it in the post. Not ready for bed, she picked up her knitting. She was making a sweater for the baby her dear friends, Josette and Felix, were expecting. Suzanne was very happy for them and told them how fortunate they were that the baby would be born during peace time. She enjoyed knitting and thought about the visitors coming during the next few weeks. They would bring little gifts for the children, and they could all really celebrate their first Christmas after five years of war.

As the holidays brought family and friends to rue Virgile, Suzanne grew ill. She had a terrible grippe and the children began to get sick also. She forced herself to shop and prepare some of the traditional holiday foods. Eva was in bed for a few days, but not nearly as sick as she was. Only Francine was healthy, and she was busy working and going out celebrating the holiday with all of her American friends. Francine learned she would keep her job with the American office for another six months, and she was ecstatic.

Lying in her sick bed, Suzanne became depressed wondering if Jack would be with them next winter. Jack had promised her that he would find a way to come back to Belgium. He mentioned that he had written to the Merchant Marine office in Washington D.C. to see if it was possible for him to get work as a seaman. If he didn't hear from them soon, he would go to the shipyard in Philadelphia after New Year and inquire about working on a ship bound for Antwerp. Jack reassured her in each letter telling her that as each day passed his love was stronger than the day before and nothing would keep them apart forever.

He sent her a second package for Christmas including more cigarettes and nylon stockings. Finally! Jack couldn't wait till she got it and was sure the stockings would be her favorite gift of all.

New Jersey had gotten a lot of snow, but the highway in front of his parents' home was clear. He often went to the downtown and would take his mother at least once a week to do the shopping. They would often go to the movies together. Jack had taken several photos of the house and his parents, and his mother took several pictures of him. He had a second set of prints made and mailed them all to Suzanne so that she could see what it was like at their house.

Jack went out a couple of nights a week. He would usually see a film and then stop in at one of the many taverns on Landis Avenue or Delsea Drive. There were still a lot of men and even some women in uniform and he found himself talking with many of them knowing they had experiences they could share. Jack had never been a big drinker, but some nights he got tipsy especially if he started feeling sorry for himself.

Suzanne and Jack spent New Year's Eve apart. Each of them surrounded by family and friends and each of them felt terribly alone. They wrote to each other at midnight so they would feel closer. The lovers reminded each other that their love was strong, and that they had to do everything possible to be together and that they would never again be apart at Christmas or New Year's. They shared photos and each looked at the growing collection of pictures from the years before they knew each other, photos of them together during the summer of 1945 and the most recent pictures taken since their forced separation.

Jack got a telegram from the Merchant Marines on January 4 telling him to go to their office in Wildwood, New Jersey. He immediately wrote to Suzanne and mentioned that perhaps he would be in Belgium before the month was over!

The trip to Wildwood didn't amount to much and Jack headed for Philadelphia on January 7. He immediately joined the Marine Union and was told he could get work right away. Jack explained that he only wanted to work on a ship destined for Antwerp or possibly LeHavre. He signed on for the engine room having learned during the years before the war that you worked five and half days in the engine room and all seven days as a deck hand. Jack was told he would have to show up each day at the shipyard to see the list of vessels and their assignments and sign on for a job then.

On his drive home, Jack was happier than he had been in weeks. He felt that he would get a ship soon and would be back in the arms of his beautiful Suzanne. Knowing it would be a temporary visit didn't matter at this moment. Being with her was all he cared about. Before the war a merchant marine could arrive in a country on one ship, take time off and stay in that country and then pick up another ship to go home or to another port. That isn't the case now, Jack was told. He would have a couple of days off while the ship was unloaded and reloaded with cargo and would have to return to Philadelphia. It didn't matter.

Jack gave all of this news to Suzanne in a letter, and near the end of January he still had not found a ship to Belgium. He wrote to Suzanne that when he got a ship, he would mark the back of the envelope with a little "x" on it and she would know he is on the way!

The lovers wrote letters to each other at least three times a week. They filled several paragraphs with words of love and lust for each other and with memories that were etched into their minds forever. They also told each other of economic crisis that was occurring on both sides of the Atlantic Ocean. Food was available, but prices were exorbitant! There were strikes in America all of the time, and there were Fascists rearing their ugly heads in Washington.

Suzanne continued in her attempts at finding documents that would prove that Maurice Morgen had perished in Auschwitz, and she also tried to collect the widows of war pension. She was very worried that she would run out of money. It was almost impossible for her to find customers for her beautiful woven scarves, but she kept making them hoping that Sloma would get his shop open by spring.

Jack's letters in French were better all of the time. He used a French – English dictionary and studied the grammar and wording in Suzanne's letters. He knew his speech would be far better when he returned to Brussels. Suzanne, on the other hand, had abandoned her English lessons. She didn't have enough time in the day. The housekeeping, children and her weaving projects used up the entire day, and she saved the evenings to write to Jack.

Jack went to Philadelphia nearly every day. He only missed if he didn't feel well or had to help his father with the farm. There were ships departing each day, but none for Belgium or northern France. Jack planned to speak to Fred Caron when he got to Brussels to make sure he could assist in the setup of the tire importing business Jack planned to establish when he could live in Belgium permanently. He had abandoned the idea of Suzanne and the children coming to the states to live. Neither of them knew when Suzanne would be free to marry, and her mother protested any mention of her departure. Jack had really enjoyed his three months living in Brussels and decided he could try his luck with the import – export business.

At the end of January Sloma asked Suzanne to take another business trip with him to the North Sea towns to look for a shop to rent. They were both discouraged to find that many streets were still filled with debris from the war and that the beaches were still being swept for mines. Sloma had paid for two rooms at a nice seaside hotel so that they could search for two days. After they had had supper, Suzanne told him she was tired and was going to her room. He walked with her and when she went into the room, he stepped inside and shut the door behind him.

Suzanne was startled and said, "I really don't want to talk any more this evening, will you please leave me?"

"I will but only after I make you an offer," Sloma said softly.

Suzanne crossed the room and sat in the chair next to the window. There was only one chair and Sloma sat on the edge of her bed. "I want to sleep with you, Suzanne."

Her mouth dropped open, and Sloma raised his hand and motioned to her. "Don't say anything until you hear me out.

"I have not had the love of a woman for a long time. My wife shuts me out, and I have long admired you, Suzanne. I know I am not handsome or your image of a lover, but I have money. I have plenty of money and I will give you enough to live on. You only need to be with me a couple of times each month.

"Well, what you think of my offer?" he asked.

Suzanne was horrified and couldn't believe what he had said. She stood up and walked as far from him as she could get before answering. "I want you to get out of here. You disgust me," she said in a low, hoarse voice. "That you even think there is a possibility that I would be your lover is sick. Yes, you have money, and you think it is so important to me. How can you even think of this? You were Maurice's friend!" she shouted.

"Now," Suzanne continued, "get out of this room. I will be on the morning train to Brussels, and I never want to see you again. Do you understand?"

Sloma got up and moved toward the door. "I'll do as you ask, and we'll never speak of this again. Everything can be the same between us as before." He walked out of her room.

Suzanne began to cry. He had stunned her and upset her. How could this man have such little regard for her and for her late husband? She understood that Sloma would not speak of this again, and she would have to hold her tongue because her mother received a lot of work from him. Eva was an excellent seamstress, and Sloma referred many of his clients to her. Oh, Jack, she thought, you must get back to me soon. I'm not strong enough to keep going on my own. Then she prayed to God, that he would send Jack to her right away.

The cold January weeks passed by slowly on each side of the Atlantic. Affordable food was scarce and everyone did the best possible with what they could find and afford. Suzanne had written to Jack about Sloma and he was furious. He assured Suzanne that when he returned permanently to Brussels, he would make sure that he made enough money for them, and they could tell Sloma to go to hell!

Their letters were filled with promises for a happy life in the future. Jack told Suzanne that he had waited for his entire 27 years to find a girl like her and to love her more than he could ever express in words. He could wait for as many months necessary for them to be reunited. Jack told her that she was his wife and the only thing besides the ocean that kept that from being true was a piece of legal paper. Suzanne had written that some couples were having religious marriages even though they could not get a license for the required civil ceremony that made a marriage in Belgium legal. Not being religious, Jack reminded her, they could live as a married couple until the time she received the papers needed so they could get married at city hall.

As winter progressed into February, Jack still had not been able to get a ship bound for Antwerp. He told Suzanne that he might get on one bound for Holland or France and then go AWOL so that he could be with her. Suzanne replied that it didn't matter if they could only be together for one night because that night would be paradise. She told him that he must keep trying to come to her, and that there was no greater love in the world than the love they had for each other.

In their exchange of news about each other's families and friends, Suzanne told him that Sloma was quiet and sheepish around her, and he realized she hadn't told anyone about his proposition. She assumed that Sloma had thought a bit harder after she rejected

344

him and that he remembered it was she who had made him, his wife and two daughters' false identity papers and that Eva had arranged for them to rent a little house in the Ardennes to wait out the war.

Jack wrote that his parents were celebrating their 32nd wedding anniversary and loved each other as they did on their wedding day. His parents looked forward to meeting her and the children and always sent their best regards to Suzanne and her family.

The winter months added to the mounting depression that hung over them like a dark, voluminous cloud. The lovers emerged from their self-pity with the arrival of each letter and then were engulfed by sorrow soon after. Suzanne worried mostly about not being able to find work or an outlet to sell her weavings or her designs since the economy was terrible. The government spewed a lot of propaganda about the greatness of peace; but all over the country its citizens still suffered from shortages. Jack was consumed by his quest to find a ship destined for Belgium and with spring on the horizon he would have to help his father with one thousand chicks they ordered for April 1. If he couldn't be on a ship very soon, he would have to wait until after he could raise the chicks and sell them for meat birds on the market.

This time frame alarmed Suzanne. She worried that if Jack stopped trying to get to Belgium to raise the chickens, he might lose interest in her. This was foolishness on her part, Jack told her, and she had to remember that nothing, absolutely nothing, would keep them apart for more than a month or two. He promised he would be in Belgium by summer no matter what he had to do to get there.

Suzanne had promised Jack that she would look into the possibility of getting passports and going to America. Indeed she did inquire at the embassy and was given a list of what would be required from her. She could produce everything except proof of Maurice's death. The consul informed her he had never had a request that included the children of the presumed deceased and didn't know how to answer her. He said that he would research her situation.

Eva became afraid that Suzanne might find the path to gain passports and would leave her forever. Meanwhile, Francine spoke of marrying an American and living in the United States, also. Eva's drama was filled with anger, sadness and guilt directed at her eldest daughter. Francine was never fully aware of the scenes that were played out to make Suzanne suffer with remorse.

Jack received his fiftieth letter from Suzanne early in March and felt the need to find his way across the ocean into her waiting arms overwhelming.

Cheri,

Here is my 50th letter, and like you I wish I hadn't written this many and that you were here. Darling, I have high hopes and want to hear your good news soon.

I'm alone with Nadine right now. Maman went into the city. Maman is strange. She acts like she is angry when I write to you. She sees all of the research I am doing to get the papers so that I can go to America and she wonders what I will find there. I know there are problems in all countries and it is not paradise. But for me, America is you and our happiness when we are together. It would be easier if you became Belgian and lived here and we wouldn't all have to leave here. But that is not easy either and our separation is what is important now. Oh, cheri, if you could live here with me! But I know how difficult that is! Jack, I can't live separate from you anymore. Life is so difficult!

At the bureau for repatriation, yesterday, they told me they have the names of 15,000 dead, and there are another 32,000 lost. Therefore, it's about half that have died for sure. If Maurice's name were on the list, it would be simpler. And there is still the issue of the children.

Maman's latest idea is that you can stay here and set up a business while waiting for me to be able to go to the US. She thinks everything is so expensive in the US. Prices here are normal again and life is easier. But I know how much you love America and want to stay there. The fortune teller also said we will have news of Maurice. Maybe his name will be among the 15,000 that arrived at the repatriation office. It will be easier for us, cheri. I don't like talking about all of these things.

You know, I talked with someone who had been with him at Breendonk and that he had received before leaving for Poland the photos I sent him of Nadine when she was 3 weeks old. He was terribly sad. Sometimes I reproach myself for forgetting some of this. I am terrible, I think, but human. It is almost 4 years since he is gone. And life goes on.

Forgive me for saying all of these things but I write what I am thinking. I love you and you are also my friend. A good friend one can tell everything to. My Jack, I don't always have good thoughts. This war gave much suffering. One must chase these thoughts away. Good night, my Jackie.

Jack wiped away the tears that fell onto his cheeks as he put the letter down. His beautiful, wonderful Suzanne had suffered so much. Much more, he thought, than he had as a soldier engineer. She had the burden of keeping her family safe and had tried to save her husband from his doomed fate all the while creating forged identity cards for Allied Paratroopers, Jews and friends. Jack vowed to himself that he would stop asking her to try to come to the states. He needed to get to her, marry her whenever it was possible, and make a safe life for his new family.

Finally Together

As winter finally gave way to an early spring in March 1946, currents of fear ran through the minds of Europeans and Americans alike. Jack and Suzanne asked each other their thoughts in the letters that kept going back and forth. Churchill railed against Russia every day and Suzanne was so afraid that war would break out. Jack told her that he felt as if Churchill had become a dictator and was afraid that his rhetoric would begin a new war. The two lovers' anxiety grew as they felt the threat of war would keep them apart for longer than they could endure. There were strikes in America all of the time, shortages and the cost of necessities were sky high. Suzanne agreed that most prices were high, but Belgium was in much better condition than its neighboring countries and news from Greece was of extreme hunger. But the letters were always filled with bits of optimism and each of them encouraged the other with tender words as their love grew stronger each day.

Jack continued his search as a seaman and took a temporary job working on a ship in port that was rumored to be going to Belgium. During the same time Suzanne showed her line of beautifully woven textiles to shop keepers throughout Brussels, but no one was buying. The economy struggled terribly and Suzanne even lost her market for gold and jewelry as prices plummeted. Finally, while visiting Josette and her little son, Michel, she learned of a proprietor who was very interested in her work and wrote to Jack that her hopes were high.

Jack was happy to receive her good news and wished he could write back that the ship was destined for Belgium. It was not. It was headed for Africa so he quit and renewed his marine union card. There were several men ahead of him for the next ship. He wrote to Suzanne that he would work on the farm for about ten days painting the exterior and making repairs on the house for his parents. Suzanne was able to send him more good news; she finally received her pension for

348

Maurice! Two thousands francs per month and they sent her three months at once. She felt she was temporarily saved from running out of money.

Suzanne informed Jack that the doctor had recommended that Serge spend three months at the seashore in a medical boarding house in the town of Le Zoute with nurses and a teacher. His frequent earaches and other sinus problems had never been totally cured, and Suzanne accepted the doctor's recommendation. In early March she reluctantly put him on the train and planned to visit with him every Sunday. Jack was worried about this situation not understanding the medical theory, but was reassured by Suzanne that the sea air would be a healthy environment and good food would be plentiful for him and the other children in residence.

On April 9 Suzanne received the letter she had prayed for with the little "x" on the back of the envelope. She could hardly keep herself from ripping it open and held it next to heart for a few moments and then went to sit at the table and carefully open and removed it from its sleeve.

April 5   Friday   6:30 pm
My beautiful wife,
At last, I have a ship! Cherie, can you imagine the happiness we will have soon? Cherie, I have a ship for Antwerp … the S.S. Calvin Coolidge. It leaves in about 10 or 12 days. We will have to load coal as our freight and then make a voyage of about 17 days.
But you know, I had luck. My work card was from March 20 and there was someone with a card from March 13. So, I talked with him and he gave me his place! Cherie, I hope so much that it all works out. I don't want any difficulties right now. Sometimes they get a change of orders but I think it will be OK. I hope to be with you the 5th of May. What happiness we will have,

darling. It's finally happiness for us, I think, after the terrible separation we've endured.

Cherie, I feel that I am almost in your arms and I feel your lips. I feel so happy. I love you, my adored, with all of my heart, Suzanne. Be well. I am coming to your arms, it's like a dream!

Cherie, write to me anyway until you know I'm at sea. If I don't get your letters, I'll read them when I return.

I did the cards but they say the same thing as usual. I really have luck today! Cherie, our day of happiness is coming.

The house is almost done except for the back. It's all white with blue window trim. I can finish it tomorrow and on Sunday I'm free!

I hope I will have a lot of time with you but we'll see later. Be patient, I'm coming to you.

We will receive 1000 chicks on Monday and my parents will take care of them but I know it's a lot of work. But we will be together and that is what I have dreamed. Our love is like the great loves in history.

There is a new moon tonight and when I get to you we should have a beautiful full moon. We will have more happiness than before. Cherie, I want to marry you when I get there. I know it will take longer and I will wait. You know I am sincere. I don't think I can sleep tonight. The days will pass more slowly than before.

Darling prepare our nest, we are like two birds. I'm going to say goodnight and I'll be with you soon. Say hello to the family and kiss the children for me. I love you, my baby.

PS Send me 100 francs, I may need them when I get off the ship.

Luckily, Suzanne received this letter in four days and she immediately responded.

I received your letters 66, 67 & 68! I am so happy, happy when I saw the little cross I opened that letter right away. I await you, my cheri, I'm so happy that you have *a ship. I will send you the 100 francs right away. I'll write more later, I'm afraid my letter will take too long.*

What a wonderful thing that the ship is sailing for Antwerp so that we can be together longer, I hope. I wish you a bon voyage, my love. I will pray for you.

If it's possible, telephone me when you arrive in Antwerp so that I can wait for you at home. I will be so sad if I am not here because of shopping errands when you arrive.

Yes, I'll prepare our nest, my dear love. I'll see you soon! The days will seem long while we wait, but we have a marvelous spirit - like our love. Good bye, my husband. I embrace you with all of my force. You will see how I love you! Your Suzanne, so happy.

Jack slept on the SS Calvin Coolidge at night and worked in the engine room during the week. The crew shared quarters with only one other man, and the cook fed them well. They were docked in Camden, New Jersey across the river from Philadelphia while awaiting their cargo of coal. Unfortunately, a strike of tugboat crews held them up for several more days. As each day passed, Jack was always afraid that something else would go wrong and the ships destination might change.

He went home the following weekend to help his parents for the last time before sailing. A thousand chicks had been delivered while he was gone, and he found them to be quite beautiful. Their fluffy, pale yellow down feathers looked like a golden carpet in the chicken coops where they were housed. Jack's mother assured her son that she and his father would be able to feed, water and check over the chicks as they grew. Vera hoped he would be back in time for them to go to the market as meat birds and they would see a nice profit that would pay the bills for several months.

Jack finished a few last repairs around the house that weekend and enjoyed the company of his mother and father. He spoke about Suzanne and how deeply in love he was, and they both told him they would be happy to welcome her as their daughter. Jack made sure he told Suzanne their feelings often in order to help her when the time came to leave Belgium and her mother forever.

Marx and his wife and their new baby girl had made a visit to them for a day and this gave a great deal of joy to Vera. The first grandchild! Her name was Sandra and she was very small with dark hair and a complexion that reminded Jack of his mother's. Her eyes were a very deep brown, almost black. Jack let them know that Suzanne had sent her best wishes, and that she had written that she was making a dress for the new baby and he would bring it back with him.

Deep in Jack's heart he hoped that he would find a way to cut through all of the red tape that kept the lovers from marrying. If he could marry Suzanne while he was in Belgium, he could send for her and the children after he shipped home on this work assignment. His only hope would be to make inroads at the American Consulate while he was there and for Fred Caron to get a declaration of death so that Suzanne could be set free. He vowed to himself that he would do his best to make their marriage a reality. Jack wrote in each letter to Suzanne that their love was infinite and that one day they could be free and would marry and be a family forever.

The war had really changed Jack. While he was in England, he didn't feel the war had really changed him. The Army wasn't that different than the C.C.C. or his time with the Bermuda Base Contractors. All the rules and regulations along with the training just made you tougher and ready for almost anything. After entering Normandy with his company of advance engineers and being in harm's way as they cleared mine fields, blew up bridges and rail yards only to rebuild roads, tracks and new bridges made him into mature man. Their unit had been fortunate not to have had to supply the front lines immediately after being engaged in battle, but Jack did see some of the men in the 347th injured by explosives, mines and heavy equipment. The drudgery of working without much sleep and eating mostly rations toughened him. Looking at the bodies of dead German soldiers around St. Lo and Cherbourg reminded him of the reason they were in France.

Jack was grateful for the friendships he shared with Steve, Carl and especially with Phil. They were like brothers and being a foursome of best friends made their time in the war bearable for him. He often worried about Phil and kept up a correspondence with him. Phil had married Marilyn as soon as he was discharged from the Army. Jack hoped Marilyn knew what a good man she was getting in Phil. He had been loyal to her in England in France and Belgium, and he hoped they would have the life he wanted so very much.

When Jack and his buddies had randomly entered the Corso nightclub in March of 1945 and his eyes immediately found Suzanne, his life did change. As Jack often thought about that initial meeting, he realized that he saw a woman like no other he had ever seen. Of course her beauty was part of it, but there was something else. Her height, slender figure and dark wavy shoulder length hair looked alluring in the Russian blouse with knee length skirt and high heels. As he had walked towards her he saw her beautiful pale complexion and sparkling blue eyes. She wore very little makeup. A touch of rouge and lipstick. Her beauty and hesitating smile on her face captured his imagination immediately. He hadn't looked back at his friends as he approached her and instantly asked her to dance. When she accepted, Jack knew he had only one chance to make the right impression on her.

Since that time they had often talked or written about their instantaneous love for each other, but realistically he wondered if that had been true. In that one moment he knew that Belgian woman was special and that he wanted to find out more. Now, he was certain he had done the right thing. Her loneliness and suffering for years had made Suzanne vulnerable to his advances and Jack knew she wanted some happiness, even if it would only be for one night. How wonderful for them that it had grown into the best times of their young lives, and now he wanted to give this woman and her children a new life and to finally begin a meaningful life for himself. Jack knew that his years of traveling the world, working only to get by, gambling and womanizing were all a part of his past. His future would be filled with hard work, taking care of a family and loving the most wonderful woman in the entire world.

****

The SS Calvin Coolidge pulled into its berth in Antwerp, Belgium on May 4, and Jack was at the head of the line to take his leave of the ship. The voyage had taken two weeks and the ocean had been fairly calm. When he learned of their departure on the Delaware River, he got permission to go ashore and sent a telegram to Suzanne letting her know that he was really on his way and they would be together very soon.

Jack had been given a four-day pass and he didn't want to waste one minute of it. As soon as the gangplank was lowered and the ship cleared customs, Jack ran off the ship and asked a passerby where the nearest telephone was located. He headed down the street towards a café and found the phone booth.

"Oui," the woman's voice answered.

"Suzanne, it's me, Jack!"

"Oh, Jack, Jack! You're here!"

"I just got off the ship and ran to a café to phone you. I'm going to get a taxi right away and go to the train station," Jack said.

"How are you my darling?" Suzanne was breathless.

"I'm fine, Sweetheart. Let's not waste any time. I'm coming to you, bye baby. I'll be there very soon. I love you!" Jack exclaimed.

"I love you," Suzanne said.

Jack put the phone back into its cradle and asked the waiter to call him a cab. Five minutes later he was on his way to the station.

Suzanne had been sitting in the salon keeping an eye on the window to watch for the taxi. She was trembling. When she realized Jack had hung up the receiver on the phone, she slowly put hers down and her mind began to race. She wanted to wash up and dress and make herself as beautiful as possible to greet him at the door. Serge was in school, and Nadine was playing in the yard at her mother's. She ran outside and into her mother's kitchen.

"*Maman*, Jack's here!" she shouted.

Eva looked at her for a long moment and said calmly, "Good, I'm happy for you. Will he be here soon?"

"He's on his way to the train station in Antwerp," Suzanne said. "Maybe he'll be here in two or three hours. Oh, *Maman*, finally," Suzanne's voice was raspy as she choked back tears of joy.

"*Maman*, will you take care of Nadine so that I can wash and dress properly to receive Jack?" asked Suzanne.

"Yes, of course. Nadine is right here in the garden. I'll tell her to stay and to leave you alone. I'll tell her there'll be a nice surprise later," Eva said.

"Thank you, *Maman*," Suzanne said. "We'll come over after Jack arrives. Maybe he'll need to wash up, or whatever. We'll see, all right?"

"Yes, Suzanne. Go on." Eva had secretly hoped that the ship would never arrive or that it had been rerouted to another country.

Suzanne leaped to her feet when she heard the door of the taxi shut and she flung open the front door. Her heart was in her throat as she looked at his tall, lean body wearing dark brown trousers and a beige shirt open at the neck. He had a duffle bag over his shoulder and was opening the little garden gate that led to the front door. As he saw her, a huge smile spread across his face, and he rushed into the doorway right into her open arms. After one long deep kiss, Jack gently pushed Suzanne into the salon, dropped his bag on the floor and kicked the front door shut so that the neighbors wouldn't have a show. They were in each other's arms, clinging to each other. They kissed over and over again as if he had been her long, lost husband returning from the war. Tears were streaming down her face and Suzanne could not control the wave of emotions that overcame her.

Jack cradled her for several minutes cooing soft words into her ear. "I'm here now, Sweetheart. I'll take care of you. We'll find a way, and we'll be married, I promise."

At last Suzanne regained her self-control and a big smile was on her face. "Oh, Jackie, I am so happy. I just can't believe that after more than six months, we're finally together. You are so brave, darling. You cross the ocean to be next to me. Oh, how I love and adore you."

"I have a four-day pass, darling," Jack said. "We must spend every minute together. But I also want to try to talk to the Consulate about us getting married."

"Oh Jack, only four days. We will just be starting to be happy and you'll have to leave again," Suzanne almost began to cry.

"Sssh," Jack whispered as he held her more tightly. "Don't think about that now, baby. Let's just live every minute we can, okay?"

"Okay," she replied in English.

Suzanne and Jack sat in the garden with Eva and Nadine, who was thrilled to be in the handsome American's lap. Eva had given him a warm greeting and had insisted on preparing him a plate of food since he had missed dinner. Jack protested for a minute not to cause his future mother-in-law extra work, but quickly gave in to a stomach that was growling with hunger. Suzanne carried a tray of coffee to the garden and they sat there soaking in the warm May sun.

356

"Did you bring me a present, Jack?" the precocious little girl asked.

"Nadine!" Suzanne interjected, "it is not polite to ask about a present."

Jack smiled at her and stroked her curly blond hair. "What would you think if I brought you a doll?"

"I hate dolls!" Nadine said with authority.

"Nadine!" her mother scolded.

Jack laughed and then tickled the girl's belly. "I did bring you a present, and it's not a doll since I know you don't like them. You'll have to wait until Serge comes home from school and then I'll get them out of my duffle bag."

Nadine clapped her hands in joy as Suzanne looked at her and shook her head. "I'm sorry she has no manners, cheri, but it is difficult to cope with everything in this stressful time since the war is over. I don't have the time to constantly remind the children."

"It's all right, Sweetheart. She's just a little girl." Jack finished his coffee and lit a cigarette and let Nadine blow out the flame on his lighter. "What happened with Serge's stay at the seashore? You brought him home sooner than I thought."

"Yes, he was only there one month," Suzanne began. "He was doing very well and gained a kilo during that time. But then I found out that two older boys had been allowed to play on the beach, and they were injured by a mine! When I learned about it, I went there and removed him. I had been guaranteed that there was no longer any danger, but obviously that wasn't true."

"Thankfully you found out before it was too late. Please don't send him away again, Suzanne."

Eva looked at Jack and wondered what right he had to say anything. She was about to say something when Suzanne spoke quickly.

"I won't," Suzanne said. "If he needs to go to the seashore, we'll go as a family. We will be a complete family again soon, won't we Jackie?" she looked adoringly at him.

Just as Eva was again ready to speak, Serge came running into the back yard from the side of the house. He quickly took in the scene in the garden and yelled, "Jack, Jack you are here!" The boy ran over to him and put out his hand to shake.

Jack shook his outstretched hand and then pulled him closer and gave him a hug. "Oh, Jack, I have missed you! We had such fun when you were here last summer. Will you be here for the whole summer?"

"I'm afraid I won't be here for long, Serge, and I'm very sorry but the law doesn't allow me to stay without the proper documents and I can't get them."

Serge looked crestfallen.

"Serge, I told you Jack would only be here for a few days. We are going to ask questions to see if he can come back very soon and stay as long as we want; all right darling?" Suzanne tried to soothe his anxiety.

"I want to go to America on the ship with you, Jack!" Serge shouted.

"Well, that isn't possible. My ship is a freighter and they don't allow passengers. Only working guys like me. Listen, Serge, I promise that I will come back, or you and your mother and sister will come to America before this year is over," Jack said with confidence.

Serge had a puzzled look. He liked the promise but exactly when would the year be over?

Jack could tell what he was thinking. "Before Christmas. I promise."

Suzanne smiled in her own relief at hearing the words. The promise.

They passed the afternoon in the garden with Serge interrogating the man he hoped would be his father one day. He wanted to know everything about New Jersey and if there were cowboys living there. There was a lot of laughter and joy in the family that was getting reacquainted after their recent six-month separation. Eva kept quiet and wondered how she could keep her daughter from leaving their home and taking away her grandchildren. She was relieved that Jack was

358

only going to be here for a few days and maybe the next separation would be longer and he would lose his enthusiasm. Men were selfish, she thought to herself, and this American will eventually grow tired not being able to live legally in Belgium and her daughter not being declared a widow so that she was free to marry and to move away.

Bittersweet Return

"Suzanne, I'm coming back!" Jack shouted into the phone.

"What?" she couldn't imagine what he was saying?

"My ship pulled out early," Jack said. "They said they called your house, but we never got such a call. Anyway, I reported to the authorities, and I'm at the Consulate in Antwerp right now. The vice-consul, Mr. Anderson, has told me that I can go back to Brussels! The shipping office will let me know when the next ship bound for New York or Philadelphia comes into port."

"Oh, my darling, I can't believe it. How wonderful. Finally we have some luck!" Suzanne was instantly alive with anticipation.

"Listen, Sweetheart, since I'm here at the Consulate I'm going to ask questions about our marriage and you and the children coming to the U.S.," Jack said. "This Mr. Anderson is a really nice man, and I think he'll try to help us."

"Yes, Jackie, do what you can and then hurry," Suzanne said. "Get on the soonest train coming back here as possible! Oh, Jackie, I'll make sure the children are at my mother's when you return."

"Okay, baby. I'll be there soon. I love you." Jack said.

Suzanne sat on the divan next to the small table with the phone. She touched the fabric with her fingertips in a caressing fashion and thought about the rainy afternoon Jack and she had spent sitting on the divan. They looked at photos of her family from years past, and she explained about her ancestors and relatives that had all lived in Villers le Peuplier until her mother had left after her father's death. Jack listened and tried to comprehend that she knew that her family, the Dejardins, had been in the same village since the 14th century. Many of them lived in houses that were four and five hundred years old! Jack told her about his parents and why his mother had left Russia to care for the children of her older brother who had come to New York at the urging of his wife who died only a few years later. Jack was named after this uncle, Yakov, or Jacob in English for he had died not long after his wife.

There was so much to learn about this American man whom she loved, and there was never enough time to talk and learn about each other. They had passed their days with the children and had also visited briefly with the Picavets. Their nights were spent alone, and they made love almost endlessly and would often go to the window and look for the moon. It was not yet full like the moon of their first night together. The lovers felt as if they were the only couple on earth where the moon shone. Suzanne's body shuddered as she remembered how her emotions after their love making and that first time she truly felt as though she would die from the ecstasy. She prayed that Jack felt as strongly as she and that she would remain the only woman in the world for him.

She thought about Maurice and how she had loved him and how fine a young man he was. He had been sweet and loving and very polite and proper with her. Suzanne had never experienced the same overwhelming sexuality as she did with Jack. She said a little prayer for God to forgive her for thinking this way about Maurice. He had given his life for his family to the filthy *Boche* and had suffered months at their cruel hands until they murdered him and the millions of other Jews from Europe. Perhaps, she thought, I was too young and inexperienced for Maurice. He wanted to make me happy and was always so tender.

The ringing phone jolted her from her thoughts and she picked up the receiver. *"Oui."*

"It's *Maman*. I just want to know if you want to have supper with us tonight."

"Oh, *Maman*, no I can't," Suzanne said. "Jack just phoned and his ship left Antwerp a day early and he will have to wait for another ship. He's coming back here. Isn't that wonderful, *Maman*?"

Eva didn't answer right away and finally managed to utter, "Yes, of course, Suzanne. Do you know what time he'll be arriving?"

"No, he's at the Consulate and says there is a very nice vice-consul who is going to try to help him get answers about us getting married. When he's finished there, he'll take the train to Brussels," Suzanne said.

"Send the children over before supper," Eva said. "They can eat with Francine and me."

"Oh, thank you, *Maman*."

The couple had a total of sixteen days together until Jack had to board his ship bound for New York. He was fortunate that the authorities believed that he had not received the phone message of the early sailing of the SS Calvin Coolidge and that he would receive all of the pay to which he was entitled. Jack was also lucky that Mr. Anderson at the American Consulate had tried to find a way for him to marry Suzanne, but it would only be possible with a death certificate for her first husband. Mr. Anderson also helped Jack gather a great deal of information on how to establish a legal importing and exporting business between Belgium and the United States, which encouraged Jack to begin planning in sincerity his business with his brother. If Suzanne couldn't get the death certificate for many more months or even years, he wanted to be living in Brussels with her and earning money at his own enterprise. Fred Caron had also promised Jack that he could help him with much of the red tape he would encounter when he began the business.

Mr. Anderson encouraged Jack to call on him any time to discuss his future plans. Anderson said he believed passenger voyages would be allowed between these two countries before the year was over. If needed, he would write a letter recommending the approval of a visa for Jack to live in Belgium. Suzanne and Jack reveled in this news. Jack told Serge he was very confident that he would be able to keep his promise to him that he would be back for Christmas.

Jack's ship took more than two weeks to arrive in Boston. When it pulled in, he could see the Calvin Coolidge and got leave to go ashore. He went to the Coolidge and was able to retrieve the baggage he had left on board, and got a ticket he could show the union paymaster to receive his wages. The next couple of days were uneventful before they arrived in New York Harbor. Jack took the train to Forest Hills and knocked on the door of Marx and Lena's apartment at eight o'clock in the evening. Lena fixed coffee for them and served chocolate cake she had made earlier in the day. The baby was awake and Jack was surprised by the amount she had grown. Her hair was red and curly, and she was a lovely little girl.

Lena unwrapped the package Suzanne had prepared for her and took out the lovely hand-knit, pale pink dress. "It's beautiful, Jack," she was genuinely happy. "Please tell Suzanne that we thank her. It's the perfect size and such a pretty dress. How nice of her to think of us."

Jack told them how wonderful Suzanne was and that her children were great kids, and that he was looking forward to being their father. Lena and Marx said they understood what a terrible time Suzanne and the children must have had during the war and hoped they would meet her soon when she could be Jack's wife.

When Jack returned to his parents' home he immediately began working on the farm. Feed for the chickens was scarce, and he began searching and buying hundreds and even thousands of pounds whenever he could to make sure the birds were well fed and fat for the market. On one trip to the feed mill, Jack met the owner of a small transportation company that hauled chickens to the New York market. He offered Jack a job driving one of his trucks and paid him $1.00 per hour. Jack knew he could save all of the money from the job, and he and his parents could live off of the sale of the birds.

He wrote about all of this in his letters to Suzanne. The summer heat made the work difficult. Jack worked several hours each day driving along U.S. Highway 1 through northern New Jersey and into the markets in lower Manhattan. He arrived back in Vineland in the evening, took a bath, ate a late dinner his mother prepared and went to bed early to read or re-read Suzanne's letters and to write to her.

Suzanne's days were busy with household chores and taking care of the children. The weather had turned cool and rainy right after Jack had left Brussels and she told him how happy she was that their days had been filled with sun and that they had enjoyed their long walks in the woods and gardens around Mortebeek and in the city.

A month after Jack's recent departure from Europe, Serge's seventh birthday was approaching. Suzanne told Jack that she had invited their good friends and included Monsieur Sloma because he was the boy's godfather. Francine had been working in France and wasn't able to return for the birthday party. Ivan was still acting strangely and kept away from all of them, she wrote. Suzanne wondered in her letters what a strange wife Ivan had that had changed him so much. She realized how much pain her mother had from this separation and the anticipation of her departure for America would only add to Eva's misery. Some days Suzanne felt a great deal of guilt, but didn't express it to Jack other than to encourage him to keep finding a way to come back to her and start his business in Brussels.

Suzanne never stopped asking officials if there was any news about the laws regarding the wives and husbands who were waiting to know what became of their spouses. If they were never to know, the law must provide a way for them to continue with their lives. The answers from the ministers and clerks were almost always the same. Polite answers telling her that this will take time and that it was only one year since the end of the war. What did they know of what one year meant, she wrote to Jack? One year was like a lifetime to them! They could be married. She could go to America.

Yet their days were busy and their letters kept their hopes alive. Their reunion in May had made it very clear to both young people that they would wait as long as it would take to be together again. Jack continued to work as much as possible to save money for his future family in order to build them a new house. He told her that they might have to live with his parents for a little while after paying for the voyage to the United States for the four of them and that his parents told him that would be fine. Suzanne worried that the children would get in the way and that his parents would grow angry with them.

They bolstered each other's hopes in every letter and told one another not to worry about foolish little things. When love was this strong, they could overcome any obstacles that they would have to face, Jack would write. Suzanne's courage was often undone by her mother and even her sister at times. They would tell her that Jack was probably not the right man for her and that he was too young to take on a big family. How would he ever be able to provide for them?

In late June, Suzanne received a letter from Jack telling her that he knew a jeweler that wanted to buy diamonds. Jack told the man he could get the diamonds from someone in Belgium. Her beloved man was very excited as he described the possible profit of 200 to 300 percent on diamonds turned into rings and sold to an anxious American market. Americans were getting engaged and married as fast as they were when the war began. The jeweler told Jack he could probably sell a thousand rings during the Christmas season.

When Suzanne read this, she was stricken with fear. To her diamond dealing was synonymous with disaster. Maurice wouldn't leave his diamond trade in order to hide from the Gestapo. He had foolishly thought that having wealth would give him a bargaining chip with the Germans. How wrong he had been, and Suzanne felt that gems and the individuals Maurice had done business with was the reason he was caught. Jack's desire to make fast money with diamonds frightened her and she wrote back instantly.

After two more letters regarding the diamonds, Suzanne did as Jack asked and found the best prices for diamonds between 25 and 60 points that were the most popular in America. She received the next few letters from Jack with American dollars and was able to buy two good diamonds of about a half carat each. Although it took Suzanne quite a while to find a reliable dealer to sell her excellent quality stones, she finally mailed them and awaited further instructions after apologizing to him for agonizing about dealing in diamonds.

Suzanne heard the telephone ringing slowly waking her. When she realized that she was awake and the ringing wasn't a part of a dream, she jumped out of bed and ran as fast as possible down the stairs where the sharp sounds pierced the early morning darkness. As she picked up the receiver Suzanne saw the clock and it was only four o'clock in the morning and fear invaded her senses as she spoke, *"oui!"*

"Suzanne, it's me, Jack!" he cried into the phone.

"Jack, oh Jackie, why are you phoning? What is wrong?" her voice expressed panic.

"*Cherie*, nothing is wrong. I love you, I love you, Sweetheart."

"Oh, Jack, I love you my darling. Are you sure nothing is wrong?"

"Only that I have been so sad and crying almost every night," Jack said. "Your letters have been filled with so much sadness and worry lately that I'm afraid you won't wait for me."

"Jack, I will wait forever, my love," Suzanne said. "Please don't be sad. Please, just find a way to come back to me, my love."

"Suzanne, I am trying. I will get a passport, and I will come. I just needed to hear your voice, Sweetheart. Listen, I can only talk till the operator cuts in after six minutes. The call costs a lot of money, *cherie!*"

"Yes, darling," Suzanne said. "I love you so much. The children miss you, Jack. Serge wants you to be his Papa."

"Kiss them for me, darling...."

"This is the operator. Your time is done."

"Goodbye, Sweetheart. I love........."

Suzanne heard nothing else. She understood the six minutes were done. Oh, how he loved her, she thought. Dropping the receiver in its cradle, she wrapped her arms around herself and realized she was cold in the early morning and ran to bedroom and fetched her robe and slippers.

She made herself coffee and went to the table with pen and paper to express her feelings to Jack. Hearing his voice had surprised her so much, but she knew he had difficulty understanding her because she had been talking too rapidly. Suzanne wrote loving thoughts in this letter and explained that she was certain their love was bigger than any other in the entire world. Patience; they must have more patience.

****

The summer months continued to pass and Jack worked as much as he could on the farm and continued to repair his parents' home. All the while he wrote letters to Washington D.C. inquiring about living and working in Belgium as a civilian and never received a reply. In August he changed some of his tactics and corresponded with the Belgian Consulate in New York and with the U.S. Passport office there. He was told he could apply in person for the passport and it would take about ten days. The Belgian Consulate replied that he could receive a two month visa with his passport and then apply to extend the visa once he was in Belgium. If he had a

367

letter stating the date of his future wedding, there would be no problem in giving him a six month extension.

Jack was joyous and quickly wrote the news to Suzanne and asked her to get a letter from the synagogue acknowledging a wedding date in December. He and Suzanne had discussed the possibility of a religious ceremony without the legal civil marriage that the country required when he was with her in May. He hoped that the religious ceremony would satisfy the consulate since that was all that was required in the United States.

Jack put himself into full motion planning his trip to New York to complete all of the necessary paperwork and to convince his brother to go into business with him. He wanted to have the framework of the importing and exporting business worked out and would consider the diamond market as part of it if the gems turned out to be as profitable as he hoped.

Marx greeted his younger brother a few days later and was glad to have him staying over in their apartment. Jack had to sleep on the sofa but his sister-in-law made him as comfortable as possible for the better part of a week.

Over supper the first evening Jack filled the couple in on what he had been able to accomplish earlier that day in Manhattan. "I completed the application for my passport, and I'll come back for it so I can drop it off at the Belgian Consulate to apply for the visa," Jack reported happily.

"Are they giving passports to every country?" Marx asked.

"No. There are still many restrictions on eastern countries and no one is allowed to go to Italy yet," Jack said.

"Well, what's next?" asked Marx.

"Tomorrow I'm going to a travel agent in the city and I'm going to find out about shipping my car when I go. Suzanne found out that new model Chevrolets cost about 90,000 francs! That's four thousand bucks!" Jack cried.

"I hope it doesn't cost too much to ship your car. Are you sure the old thing is worth it?" asked Marx.

"Sure. I've got to have a vehicle there," Jack said.

"Why, it's like New York, right?" Marx was puzzled. "You got buses and trains to go around."

"Yeah, yeah; but I want to have my own car so I can do what I want," Jack said. "Listen, Marx, while I'm here I'm going to figure out all the legal stuff I need to do to set up the import – export business. I have to have my own business in Brussels. Suzanne wants me to work as a civilian for the Army like her sister does. She works in Liege and makes about $250 a month, but I don't want a desk job and I don't want to have anything to do with the Army!"

"Don't blame you, brother. You know what? You're entitled to all the GI benefits they are offering, and I can't get any of it because the Merchant Marines aren't veterans!" Marx sounded angry.

"That's wrong. You risked your life every time you went to sea. You wait; they'll change that someday. Anyway, what do you want to do? Go to college?" Jack teased his brother.

"No, but suppose I did, huh?" asked Marx.

"Yeah, yeah; well you don't. Marx, I told you before I want you to be the agent here in New York for the business and I might want you to come over to Belgium now and then to bring diamonds back to the states," Jack said.

"Diamonds? What are you talking about?" asked Marx.

Jack explained his dealings with the gems and the jeweler in Vineland and how profitable he expected it to be. "You have a problem getting on a passenger ship to make some good money?"

"No. But I have a wife and baby and I have to have a steady income," Marx was emphatic.

"Yeah, and I'm going to have a wife and two kids in a few months," Jack said. "Listen, I'll guarantee your income when we start this up. Leave it to me. You always left the real planning to me, big brother."

"Okay, Jack. We'll see," Marx said. "You find out what you need to, and I'll get a passport so that I'll be ready." Then in a low voice so that Lena wouldn't hear him from the bedroom, he said, "The little woman isn't going to like it, but I'll do it if there's good money in it."

Jack nodded at him as he lit another cigarette, and they continued to talk at the little kitchen table about old friends from New York and what they were doing with their lives. They talked until after midnight and finally Jack settled in on the sofa while Marx joined his wife and baby in the bedroom.

Reward at Last

Suzanne and the children arrived at the seashore with a long-time friend of the family, Madame Schugoulit. She owned a shop in Brussels and had met Eva before the war. Being an excellent seamstress, Eva had often made the woman dresses and suits and did so for her sister at times. After the war ended, Madame Schugoulit came to visit the family on rue Virgile. She had been in hiding and had not been found out. When she learned of Maurice's deportation to the death camp, Madame Schugoulit had great empathy for Suzanne and began to spend time with her. She was several years older than Suzanne and acted like an older sister. Often she made very kind gestures and brought gifts of lovely material so that Suzanne could design and sew herself new dresses and outfits for the children.

Madame Schu, as Suzanne liked to call her, knew important people and was involved with finding a lawyer to help Suzanne get a certificate of death so that she could get on with her life. Together they recently had applied for all the necessary legal documents that were the framework of Maurice's life in order to finally get a declaration of his death.

Suzanne kept Jack informed of her progress with the legal process and was ecstatic when he reported that he felt he might be able to leave the United States at the beginning of October. Jack, too, was up to his ears in legal paperwork, and they both hoped it would be over soon.

Suzanne told her friend that she could not afford a vacation with all of the complications in her life. Madame Schu insisted, telling her to think about the children and how they would benefit from the good fresh air and healthy food they could expect to find there. Suzanne hesitated at accepting this charitable gift, but Madame Schu pressured her and said she would rent a small apartment and they would have a wonderful holiday without a financial burden to her. Suzanne finally agreed and told her she would repay her one day.

"Don't be ridiculous, my dear," Madame Schu told Suzanne.

"I would be able to pay, but you know they have stopped the pension for Maurice, and I don't know what I will do until Jack gets here permanently," Suzanne said. "I am so afraid at times. No matter how much I weave, I can never make enough money with it."

"I know, Suzanne. I want you to put all of those worries out of your head for a while. Concentrate on having a good time and we'll even look for things you will want to buy for your marriage to Jack," Madame Schu said.

Suzanne smiled and agreed that she needed to rest and to enjoy herself. They began their vacation on a very warm and sunny September 1st, and Suzanne's first order of business was to phone her mother and give her their address. She had left explicit details for Eva to forward all mail from Jack to her immediately and that if any official documents arrived she should phone her. Jack had let her know that he was worried that if something important happened while she was on vacation he wouldn't be able to reach her. Suzanne assured him that her mother would contact her and that she hoped he understood how much she needed to be away from Brussels and all of her troubles and worry.

It was midnight on Sunday, September 8th, at the North Sea resort town of Le Zoute, and it had been cold and raining the entire day. Suzanne sat alone in her bedroom writing to Jack. Since his visit during the spring Suzanne had asked her beloved to rendezvous with her each Sunday. She would write to him at midnight and Jack would write at 6 o'clock so that each of them would have nothing on their minds but each other. Each of them felt closer to the other at this particular moment, and Suzanne told Jack that sometimes she almost felt his arms wrapped around her in a soft embrace. Jack would kiss her photo as he began each of his letters every Sunday.

Suzanne had a letter Jack had written in late August telling her that he had visited with a tire manufacturer in New York who was willing to work with him and Marx in an exporting business. The news was very promising to Suzanne, and as she answered she encouraged him to pursue the idea. She felt that it was a safe business and one that should prosper. Jack also told her that Marx was definitely going back to work as a seaman to earn more money, and he would gladly transport diamonds for him. Jack also reported that he had received his passport and would find a passenger ship as soon as his visa was approved. Suzanne kept her thoughts positive and urged Jack to hurry and get all of the documents he would need to set up a legitimate business in Brussels.

Suzanne ended her letter to her lover.

My Jack, it is almost midnight and you are writing me also. Take me in your arms and hold me tight. Only a few more Sundays until we are together! I love you, my husband, and soon we will be husband and wife in front of all of the world. In our hearts we are married for a long time. I love you since the first day and yet I never dreamed we would one day be married.

Goodnight my love. Don't be sad, we will realize our hopes soon. I love you.

Suzanne was putting away the breakfast dishes when Madame Schu came into the apartment with mail.

"Here, Suzanne, is a letter from your mother. "

"Thank you. I hope there is good news!" she spoke excitedly as she slit open the envelope with a knife.

"What does she say," Madame Schu sounded impatient.

"Oh, it's wonderful! Please wait a moment," Suzanne exclaimed as she continued to read.

"The death certificate has come for Maurice! I can't believe it. Maybe *Maman* is wrong. Maybe it is only the "presumption of death," Suzanne wondered aloud.

"Even so, my dear, that will be progress," Madame Schu said.

"Yes, you're right. Why do I always worry that it is the worst news?" asked Suzanne.

Madame Schu laughed and gave Suzanne a little hug. "Does Eva say anything else?"

"She didn't send it to me in case the letter got lost," Suzanne said. "That was a good idea. Oh, now I can't wait to go home and read it for myself! I have to write to Jack immediately and tell him of the hopeful news."

By the time Suzanne and the children returned to their home on September 15th, there was a great deal of news to discuss with her mother. Eva was happy to see her daughter and grandchildren. They enjoyed dinner together and sent the children to play with the neighbors since it was a warm afternoon. Suzanne scrutinized the "death certificate" and found that it was only a presumption of death. She did not abandon her happiness because, finally, there was hope that all would be settled and legal.

Eva was surprised to learn that Jack was going to book his voyage to return by mid-October. To her it felt like the beginning of the end. She began to complain to Suzanne that her son rarely spoke to her, that Francine was intent on marrying an American and that Suzanne was still planning to take her grandchildren and flee to the United States! Suzanne begged her to think about the happiness Jack provided her and the children and that she would be cared for and loved, and Serge and Nadine would have a father to raise them. Eva maintained that she had nothing against Jack and didn't understand why he would not want to marry and stay in Belgium for the rest of his life.

374

Suzanne didn't want to hear any more from her mother. She had done as her mother wished for her entire life. "*Maman*, I am going to be 29 years of age in a week, and I think I'm entitled to some real happiness!"

"You are, but if you leave, what will become of me?" Eva's tone was shrill.

"You will be fine, *Maman*. You have a pension and you have your work," Suzanne said. "I have nothing. I am totally out of money. I'm trying to sell all of Maurice's jeweler's tools and his suits and tuxedos just to put food on the table. You know they stopped giving me his pension since he was a foreigner. What kind of government do we have? What can I expect for the rest of my life?

"You want me to give up a man who loves me and the children so that I can stay here with you?" Suzanne began to cry not being able to hold in the emotion any longer.

"No," Eva shouted, "I don't expect you to give him up; I expect you to live with him next door to me so I can rely on you. You are the eldest. You owe it to me. You and Francine who only think of yourselves! I should have killed you when you were babies rather than have to suffer at your hands now!"

Suzanne was speechless for several moments. Her tears intensified and rolled down her cheeks and dropped onto her lap. Finally she choked them back and wiped the tears away with the back of her hand. Her voice trembled as she began to speak, "*Maman*, I cannot believe what you have just said to me. It is the most cruel thing you have said to me and you have said terrible things to me all of my life."

Suzanne stood and continued, "Maurice wasn't good enough because he was a Pole and a Jew. He was good enough when he was making a lot of money and helped you out whenever he had extra. But when he was arrested, you only knew that our suffering during the war would all be as a result of him. Now, Jack is no good, because he wants me. He wants the children! Do you know how many men want a woman who has two children that aren't his? Not many, *Maman*. And, Jack wants to adopt them. They will be his children!

"I can't help what happened because of the dirty Germans, *Maman*. I didn't make this mess yet I have suffered plenty. I have risked my life working for the Resistance and helping to hide Jews. You helped, too, *Maman*. What is wrong with you now?" Suzanne felt as though she would collapse and grabbed the back of a chair.

Eva looked at her and there was a long silence. She knew Suzanne was right but she just couldn't bear to think that her children and grandchildren were going to leave her.

Finally Suzanne spoke again. "Obviously you are not going to apologize to me. Think about what you have said, *Maman*, and don't talk to me again until you understand how I feel. How the children feel, too." Suzanne turned and walked out of the back door.

Suzanne ran into her house and sat down heavily at the table. Her tears were done, but the sadness weighed heavily upon her. She took out her writing materials and told Jack to hurry and come to her. Suzanne promised him that Fred Caron would be able to get his visa extended; after all, it was Fred who was able to obtain the 'presumption of death' for Maurice. As she wrote, she poured out her heart and told him she could wait to be able to come to America after they were married. His love was the only thing that sustained her. Without him her life would be over.

****

Jack received word that his visa from the consulate was ready and immediately went to New York. After picking up the documents, he went downtown and walked into the Thomas Cook travel agency to book passage on a ship sailing for Antwerp. One hour later he had an invoice marked paid for a ticket on the *Union*

376

Victory sailing on October 11. He almost danced on the sidewalk as he strode out of the agency!

The price for diamonds dropped in the United States, and Jack realized that the Vineland jeweler didn't know what he was talking about. Jack went to New York's diamond district to see how much he could get for the two stones and was discouraged because the price was the same he had paid. He decided to keep them until the market changed. For now he had enough money because the chickens had sold for a good price. His parents didn't need to work over the winter and his plan was to return with his bride and children in the spring and work on the farm.

Jack returned to Vineland thinking he would be back in New York a day or two before his ship would sail. He worked around the house, and his parents showed him how content they were that his plans were working out. After dinner a few nights later, he was listening to the radio when a strike was announced for seaman. It can't be possible, he thought with alarm. Not something to stop his reunion with his Suzanne.

The next day a telegram arrived from Thomas Cook agency making it crystal clear that his ship was postponed indefinitely and he would receive another telegram at least two days prior to sailing after the strike was finished. Jack sank into a slight depression. He didn't have much work to do, and he wasn't receiving letters from Suzanne. He knew she must think he was on the ship sailing to her and had stopped writing. Each day he wrote to her and begged her to write to him quickly because he couldn't live without her letters.

Jack passed time by working on his business plan he would implement in Belgium if they were not able to marry right away. He felt that he would find a way to earn money with the assistance of Fred until they sailed for the United States the following spring. If there were still delays in obtaining the very necessary death certificate of Maurice Morgen, he would ask Fred to help establish his importing and exporting business.

Several days later Suzanne received Jack's letter informing her of the delay because of the strike of two unions and that it might take weeks before he would sail. She wrote to him immediately so that he would have a letter and filled him in on her news.

Nothing more had happened to set her free to marry him, but she reported that a jeweler from the city paid her 11,000 francs for the tools that were in her attic. Suzanne would put aside 10,000 as Jack requested in case there would be customs to pay when he disembarked and any other fees he didn't know about. At her wits end to find money to pay her household bills, she sold some loose gems she had saved. She paid Madame Schu for the expenses from the September holiday, and her friend was happy to get the money because her shop didn't have much business. The war was over for more than a year, but times were still difficult if you didn't have full time employment.

Suzanne told Jack that her mother had calmed down and did apologize for saying the cruel things to her a couple of weeks before. Her brother and his wife had a baby boy whom they named Ivan, also. He told Eva he would visit soon with the new baby and they were not to come to his apartment. *What a family you are going to marry into, my Jack. A brother-in-law who has turned into a stranger and a sister-in-law who is trying to get to America more than I am!*

She continued in the letter, *All that is important is that we are together. We must have patience just a little longer and we will be together forever. I am your wife already. Your Suzanne.*

Monday 6 pm   Oct 28

My darling Suzanne,
I still don't have news and I am waiting impatiently. I know that it will happen but I am nervous just waiting. I don't have a letter from you since Friday and I hope tomorrow, cherie.

378

Oh, my love how marvelous it will be when we are reunited again. Cherie, I will love you so deeply and will make you so happy.

Suzanne, cherie, I regret so much for not giving you all of my love when we were together the first time. But you know, I never thought it was possible that we would be able to marry, there were so many obstacles. But our love has surmounted all of the obstacles. Our lives haven't been easy for love to flourish; you in Europe and me here; but we are sure now that there is nothing that can stop us. Even if you lived on the moon, I will come and get you. You are my Suzanne and I can't live without you. I love you, Sweetheart.

Goodbye my love. I want to write you about the ship. Maybe tomorrow I will have news. I love you.

7 p.m.

Cherie, the telegram has arrived! I leave on Friday, Nov 1! Still 4 days before I am in route. I think we will be together or the 9th or 10th of Nov. I am so happy, cherie. Soon we will be together forever. Oh, my love, I love you. Finally all of our dreams will come true. Goodnight my love, a bientôt, all of my kisses. Jack

Reunited

Suzanne was standing on the quay in Antwerp, Belgium on the morning of November 12, 1946. Jack's ship was there. It was right in front of her, and the gangway was down. There were two officers standing at the bottom of it and she knew the ship had to be cleared by customs before the passengers could disembark. The sky was gray and it was cold but she was happy there was no rain falling. Suzanne wore her black Persian wool coat with matching hat. She had put on a pair of the beautiful nylons Jack had sent her and wore dark brown leather pumps and carried a matching handbag. She was nervous and not sure why.

Her mind wandered and she thought that perhaps Jack wasn't on the ship and wasn't coming for her after all. So much had happened to her over the last several years and the 29-year-old woman worried that she would not have the happiness she needed desperately to go on living. Stupid, stupid thoughts, she told herself. Why do I do this to myself? My great love is on this ship, and he has come to be with me for the rest of our lives.

Craning her neck to see as much as she could, Suzanne saw men in uniforms coming towards the gangway. Yes, those are the customs agents, she thought happily. The passengers will be there any moment. Oh, please God, let Jack be first!

A loud banging noise from the rear of the ship distracted her and she turned to look. It was another gangway but much bigger, and she knew the luggage would be unloaded from there. By the time she turned her attention back to the passenger gangway, she heard his voice.

"Suzanne, Sweetheart!" Jack said in English and waved with his free hand as he carried a small valise.

"Jack! Jackie!" she returned. Suzanne thought she might faint at the sight of him. Oh my God, he's here, and he's never going to leave me again. She waved furiously and smiled as broadly as possible.

380

There were only a few people ahead of Jack and she could see he was impatient to get down the gangway. Finally the other passengers were at the bottom and moved away, and in the next instant he was in front of her dropping the suitcase to the ground and sweeping her up into his strong arms. Suzanne threw her arms around Jack's neck and he spun her around and her feet actually left the ground. "Jackie...." Her voice trailed off as he kissed her deeply; more deeply than she remembered he ever kissed her before. The kiss lasted for at least a minute, and then they held onto each other fiercely. Finally Jack pushed away slightly and said, "Let me look at you. Let me feast my eyes."

"Oh, *Cheri,* it is almost too much to really believe. You are finally here," Suzanne's voice was low and filled with emotion.

"I will never leave without you again, Suzanne. Never. Do you understand?" Jack said looking straight into her eyes with his hands holding her shoulders.

"Yes, my darling, I understand. I can't ever live without you again," Suzanne said.

Jack pulled her close to him and held her for another minute and finally said into her ear, "I will take care of you and the children forever, my sweet baby. Now let me go see how long it will take for the rest of my luggage and then we'll get a taxi for the station. Wait here, Sweetheart."

Suzanne nodded. She was so overcome by emotion she couldn't speak. She watched as he walked away towards some of the ship's crew to ask them questions. Look at him, she said to herself. He's still so handsome with his dark brown, wavy hair and tall lean physique. He's more beautiful than I even remember. I am lucky and I will make him the best wife possible. My life is going to start all over again and nobody can tell me how I will live it; definitely not my mother.

They were on the train headed for Brussels an hour later. Jack had brought three large suitcases, and he told her that besides some clothing of his, the rest were filled with clothes and things for her and the children. He had bought the rubber boots she wanted for Serge and Nadine so their feet would be dry when it snowed. The rest, he insisted, will be a surprise. Suzanne squeezed his arm as they sat in the second-class passenger car. She noticed that many people looked at them, and this gave her great joy. For the last year since Jack had left after the war, she looked at couples that walked arm and arm with complete envy and became miserable. Now everyone was looking at them!

"Sweetheart, you seem distracted?" Jack queried.

"No, I'm just thinking how lucky we are, finally! It seems as though we had so many obstacles to overcome, and it's only because our love is so great that we are here right now, together," she said in a low voice so others wouldn't hear.

"Yes, Suzanne, we are lucky. Others were lucky much before we were. You're right, if we managed to wait for an entire year to be together, our love will last forever. Nothing and no one will ever come between us again. I don't want you to worry any more. I'm here and we'll make our plans, and our lives will be together. Now, tell me if you have any news about the legal papers so we can get married."

"I'm afraid that there is nothing yet. Fred keeps trying for me, but nothing. I haven't seen the lawyer again because I have no money to pay him," Suzanne suddenly sounded sad.

"I'll go to the lawyer with you. We'll get to the bottom of this. Are there other women like you still waiting? For what? If Maurice hasn't been found by now, then for sure he must be dead. Don't worry, Sweetheart, Fred will help and I'll go to the American Consulate for help, too," Jack put his hand under her chin and looked deeply into her eyes.

"Yes, Jack. Now everything will fall into place. We have each other and we will have our happiness; that is what really matters."

They continued to talk about the future including plans for their wedding. They had written each other so often about how the marriage would take place and who would be their witnesses that it seemed so natural for them to fall into conversation about their nuptials. When they arrived at the Gare du Midi, Suzanne hailed a taxi while carrying one of Jack's bags as he came up behind her juggling three suitcases. The driver loaded them in the trunk and they arrived at 31 rue Virgile in twenty minutes.

Suzanne opened the gate and the driver helped Jack with the luggage and placed it in front of the door. She unlocked the door and they brought in the bags. "Jackie, let me go tell the children you're here. They can't wait to see you."

He grabbed her and kissed her and then released her. "I wanted to kiss you here! In our house, Sweetheart," Jack was choked with emotion. "Go, get the children."

She ran to the back door and went next door to her mother's. "*Maman*, we're here. Serge, Nadine, come along!"

"Why don't you bring Jack here?" Eva wanted to know.

"We'll come over in a little while," Suzanne said. "I want the children to have time with him. He will be their papa."

"All right. I will have dinner ready for 12:30, Suzanne," her mother said.

"Thank you, *Maman*. Come children," Suzanne said.

Serge and Nadine ran ahead of their mother and through the back door. Jack had taken off his winter jacket and was standing in the dining room. "Jack, Jack," they both cried.

Jack scooped Nadine up with his right arm and encircled Serge's shoulders with his other. "Oh, how you've both grown. Nadine, your four years old!"

"No, Jack, I'll be four in two weeks!" she shrieked and wiggled out of his grasp. Serge shook his hand like a big boy and Jack lifted him up.

"You are so tall. I bet when you grow up, you're going to be taller than me," Jack said.

Serge nodded and said, "Yes, I will. I eat whatever Mama makes for me, and I am growing."

"Is your mother coming over, Sweetheart?" Jack asked.

"No, I asked her to give you some time with the children," Suzanne said. "We'll go over in about an hour for dinner. Do you want to go upstairs and wash up?"

"No, I had a shower on the ship. Maybe Serge will help me take the luggage upstairs, and then I can unpack some of the surprises I have in them," Jack said winking.

"Did you bring us presents, Jack?" Nadine asked loudly.

"Of course I did. Didn't I bring you presents last time?" asked Jack.

"Yes, but this time you are not leaving and you are going to live here and be our papa," replied Nadine.

"You're right, but I brought you presents anyway!" Jack laughed.

"All right, Serge, help Jack. You can carry the small bag and I'll take one of the large ones," Suzanne gave orders.

"No, darling, Serge and I will handle everything. I'll be back downstairs in a lit bit."

"Can I help, too?" Nadine wanted to know.

"Sure, you just come upstairs last and help me unpack," Jack said.

Suzanne smiled at him and at the scene that played out in her house. *Their house*, as Jack had said. She let them go upstairs and took off her coat and hat and went to the mirror in the hallway to fix her hair. Looking at her reflection after a moment, she could see her happiness. My God, she thought, the worse is over. We may have to wait, but he's with me. Jack completes my life and he will take care of us. I am sure of it.

****

"Thanks Fred, I really appreciate everything you've done to help us get started," Jack said shaking hands with Fred Caron in his office.

"It was my pleasure, Jack. You and I only know each for a short time, but Suzanne is one of the finest women I've ever known. You both deserve a life time of happiness and, hopefully, prosperity," Fred replied with genuine sincerity.

"Without you we would never have been able to open 'United Rubber and Tire, Company'. I've got quite a few clients waiting for their shipments from the U.S. You know, Fred, when Belgium falls in love with the automobile like we Americans have, I'll be a rich man," Jack said.

"I hope you're right, Jack." Fred patted his American friend on the back as they walked to the door.

Jack turned and said to Fred, "Don't forget, Saturday night. You and Marie are having supper with us in the city. Suzanne has picked out a fine restaurant for us to celebrate."

"We won't forget. The only thing we want to celebrate more is your marriage," Fred said.

"Not any more than I do, Fred, but you know as well as we do that it may still take months."

Fred nodded and they shook hands again as Jack left his office in the building near Place Louise. Jack walked outside and lit a cigarette as he walked towards his car parked a few space away. It was clear, but cold, this last day of March 1947. Jack leaned against the passenger side of his car to finish his cigarette and thought about the progress he had made since arriving in Belgium less than five months before.

After a week of celebrating his return with family and friends, the lovers settled down to planning their future. They had no idea when Suzanne would be free to marry and so Jack proceeded to set up the tire importing business. Marx had arrived in Brussels two weeks later and Jack was pleased to introduce him to Suzanne and her family. He stayed with them for a few days before he had to return to his ship. Marx promised to contact the American sales office for United Tires and start the wheels of importing in motion.

Jack had enough money to pay Suzanne's household bills for a few months while he worked on all of the details to establish their business. The couple planned their wedding details and Jack showed Suzanne the wedding ring he had had made for her in the United States. It was gold with a palladium inset that was engraved with small hearts. Suzanne was moved by his romantic side. He was much different than Maurice who had been a true romantic, yet Jack would often surprise her by doing and saying things that didn't seem to fit the mold of the American GI.

Their nights were spent making love or sleeping wrapped in each other's arms, and they enjoyed the cold, dark winter months totally immersed in their love. They listened to the radio, and Suzanne would get Jack to dance with her to the jazz they both adored. They visited with friends and family at each other's homes and tried to keep their spending to a minimum so they wouldn't run out of money before the business could open.

Jack spent late afternoons and a lot of time on the weekends playing with Serge and Nadine. It didn't take long for them to begin calling him Papa. Their new father would tell them stories about his time as a cowboy in Montana, and Serge insisted that he, too, would become a cowboy in America when he was grown up. Serge showed Jack his collection of Tin Tin comic books, and Jack enjoyed reading them. He told Suzanne that he could improve his French by reading the comics!

Jack tossed the cigarette butt into the gutter and went around and got in his car. Fred had loaned him the money to buy a used Chevrolet, and Jack planned to pay him back as soon as they began to collect on their first invoices. When he got home he was happy to find

Suzanne at the table working on some of her textiles. She smiled as he came in.

"How is everything with Fred?" she asked.

"Oh, he's fine, and all of the papers are done!" Jack reported happily.

Suzanne got up from the table and moved into Jack's arms. "Wonderful news, *Cheri*. How long do you think before you can start importing?"

Jack held her closely and answered, "Only a matter of a few days and I'll be able to telegraph Marx. He'll have the tires on board a ship within a couple of weeks. I should be able to deliver the first orders by Easter!"

"Oh, Jackie, I know the business will be good. It has to be," Suzanne said.

"It will, Sweetheart," Jack said. "Now, don't start worrying. We have enough pre-orders with deposits to know that we'll have a small profit by the end of next month. These clients will make excellent references when I start going around on sales calls to establish more clients. I think I'll find a big market in northern France," Jack said with determination.

"You will; I know you will," Suzanne said enthusiastically.

Jack gave her a kiss and released her. He removed his jacket and took out a cigarette and offered one to Suzanne. Lighting them for both of them, Jack changed the conversation as he sat down.

"Suzanne, it's almost our anniversary. I hope you didn't forget, Sweetheart," he said coyly.

Suzanne smiled and sat across from him. "Of course I haven't forgotten. How could either of us ever forget that night when we saw each other for the very first time? I loved you that night. I didn't know how much I loved you, but I knew you were my love, my life."

"It will be two years, Suzanne. Two years and we're still not married," Jack said.

"I know, Jack, but in every way we are truly husband and wife," Suzanne said. "It's only the stupid laws that stop us from being married legally. It will happen for us soon."

"Well, my *wife*, what would you like to do to celebrate our second anniversary?" asked Jack.

"I'd like to go to Corso!" she answered quickly.

"Great idea! Last year we were separated by the Atlantic Ocean and had our rendezvous by letters. Do you think we'll have our beautiful full moon, *Cherie?*"

"No, the moon will be only half, *Cheri*. But it is always *our moon* when it is full," Suzanne replied with a longing look in her eyes.

Jack took her hand in his and held it tightly. "No matter whatever happens to us throughout our lives, Sweetheart, March 28 and the full moon will be ours and ours alone. We will have our wedding day and its anniversary for years to come but to me, this will always be our real anniversary. You are the only woman I have ever loved and I never want you to forget that, darling. Never. Will you promise me?"

Suzanne nodded and fought back tears of emotion. "Yes, Jack, I promise and I'll never forget."

****

By June, Jack and Marx's business was in full swing. United Tires of Benelux had entered into an agreement with Jack to be their General Agent and Marx was his partner. Their warehouse was located about 100 kilometers from Brussels at 20 rue de la Marliere in the town of Mouscron. This arrangement lowered the overhead expenses and gave the brothers a twenty-five percent of every sale plus bonus commissions once they sold 300,000 francs of product. The deliveries would all be made by other employees of United, and Jack could fully focus on sales. He trusted Marx to be able to deliver the goods to Europe.

They had tires and tubes to garages and auto dealers throughout Belgium and in much of Holland. Jack sought opportunities to expand into France. He was earning enough money to maintain the household on rue

Virgile while saving as much as possible for a future journey to the United States. Jack hoped to take a vacation with Suzanne so that she could meet his parents. For the time being, he remained confident of his continued success and decided they could live in Belgium. He had no problem renewing his visa since he was supporting himself and his fiancée.

Suzanne was delirious with joy. Her mother only found compliments for Jack now that he had established a successful business and planned to remain in her daughter's house. Eva didn't mind interjecting her opinions in their lives, but she was only a nuisance and her tongue was no longer malicious. Ivan had finally started visiting more often and his wife, Rosa, brought their little son for visits on Sundays. No one had ever figured out what was going on between the newlyweds that made Ivan a stranger, and they were all eager to leave that in the past. Francine was still employed with affairs dealing with the Americans and had met a former Army quartermaster who was dating her frequently and whom she seemed to like very much. Frank was from California and Jack enjoyed talking with him about southern California and what good times he had spent there. They both would commiserate about the lack of sunshine in Belgium while telling the rest of the family about the never ending sunny days in California.

With summer upon them Suzanne hoped to make plans to spend the month of August with the children and Jack at the seashore. She worked happily in the garden and in the house knowing she had the most wonderful fiancée to complete her needs and desires. Their love seemed to grow until she would think it was impossible to be any greater than it was until a week before Serge's eighth birthday.

The postman rang the bell when he arrived at Suzanne's door. She left the kitchen where she was preparing dinner and was surprised to see the postman.

"Hello Madame Morgen," he greeted her in his friendly manner.

"Hello, Monsieur *le Facteur*. What is it?" asked Suzanne.

"I have a registered letter for you and you must sign the receipt for me, please," the postman said.

"Of course," Suzanne replied as her heart began to race wondering what it was. She signed quickly and the postman handed her the envelope and tipped his hat as he turned and walked out through the gate.

"Goodbye," Suzanne called after him.

She went to the dining room table and sat down looking at the envelope. Suzanne was alone and was glad of it. She slit open the envelope and removed the official document from the office of the Supreme Justices. Taking a deep breath, she unfolded the document and began to read. Oh my God, she thought to herself. Finally. Tears welled up in her eyes and she let them fall with abandon. Maurice, she thought, and cried a minute longer before she dabbed away the tears with her apron. He is officially dead. One of the six million Jews that died during the six years of the war.

Suzanne had waited and wanted this official document for nearly two years even though she was positive that her husband had died in 1943 after he had written her saying 'goodbye.' Now that she held it in her hands, she was overwhelmed with grief. Thank God I am alone right now, she thought. Jack would see this as a moment to celebrate and in many ways it is for us to continue our lives together, but it is also so very sad. "Maurice, she whispered aloud, "I did love you with all of my heart, and I will always tell the children how good their father was. Now I must go on with my life and marry the man I now love. I'm sorry my poor, poor *bebe*."

She put the document back into the envelope and placed it on the mantle. Suzanne looked at the clock and was happy that she had another half-an-hour to herself. She would be composed and tell Jack that the paper they had waited for so long to receive was finally here, and now they could prepare for their wedding. When the children were older she would explain everything to them

390

and save all of the letters and papers pertaining to their father for them.

Suzanne walked back into the kitchen to finish cooking dinner. The warm and mild June weather embraced her as she stood by the open door looking out into the garden. The children were a few doors away playing with their friends and would be home soon along with their new papa who was in town doing some business errands. She stared at the empty canvas chairs and the rose bushes filled with blooms, and for a moment she saw Maurice standing there. Suzanne shut her eyes and said goodbye one last time. When she opened them she saw Jack walking towards her on the sidewalk that led from the street to the back yard. As soon as he saw her he smiled, and she looked at him with adoration and smiled back.

The Last Decision

The sun warmed her face as Suzanne leaned back in the little rowboat they had rented for the afternoon on Lake Thun in Oberhofen, Switzerland. Jack had made all of the arrangements for the hotel in the vicinity of Interlaken, the little town that was situated between Lakes Thun and Brienz in central Switzerland. He had always wanted to see the Alps and the beauty of the land that he had read about before the war. He had hoped to spend his military leave there until he met Suzanne.

Suzanne told Jack he had made the perfect choice. Hotel Elisabeth sat on an elevated piece of terrain with balconies overlooking Lake Thun. Their room was cozy and filled with sunshine each morning when they awoke and threw open the shutters. The air was crisp and clean and they enjoyed long walks along the shore and would often take the tram into the center of Interlaken to browse the shops and enjoy a meal. As they strolled through this mountain paradise they marveled at the Jungfrau Mountain that loomed not many kilometers from the lakes, and a bit further they could see the Eiger Mountain that was one of the most well-known of the Alpine mountains.

It was late June 1948, and the couple decided that this would be their true honeymoon, albeit nearly a year delayed. Jack stopped rowing for a moment and removed his shirt tossing it to Suzanne.

"It's getting hot and I'd like to get a tan from this glorious sun," he said to his wife.

Suzanne smiled and folded the shirt keeping it in her lap. She looked at his lean body and muscular arms as he continued to row and again thought how lucky she was to have met her American and to have married him. What a struggle it had been, she thought. She remembered how anxious they both had been waiting for her to become legally free to marry. They wasted no time making the final preparations for their marriage, and

392

Suzanne let her mind drift back to July 23 of the prior year.

Her suit had been made by Eva months before the wedding after she had found a wonderful fabric and decided it would be perfect for the outfit she had designed herself. Suzanne wore an exquisite white silk blouse under the beige wool-crepe with large, white polka dots double breasted suit. The fitted bodice accentuated her trim figure and illuminated her fair skin and long blonde hair coiffed in soft curls away from her face and falling to her shoulders. The 29-year old bride wore white leather pumps and stylish matching handbag and a wide-brimmed white felt hat. A lovely orchid corsage graced the small lapels on her suit.

Jack was extremely handsome in his brown wool suit with a wide pinstripe in the fabric. His crisp white shirt was set off by his dark maroon tie and breast pocket handkerchief. His dark brown hair was a bit unruly with the mass of curls and waves that added to Jack's good looks and had been disarming to countless women since he was a very young man.

As Jack waited for Suzanne to come downstairs he hardly noticed Francine and Eva rushing about the house placing china and glasses appropriately on the buffet for the guests they would receive later that day. The house was filled with vases of pink tiger lilies and greenery. Suzanne had chosen them since they were in season and did not want to have anything similar to her first marriage. Serge and Nadine had been ordered to Madame Temperman's house to play inside and told not to get dirty. They would be dressed in their good clothes for the reception.

As Suzanne reached the landing on the stairs, Jack looked up from the divan in the salon. A big smile immediately brightened his face, and Suzanne continued her descent. "You look beautiful, Sweetheart," Jack managed to utter although his voice choked.

"Thank you, *Cherie*. I'm glad you think so," Suzanne said.

Jack kissed her cheek not wanting to smear her lipstick and whispered in her ear, "I love you more than I can ever tell you."

"I love you, Jackie. Forever."

He let go of her and asked, "Are you ready to go?"

"Yes. Goodbye, *Maman*. We will see you at the restaurant at 12:30."

They went out the front door and climbed into Jack's Chevrolet to drive to City Hall only a short distance away in Anderlecht. There, Josette, Felix and Madame Schu were waiting for them as their witnesses. As they got out of the car, Felix told Jack that the photographer had arrived and was getting his equipment to set up outside of the building.

The bride and groom climbed the granite steps to the entrance, and their friends were right behind them. Josette took an opportunity to squeeze Suzanne's arm affectionately when they were all inside, and Felix went to talk to the clerk announcing their arrival for their 11 o'clock appointment for the marriage. Madame Schu told Suzanne how lovely she was and how very happy she was that the day had finally arrived for them.

When they were all ushered into the magistrate's office, the clerk asked the couple to be seated and explained the documents they were about to sign. Upon completion the magistrate came into the room in his official robe and greeted each member of the wedding party with a handshake.

They took their positions and the magistrate read from a small book to perform the wedding ceremony and to ask the bride and groom to repeat their marriage vows. Each of them did in a clear voice while looking into the other's eyes. Only ten minutes after the magistrate had begun, he finished by announcing them officially husband and wife. Jack kissed Suzanne tenderly and she clung to his arms for an instant longer. As they pulled apart they were smiling, and each of them was embraced in turn by their friends. Thanking the magistrate they all left the building.

The photographer was waiting with his camera and tripod and posed the couple and took several photographs. Suzanne was filled with happiness as the sun shone upon them. She knew in her heart that all of the terrible times were behind them and that she and her husband could look forward to a life filled with their hopes and dreams. Suzanne knew there would always be plenty of hard work ahead for them as a family, but they would be working together and she didn't have to face the unknown by herself.

"You're awfully quiet, Sweetheart," Jack said as he took a break from rowing.

"I'm enjoying the beautiful scenery and watching you row!" Suzanne replied.

"It is beautiful here, isn't it? I think it is the most beautiful place I've ever seen, Suzanne," Jack said.

"And it's even more wonderful because it's our honeymoon," said Suzanne.

"Are you sorry we didn't have our honeymoon right after the wedding?" asked Jack.

"No, Jack, of course not. We didn't have any time to plan it and the business was so new, you couldn't leave then. Anyway, we had the seashore that summer with the children! It was fun; especially when Josette and her family joined us," Suzanne remembered happily.

"It was fun, and I could still keep in touch with my clients," Jack said.

"I'm so proud of what you've accomplished so quickly, Jackie. You're a fantastic husband!"

"I want to make you happy always," Jack replied and then asked, "Am I a good papa?"

"Of course you are. If only my mother wouldn't interfere and tell the children they don't have to listen to you when you reprimand them," Suzanne looked sour for a moment.

"I can handle your mother and the children. Now, what are we going to name the little one that's coming, hmmm?" asked Jack.

Suzanne rubbed her small rounded belly and answered, "Jackie, of course."

"And what if it's not a boy?" Jack asked coyly.

"Jacqueline. Why not?" Suzanne wanted to know.

"I don't know about that, Sweetheart. You know when you're Jewish you don't name a child for someone living; you honor someone who died."

"I know that, Jackie, but I love your name. I love you," Suzanne said.

Jack laughed and picked up the oars. "I think we better head back to shore; it's getting late."

"Yes. Jack?"

"Yes, Sweetheart."

"We'll figure out a name later. It's only June and we have to wait until January. Imagine.... this baby will be almost ten years younger than Serge. I hope the children are not going to be jealous," Suzanne sounded worried.

"Listen to you. You're already worrying about something that hasn't happened. You need to stop doing that. Hasn't everything worked out quite well for us?" Jack chided her.

"Oh, it has, Jack. You know me; I can't help it," Suzanne answered with a smile and a little laugh. "I promise that I will try not to worry."

"That's better," he replied. "Let's get back to the hotel and take a nap. I haven't worked this hard in ages!"

"I'm all for going to bed, Jackie, but maybe not to sleep," Suzanne answered with desire in her voice.

"You don't have to convince me!" Jack said as he rowed harder. They both burst out into laughter as he made his way to the boat house on the shore of Lake Thun.

****

They were back at home in July and happy to be with Serge and Nadine. The weeks of summer passed quickly as they socialized with their friends and Suzanne's family members from the Ardennes and

Villers. Jack enjoyed his in-laws, and his friendship with Fred and Felix was more mature than any of the friendships he had as a young drifter and as a GI. They were good men who had faced difficult times with bravery, risking their own lives for Resistance of Belgium.

Yet there was a small piece of Jack's heart that felt empty. It had only manifested itself after Suzanne told him she was pregnant. They were both thrilled to be having a baby of their own, but Jack felt twinges of sadness when he thought about his parents. They would be grandparents without ever getting to know this child. Although Jack had missed and yearned for Suzanne each day he had been separated from her when he was living with his folks, he now realized that he often missed being in the United States. He was an American, and he liked American ways and customs. Everyone here had been terrific to him, but he thought more and more about moving his family to the U.S.

Suzanne walked into the garden having finished the dishes from dinner. The children were playing with the Temperman children, and she was happy to take one of the canvas chairs and relax next to her husband. Jack reached for her hand and held it tightly.

"What is it, *Cheri?*" she asked.

"Nothing much, Sweetheart. I was just thinking about my parents and how alone they are," Jack said.

"Oh, Jackie, don't be sad. They are used to be living by themselves. I'm sure they see family sometimes, don't they."

"Once in a while they go to New York and visit with my aunt and uncle," Jack said. "Life hasn't been easy for my mother, you know."

"Yes, I know, Jack. Your father is not a well man, and your mother has always worked very hard. I am sorry that it gives you pain, Jack. Why doesn't Marx visit them more often?" Suzanne asked.

"He's busy with our business and with the other job he took. I wish he would move to Vineland so that he could be close to Ma and Pa."

"Maybe he will, *Cheri*." Suzanne felt his sadness and became a bit afraid of what he might say.

"In Ma's last letter she told me that Pa isn't doing very well with his health. Suzanne, remember when we talked about living there and buying our own land and building a house and having a farm?"

"Yes, of course, Jack, but that was before you established the importing business. Aren't we doing well enough?" Suzanne voice trembled just a bit.

"Sure. We're doing fine for now, but it's not totally my own," Jack said. "I just want our baby to have a chance to know my parents, too, Sweetheart."

"Oh, Jackie, if my mother hears this, she'll start all her hysterics again. I don't know if I can bear it," Suzanne said.

"Look, Suzanne, we don't have to decide now. We can't go anywhere while you are so close to having the baby. But let's think about it, Okay?"

She only nodded at her husband. Suzanne didn't want to leave her beloved Brussels to live on a farm in New Jersey.

Jack took her hand again. "Sweetheart, remember what we always said? We will be happy no matter where we live as long as we're together. You and me and our children."

"Yes, Jack, I remember and you're right," Suzanne said. "As long as we're together nothing else matters."

Suzanne thought to herself. He's right; I live for him and the children. What has my mother done to make me happy? I have no right to be so selfish. America is a great country, and I would get use to it. I can learn to speak English. The children will probably be better off being Americans. It's the most powerful country in the world.

She squeezed his hand and looked straight into his eyes as she spoke. "Jack, if you think it is the right thing to do; if you think we will all be better off in the United States, then we should do it. We should move there."

"Sweetheart, oh, Baby, you mean it?   Really?"
Jack's heart leaped.

"If it is the best decision for us, then yes.   But you
must be sure that it will be the right thing to do," Suzanne
spoke with real conviction.

"We'll decide together.   I'll figure out what it will
cost to start our lives over in the U.S.   We won't say
anything to anyone until we can make that decision,"
Jack sounded so excited.

"No, we mustn't tell anyone," Suzanne squeezed
his hand again then relaxed in her chair.   She felt better
now.   There had been a huge release of emotion and
perhaps a new life in America would be best for all of
them.

Jack entered the house through the back door in
late October and found Suzanne in the dining room
knitting as she sat next to the stove.   He leaned over and
kissed her on the cheek and the neck from behind her.

"Ooh, you're so cold, *Cheri,*" Suzanne remarked.

"It's too damn cold for this time of the year.   No
Indian summer in Belgium, that's for sure," Jack
muttered.

He hung up his jacket and sat down near her to be
close to the warmth of the stove and withdrew some
papers from his pocket.   "I have some news,
Sweetheart."

"Oh.   You don't look happy.   What is it?" she
asked putting down the knitting.

"The Belgian government has put restrictions on
importing some products.   The number one ban is on
tires," Jack said glumly.

"What?   How can that be?" asked Suzanne.

"Michelin is cranking out tires just as fast as
Firestone and Bridgestone in the states and Belgium
wants to buy from France and the factory they have set
up here," Jack stated the facts.

"Oh, Jack. What will happen with our business?" Suzanne asked.

"Well, it's a good thing we're importing many other items now," Jack said. "We should make enough money to see us through for a while, but I'm not sure what the future holds."

"I see," Suzanne paused for a few moments. "Is it time for us to start our new life, Jack?"

"I think it is, Sweetheart. Does it make you sad?"

"No. We said if it is the right thing to do, then we will do it. As long as we are together, Jackie, that's all that counts," Suzanne said.

Jack stood up and helped Suzanne to her feet. He took her in his arms and held her as tightly as he could. "Sweetheart, you are amazing. I love you so very much. You know, we didn't really have to make this decision, did we?"

"No, Jack, fate determined our future, and we must think it is for the best. We will be happy in America."

"It is fate," Jack reiterated. "We won't travel until the baby is a few months old; next summer when the ocean is calm and the sailing will be easier. That will give us plenty of time to prepare, and for me to ask my parents to start getting ready for us to arrive."

"Yes, *Cheri*. When will we tell the children? When we do, the whole neighborhood will know," Suzanne laughed.

"Let's wait until after New Year, but I think we should tell your mother and then the children before our baby is born," Jack said.

"I agree. Oh, Jackie, it will be fine. I remember I would have boarded any ship that would take me and the children to be by your side after you returned to America when the war was over. I can certainly do it now when we are married and are a real family. Remember, Jack, I told you I would love you forever."

"I will never forget, Sweetheart." Jack held her in his arms and knew that it was not too late to start all over, once again.

Made in the USA
Charleston, SC
02 April 2013